If you cannot pronounce the word "Appalachia," and you don't know the difference between a pee-can and a pecan, you will love reading my stories.

Wait 'Til You Hear This One

Copyright © 2017 Patricia Estep O'Neal

All rights reserved. No part of this publications may be reproduced, stored in a retrieval system, or transmitted, in any form or by any means, electronic, mechanical, photocopying, recording, or otherwise, without the prior written permission of the publisher, Patricia Estep O'Neal, Lexington, Kentucky, U.S.A.

Print ISBN: 978-1979830157

Cover painting by Mollie Radden

Back cover photo courtesy of the author

First Edition

WAIT 'TIL YOU HEAR THIS ONE!

HUMOROUS ESSAYS

PATRICIA ESTEP O'NEAL

This book is dedicated to my entire family—my parents, six sisters, two brothers, and my children, Jan and Greg. Without them there would be few stories to tell.

CONTENTS

Introduction	xiii
The Family Genes	1
Mama's Front Porch	4
Finding Our Roots	9
Wait 'Til You Meet My Mother!	13
A World's Fair	20
You Can Read It in the Newspaper	24
The House is on Fire	26
Uncle John	29
The Depression Years	34
Home Away From Home	40
Grandpa's Lazy Susan Table	46
"Mama, Tell Me About the War"	50
Dammit, It's My Turn!	55
The Push Mower	59
Norge Frigidaire	64
Cursing the Thrush	67
A Dose of Sulphur and Molasses	69
Sisterly Love	74
The Lumberyard	77
The Paper Boy	85
Juicy Red Plums	91
Headless Horseman	93
Going to Akron	97
Through the Eyes of a Child	100
Blue Horse Wrappers	117
Daddy's Classic Car	120
Father's Day	123
A Dress With Covered Buttons	126
The Door to Door Salesmen	130

The Blue Serge Suit	134
A Place Called Frog Level	137
Before the Dixie	143
A Piece of History	146
Don't Tell Mama!	149
Cissy Gregg's Cookbook	152
The Days of Comic Books	154
Sadie Hawkins Day	157
Love Letters	160
The Model T Ford	165
Young Love	168
Coal for Sale	170
I Want to Be a Movie Star	174
The Black Velveteen Dress	178
Meatloaf for Dinner	181
Aunt Ruby	184
Sunday in Defoe	188
A Day of Resurrection	192
My Neighborly Neighbor	198
A Birthday Present for My Mom	204
Another Birthday	208
Irresistible Sleep	212
Bittersweet	217
Golden Wedding Anniversary	221
The Old-Time Family	225
Tornado of 1974	227
Dogwood Shores	230
Drip, Drip, Drip	234
Sunshine Yellow	236
Mirror, Mirror On the Wall	240
I Thought I Saw a Mouse	243
Kentucky Horse Biscuits	245
The Hoosier Wall Cabinet	248
The Antique Baby Bed	250
Rhoda	252
Post Office Murals	256
Klondike Gold	258

The People We Meet	261
From a School Newspaper to a National Magazine	263
In Britain	267
The Old Taylor House	269
Hear the Train A-Comin'	273
House By the Railroad Tracks	278
Blessing	282
Tea in an English Cottage	286
A Church Bazaar	290
The Mathematical Bridge	294
It's Only a Sprained Wrist!	299
Savannah	304
The Queen Anne Style House	308
Follow the White Truck	314
Watch That Finger!	317
What's New Today?	320
Mountain Laurel Festival of 1936	325
If I Could…	329
Peppermint Candy—A Tradition	334
The Christmas Bowl	336
A Guiding Star	339
An Early Christmas	342
Memories of Christmas	346
The Easter Bunny	349
Hidden in a Cloud	353
How Funny Can It Get?	357
You Just Had to Be There!	361
There Goes Ms. Velma	365
Going to the Doctor	369
The Nursing Home (1996-1998)	373
A Long-Awaited Journey	380
Mama's Butcher Knife	386
Her Life in a Nutshell	390
Afterword	397
About the Author	399
Also by Patricia Estep O'Neal	401

Mammaw's House by Mollie Radden

INTRODUCTION

I was already deep into the research of my own family history. I suddenly remembered that it was in the early 1970s when a new TV series premiered called *The Waltons*, considered to be the best of the very best shows on television. I recalled seeing the first two-hour episode which starred Patricia Neal. I was immediately drawn to the series. Each week I watched the Waltons and was amazed at how much like my own family they were. Grandma and Grandpa Walton shared the same two-story white frame house just like my mother's grandmother did in their two-story whitewashed house on Cox's Creek in southwest Virginia. And each week as I continued watching the television series, I found myself uttering the words, "The Waltons have nothing on my family. I could write a story just as good."

I decided to do a little research on the writer and narrator of *The Waltons*, Earl Hamner, Jr. I soon learned that he grew up in Virginia, just as my parents did. I was amazed at how his personal life ran so parallel to mine. He was the oldest of eight children and the character, John Boy, was based on his life. I was one of eight living children also. His parents eloped, just like mine did. They were of the Baptist faith, just like mine. When he described his mother, I thought he was talking about my mother.

INTRODUCTION

Hamner told of the Depression Years, just like I did in my story. He served in World War 2, just like my brother. As I continued reading, I was beginning to feel a connection to this man. Mr. Hamner died several years ago but he left behind a great legacy. I wish I could have met the man. He was like a kindred spirit to me.

I began writing short stories about every day events in a large family and remembering more tales from my childhood and jotting them down. I found myself telling these stories and gaining popularity from others who enjoyed hearing them. They wanted more stories reminding them of their own childhood in the hills and towns where they grew up.

Today, I have compiled approximately 100 short stories about my family life. Some stories are sad, some about the days of war, everyday small town events, holidays, and others will make you chuckle with laughter. You will say, "I remember doing that!" or "That reminds me of when I was a kid."

The stories are not in chronological order. They are written so that when you break away from the book, you can return to the page where you left off and begin a new story. You will be reminded of the good times as well as the sad times in your life, then and now. I hope they leave you with the feeling "I can go home again!"

THE FAMILY GENES

We talk about our blue and brown eyes and our blonde, brown, or red, curly hair, and even that big dimple in one cheek. The genes I refer to are the ones that decide your looks, health and well-being.

I come from good genes! I've said this time and time again. There is no history of diabetes, high blood pressure, heart disease, arthritis, high cholesterol, and the list goes on. When I go to the doctor and the receptionist gives me the piece of paper listing all the conditions and diseases you or someone in your family may or may not have had, I go down that long list checking them off, one by one. No, no, no... The doctor takes a look at my checked-off list and is very impressed. "You are a healthy girl! You come from good genes." And then he comes to the item that says OTHER. That's when his mouth flies open. "Wow!"

He sees nine names under the heading of CANCER. Yes, as someone wrote in her story, the "Cancer Monster" had attacked my family. My dad died of pancreatic cancer. My oldest sister, Inez, died of breast cancer, and my sweet sister, Velma, suffered for months with ovarian cancer until her death. My mother, with colon cancer, was a survivor along with four more sisters and my younger brother, who had a tumor removed from his lung. And only a year ago, another sister, Bena Mae, passed away after years of suffering from Leukemia. Use your math…my parents and seven siblings. And then there is ME, the only member of the family who has escaped the Cancer Monster—so far!

I am not asking for pity. I do not ponder and worry about getting cancer. If it happens, it happens. I have had many trials and tribulations in my life and while stumbling through them, I learned to take on a positive attitude. Solve the problems that can be solved, and put aside those you have no control over. I learned to laugh at myself and turn a bad incident into a humorous story—that is, when it was feasible. I remember the time my craft shop had just burned. I had been open for business exactly one year. I was left with no income, no job, and not enough insurance to rebuild my business. I had already suffered the loss of my house by fire in less than a year. It truly was a dreaded day when I called my children and relayed the bad news to them; waiting three days until I could work up the nerve to place that phone call. In conversation, I said something jokingly and my son came back at me in an apprehensive voice saying, "Mom, that's not funny!" I responded, "If I don't laugh about it, I'll cry myself to death." I taught myself to think positive. As they say, "When you are given lemons, make lemonade." And that's just what I did.

One of the best things I ever did was take up the task of researching my family history. That led to writing a book, which was the most enjoyable thing I've ever done. I laughed at the dumb things I did and continually told my co-workers funny stories. I was then working in Tennessee and my friends would say, "We can't wait 'til you get back from a weekend trip to Kentucky because you always have something funny to tell." I considered that a true compliment, so I continued telling stories. In most cases, I'm turning a not-so-pleasant situation into a humorous story.

And now, I am acquiring an addiction that can only be cured if my kids take my laptop computer away from me. I keep writing silly little short stories and sharing them with a group of terrific people on Folklore webpages. My stories may not make a lot of sense to most people, but let's just say I'm having fun writing them.

It gets even better when you realize your children have grown up and reached an age where they enjoy doing the same things you like to do. Ah, what great trips we take together; nothing exotic or sensational as one might expect, but fun trips. They are fun trips because of the family and friends sharing them together. Each trip ends with a story for me to tell.

And now, I have compiled many of my short stories for your pleasure. Even in the sad and melancholy tales I seek to find a reason to smile. I have reason to smile a lot these days. I might even wake up at three in the morning and a thought comes to my mind—the makings of a good short story. I might even crawl out of my bed and head for the living room where my laptop computer sits, waiting for another story. I think about my parents and my beautiful sisters who died of cancer and I am thankful they have given me the stories to tell. As the days go by I can look in my mirror and say, "Thank you, Lord, for letting me triumph over the 'cancer monster' another day!"

MAMA'S FRONT PORCH

A generation of history could be brought to light if you had been around to hear the stories told on Mama's front porch. The porch wasn't all that big, about the size of one of our bedrooms. It was a covered porch with an awning that blocked the late afternoon sun. A glider sat against the wall at one end of the porch and a wooden swing painted white hung at the other end. No matter how many people were on the porch, the first to arrive always went straight to the swing.

Life in our Kentucky home began around 1920 when my dad worked for the Railroad Company. He had been transferred from Middlesboro to the railroad center in Corbin, Kentucky. He also began building houses and doing construction work. By 1924, he was no longer working for the railroad company. He applied his time to carpentry, building houses, churches, and schools. He went wherever there was a job, sometimes taking the family with him when the construction job extended many months and possibly years. But our family home was back in Corbin in the house he had built on Whitley Avenue. That is where nine of thirteen children were raised.

Sisters: Inez, Ada, Velma, Bena Mae, Janette, Wanda, Pat

Mama was well into her nineties when we, once again, gathered on her front porch one summer night. There were four sisters, my brother, and his wife. I would ask questions of each of them because I needed their take on incidents that took place during our childhood. I was in the process of documenting the family history. There was lots of laughter. My sister, Inez, would begin telling stories about her youth, and since she was the oldest of us all, she would ramble about things that none of the rest could remember. She would begin laughing and then tears would stream down her cheeks, making it difficult to finish her story. Another sister would begin a tale and she would get so tickled that the pitch of her voice was so high we were plugging our ears because we couldn't understand a word she said. That brought on more laughter and it took at least three tries before she could get her story told.

Don Estep

    Today, my mother and three of my sisters are gone, but I still have the recordings of our fun and laughter that summer night on Mama's front porch. It is something I will always treasure—being able to hear the voices of Mama and my sister, Inez, telling their stories of old, hearing them laugh, and remembering the tears. January 25th is my mother's birthday. It is also the day my sisters Inez and Velma were both buried. My sister, Bena Mae, died last year of Leukemia. She was also sitting on the front porch swing that night and occasionally, she would tell a story of her own. We never knew if her wild tale was real or fabricated, but everyone would be laughing before she finished. The tales went on and on with all of us laughing and trying to top the last yarn.

    Year after year, we sat on Mama's porch, talking and laughing, the chain squeaking as the swing slowly moved back and forth. I suppose we covered every subject known to man, including religion, neighborhood gossip, and everyday happenings, but very little politics which wasn't a major issue to small town folks in those days. Sometimes we just sang. Oh, yes, in the early days we sang! With seven girls and two boys, you were bound to get some good harmony. I was too young to harmonize with the others, but I loved listening. Before my older brother joined the Army Air Corps during World War II, he and my sisters often gathered on the porch to sing. One by one, the neighbors would saunter out onto their front porches to listen to the musical sounds coming from our house.

From the first warm day in spring until the last warm day in late fall, you could be sure someone would be occupying the swing on Mama's front porch. For many years, when the weather would permit, every evening after supper the family headed to the front porch to relax and watch the sun go down over the hill. Neighbors could be counted on to join us. There was always something worth reporting and laughing about. Nobody went to the trouble of making up tales; they didn't have to because the truth was better than fiction.

Elizabeth Estep

I like to pull out the old audio tapes, close my eyes and bring to life once more those happy voices, and in my mind I see the silhouette of their faces as I saw them in the soft light from the lamp shining through the living room window. They were a pretty bunch of girls and my brother was quite handsome. I listen to the recording as they each clear their throats then talk and laugh about the old days. Sometimes, everybody is talking at the same time or their voices become a bit muffled and they are hard to understand. I again listen to my tapes and shed tears of joy because I had them in my life and can hear the voices of Mama and my sisters who are now in heaven.

Those days are gone now and as the youngest of seven sisters, it's my sense of duty to review the family stories and tell them once more. But the laughter and camaraderie from Mama's front porch is missing. If I close my eyes, I can see Mama with one arm across the back of the swing and the other holding the chain as she sings to herself, "From this valley they say you are going. We will miss your bright eyes and sweet smile. For they say you are taking the sunshine that has brightened our pathway awhile."

FINDING OUR ROOTS

In wintertime when the ground was covered with snow, you could go to the top of the hill with your large handmade sled made from a piece of a cardboard box, plop yourself down, and with a push, slide down the long drifting mountainside. By picking up speed you would reach the bottom of the steep hill and ride halfway up the other side of the mountain.

Summertime entertainment was almost unheard of since there were gardens to plant and harvesting to be done. An occasional dip in the creek or trek through the woods was all the kids could hope for on a hot summer day.

This was the land my ancestors had chosen to live on after migrating from their British homelands. Ships had landed in Delaware, Maryland, and North Carolina where families began their pilgrimage, heading west. It would be a very long journey. All of the immigrants seemed to have their visions set on Oklahoma, Texas, and California. Some were settling in Missouri. It would take many months to travel across the country by pioneer wagon and horseback to the western territory, risking illness along the way, with young children and new babies putting a strain on the journey.

My paternal great-grandparents left North Carolina and trudged along for weeks and months until they came to the hills of southwest Virginia. The pioneer wagon broke down. It would be a long wait in repairing the wagon. They unpacked their belongings, planted seeds for crops, and began building log cabins. This was where they would settle and remain the rest of their lives.

I remember the first time I saw the 300-acre farm where my mother was raised. We drove over dirt roads muddled with heavy stones in our path, enough so that it appeared we would have no tires left for traveling back home to Kentucky. Everywhere I looked there were hills and woods and creeks and only manmade dirt roads to follow from farm to farm.

I was a city girl, so to speak. I had never lived on a farm. I didn't know what it was like to get up in the morning when the rooster crows, milk cows, and plow in cornfields. I looked around at the big barn that stood right at the intersection of the sign that read VA/TN Border. The barn was in Virginia and on the Tennessee side of the state line stood a two-story batten board house with a shake-shingle roof. The house was so weathered you could hardly tell that it had once been white where my grandfather had painted it with whitewash. When Grandma and Grandpa Rowlett gave up housekeeping and sold the farm, they bought a small piece of property at Middlesboro, Kentucky, and lived with my Uncle Paris, Mama's younger brother.

The farm that had originally belonged to my Great-grandmother Brooks in the 1800s, was home to my mother. I was just itching to get inside the old farmhouse and go room by room looking at the red textured wallpaper Mama had described, the two big fireplaces, and the parlor Mama had told me about, but the house was occupied and we didn't feel it would be proper to go knocking on a stranger's door. Instead, we walked down the hill to where there was an opening in the overgrown brush that took us to an area in the woods at least twenty degrees cooler than in the sunshine. Mama pointed us to the springhouse hidden among the bushes and we could see the spring water flowing quietly down the hillside. That was where Grandma Rowlett did her laundry and kept her milk and butter cool in the summertime. We found our way back through the thick brush and walked up the road to where Grandpa Rowlett's blacksmith shop and grist mill once stood.

There didn't seem to be a four-foot square piece of level ground in any direction I looked. I asked Mama where they planted their gardens. I couldn't see any flat land at all. She pointed to the top of the hill. I could then see it was a long climb to the level ground at the top where the apple orchards and vegetable gardens had been. Mama pointed in another direction to the top of another hill. "That's where the family cemetery is located," she said, "but I'm afraid if we try climbing that hill we may run into snakes." We turned and saw a lady walking across the yard with a water bucket in her hand. She was headed to the old water pump Pap (Grandpa Rowlett) had built to provide fresh water to the house. Up behind the house stood a tall post with a huge dinner bell attached to the top. Mama said Pap had placed the dinner bell there as a convenience for Grandma to call him and the working hands in to dinner.

We returned to the car and headed up the road in the direction of Big Spring Union Baptist Church, one of the small churches established by my dad's grandfather, George Washington Nevils. Winding in and out of sharp curves and over large rocks, I looked around at the woods covering the hillsides and whispered to myself, "Why in the world would anybody want to live in this hilly country where there's nothing to see except the sun coming up just before noon each day and then going down at night?"

It was 45 years later when I was privileged with a trip to my ancestors' homelands of England and Wales. I joined others on a nine-day land tour going from village to village. We traveled from London to places like Bath, England, Llangollen, Wales, and farther north to the Lake District of Grasmere, England, the home of Beatrix Potter. As the coach made its winding circuit down the mountain into Grasmere, I looked up at the mountainside. I had never seen anything so beautiful. Along the very top of the mountain the sun beamed down upon stone fencing as far as the eye could see. The fencing spread for miles and occasionally divided off into separate plots. The grass shimmered in the sunlight. Here and there cows were grazing on the hillsides and black-faced sheep could be spotted in every direction, grazing and keeping the hills smooth and clean. When I saw the long white foam cascading over rocks from the mountain springs above and flowing down into the valley, tears came to my eyes.

Virginia Mountains, Rowlett farm

It was at that very moment I came to realize why my ancestors had chosen the Virginia/Tennessee hills of Appalachia for their homes after their long and tedious migration to America. The vast expanse of hills, the valleys of beautiful colored grass swaying in the breeze, the mountain streams and springs—they were all reminders of their British homelands. When the immigrants settled in southwest Virginia and east Tennessee, they had found their roots.

WAIT 'TIL YOU MEET MY MOTHER!

Elizabeth Rowlett Estep, 1935

Mama was unique, what you might call surprisingly intelligent in her own way, while at the same time she was a simple homemaker and mother concentrating on what she was going to prepare for the next meal. She loved to cook and had been cooking since she was twelve. Most of her life she had been cooking for a large family. It was easier for her to fix a dinner for ten than for two.

She had grown up learning all the home remedies for anything that ailed you. A small metal cabinet hung on the kitchen wall that contained a few special serving dishes and iced-tea glasses, and back behind them was hidden her medicines.

Following the Ladies' Birthday Almanac for planting crops was a way of life for her. Mama never wavered from the things she had learned back on the farm in Virginia and Tennessee.

She was serious about her duties as a mother and housewife. Everything she did had a formula to it. Her way was the only right way, whether it was making beds or canning kraut. She was unmatched. She was also the neighbor who had birthed the most children. When the neighbors saw ol' Doc Smith heading towards the Estep house, they knew Lizzie was ready to deliver another baby. It took her 24 years to bring all thirteen of her babies into the world. And, as far as my oldest sister, Inez, was concerned, Mama could have quit after she was born! Playtime for Inez was sitting on the front porch, rocking the newest addition to the family.

When a person reaches a point in life where he or she becomes the caretaker instead of the child, the daily routine can become insufferable and hard to deal with. It takes more patience and compassion than you think you can muster, and there will be times you feel you can't make it another day without relief and rest. But there is always light at the end of the tunnel and humor along the way in many of these situations. You just have to look for it. You can make it through what seems like a very trying and unrewarding time, and do it with a smile on your face.

My oldest sister, Inez, became Mama's major caretaker because she lived directly across the street, making it convenient for Inez to see to Mama's needs. Unfortunately, Inez ran out of time before Mama did. She died of cancer at the age of 74. That meant the other six sisters had to take over with Mama's care. By then, Mama was 95.

When Mama was 98, she had become ill with a bout of pneumonia, which left her weak and out of sorts. She became bedfast, requiring the need for an aid to assist her twenty-four hours a day. My sister, two years older than I, had purchased a book that described signs of death. The book said the dying talk about people who are already deceased. We had noticed that Mama would awaken from sleep asking about her brothers and sisters, and talking about her 'Mama' (as in the present day) carrying a bucket of water from the spring to the farmhouse. There were memory lapses, which may have been due in part to her medication, because ordinarily, Mama's recall was very good. She would ask about Daddy. He had died in 1976. Answers to her questions were given so as not to create emotional upset. We kids were certain our mother had reached the last stage of her life and we were trying to prepare for it. Mama talked and talked, rambling on about her childhood, her courtship with Daddy and what a handsome young man he had been, her children when they were small, and my brother who was the youngest: "He was a perfect little angel."

We heard familiar stories and several, quite humorous tales she had never revealed to us before. Mama liked to talk about the past. She told one story about a preacher from her early years of marriage, Oscar Brooks, who lived across the street from us. He was a lay preacher whose wife had just died and within two months after her burial, Oscar remarried. A friend and deacon of the local church approached him one day and said, "Preacher, don't you think it's a little soon to get married again? After all, your wife was just buried two months ago!" Oscar rolled the tobacco around in his mouth, took a spit, and answered, "Well, the way I see it, Ethel's as dead as she'll ever be!" Mama held her hand over her mouth while she chuckled. Her humorous ramblings reduced the stress of the day and helped pass the long tedious hours of her illness.

One day Elsie Freeman came by to see Mama. It had been several years since they had seen each other. Elsie owned the neighborhood store where Mama bought her daily groceries for many years. Elsie and her husband, Herbert, retired and moved to a farm in the country. Her hair had turned to silver. When asked, "Mama, do you know who this is?" she curtly replied, "Of course I do! I haven't lost it yet. That's Elsie."

Mama's eyes had turned dark, which was supposed to be another telltale sign of near death. We began discussing

final arrangements and preparations for Mama's passing. Sisters took turns coming home on weekends.

During her illness, she was easy to manage. She asked for nothing that couldn't be provided. She became the gentle mother we wished for during our growing up years, instead of the one who used a switch to make us mind, taught us proper manners, and proclaimed the Dos and don'ts of our everyday life.

Also, during this period of illness, Mama had constantly complained of one ailment or another. All we heard was, "I want to go to the hospital." If we explained once, we explained a hundred times, "You don't go to the hospital just because you want to go. The doctor has to make the decision unless it's an emergency situation, and then, we will call an ambulance."

A few months prior to what we thought was Mama's bout with death, she became ill and had to be admitted to the hospital. After several hours of tests and treatment in the emergency room, she was placed in a room overnight. The next morning she decided she was ready to go home. The young intern patted her on the arm and said, "Elizabeth, you can't go home. You have pneumonia." Every day of her four-week stay, she repeated, "Get the doctor so I can tell him I'm going home today." One sister looked her square in the eyes and said, "You are not going home until you are well and the doctor dismisses you."

During that four weeks, every nurse in the ward heard the family history again and again. Mama was a talker. The staff felt as though they knew all of the children personally. They had lots of patience with her and were delighted to see someone her age with such a terrific memory, but she was taking up most of their time.

Mama may have been weak in body, but she was strong in mind. She insisted on getting out of bed. At times it was difficult to handle her and my sisters' patience began to wear thin. One day she kept kicking off her blanket. The sister on duty would straighten her hospital gown, trying to cover her naked body. Then she pulled the blanket up over her body. She pulled it in at the sides of the bed. After much frustration, my sister finally said, "Mama, quit kicking the cover off. Everybody on this floor has seen your rear end!" Without hesitation, Mama smugly replied, "Well, the Bible says, 'All secrets shall be revealed in the end.'"

It was another trying day when Mama had tested everyone's patience. My sister was trying again without success to explain why she had to leave for a few days and go back home. She needed to take care of household chores, pay a few bills, and check on her husband's needs. After repeatedly listening to "Why do you have to go; why can't you stay a little longer?" my sister gritted her teeth and in an effort to come up with a satisfactory response, calmly said, "You know, Mama, the Bible says, 'A wife should cleave to her husband.'"

Totally unprepared for the response, she heard, "Yes! And the Bible also says, "Take care of the widows and orphans." That brought about uncontrollable laughter. My sister said, "Nobody can get ahead of you." A couple of days later, Mama was dismissed from the hospital. She had grown weak from her bout with pneumonia and could no longer walk without assistance. It had already been two months since we thought she was going through the dying stages. One weekend, another sister and I arrived home to find Mama sitting up in bed. Her eyes were no longer black and glassy; they had returned to their natural blue tint. Color had come back to her face and she was expressing hunger for food. Shortly after eating, she asked for something else to eat. She was on her regular diet of enjoying foods she had not been able to chew or swallow during her illness. A week later, she appeared to be gaining weight. Her face was full and she was back to her cranky self again, demanding attention—telltale signs she was definitely getting well.

Crossing the mountain on our way home to Tennessee that following Sunday, I turned to my sister and said, "Mama wasn't dying!" Bena Mae agreed, and I suppose, due to sheer exhaustion and relief, we began laughing. We decided the medication she was taking had contributed to her hallucinations.

It was pretty obvious to us, Mama would be with us a while longer. The Grim Reaper would have to wait. Even she commented that she had had repeated dreams of my oldest sister and my aunts coming for her, and she told them, "I'm not ready yet. I've got things to do." Heaven help the rest of us kids! What did she have to do that she couldn't have accomplished in 98 years, besides purposely driving us all crazy? She often asked me, "Why do you think the Lord has let me live this long?" To avoid getting into a discussion of death and dying and feeling sorry for herself, I would respond, "I guess, so that you can drive us kids crazy." She always smiled. She took my comments in good humor.

We sisters worked in pairs. While one sister sat at Mama's bedside, another worked diligently in the kitchen preparing meals. Mama wouldn't accept anything unless it was cooked by one of us girls. According to her, "Nobody else can cook fit to eat!"

On one occasion, I was being Florence Nightingale; giving Mama my undivided attention. I decided to make a meatloaf for her. She always said I could fix the best meatloaf in the family.

For whatever reason, the meatloaf did not turn out to my expectations. Since Mama's taste buds were not up to par, I figured she wouldn't notice the difference in the taste of the meatloaf. I filled her plate with cooked carrots, mashed potatoes, coleslaw, and cornbread baked in one of her seasoned iron skillets. A small portion of meatloaf was placed to one side of the plate. Mama was being served one of her favorite meals.

Sitting beside her bed, I watched while she fed herself from the bed tray. She slowly lifted the fork to her mouth, bite by bite. I intermittently wiped her chin with a napkin, making sure there were no spills. I talked to her as she ate. When she finished, she had cleaned her plate except for small bites of the meatloaf. I took the tray and said, "How did you like my meatloaf, Mama?"

Wiping a speck of food from the corner of her mouth, she took a deep breath, drew her mouth to one side in a smirky expression and answered, "Well, Pat! I'll put it this way, I wouldn't give out the recipe if I wuz you!" Mama was definitely getting better.

A call for an ambulance brought about another emergency run to the hospital. Being bedfast had required the use of a catheter, consequently creating a kidney infection. Hospital medication caused her to be somewhat difficult to control at first. That hospital stay lasted a week with her begging to go home daily. The weird thing about Mama was that she would beg to go to the hospital for no good reason. When she got there and was settled into a room, she was satisfied and ready to return home again. I stood beside her bed trying to explain why she couldn't go. "Mama, you have a serious kidney infection." I pointed to the tubes attached to her arm and continued, "IVs are necessary and you have to stay in the hospital until the infection is gone."

My mother gave me a long stern look, tightened her lips and responded, "You ol' hypocrite! You'll tell me anything." The lady in the adjoining bed rolled over laughing. Mama reached to remove the telephone from the side of her bed and began pushing buttons. I shuffled around to grab the phone and asked, "What are you doing?"

"I'm calling the police to come and get me. I'm going home." As I took the phone from her hand, she turned and stared at the television screen, and without hesitation, she said, "Isn't that John Wayne? He sure was a good man!"

It was conceivable to say that my mother was unquestionably planning to stay with us a good while longer. At the rate she was going, she would most likely survive all of her remaining children, namely: Six daughters and one son, who all decided to make a pact: "The last one living has to take Mama!" Mama lived to be 101-1/2—still entertaining us with her challenging sense of humor and amazing recollections of the past.

A WORLD'S FAIR

How long has it been since you heard someone mention a World's Fair? I can remember when I thought it would be the most exciting thing in my life if I could go to one. I was living near Knoxville, Tennessee, in 1982 when the fair was held there. The television coverage was so excessive and exposed so much about the fair that I had no desire to go and see it in person. Somehow the passion and excitement was gone, so I made no effort to take in the sites at the fair. Today, the big gold ball still hovers over the city of Knoxville.

IT WAS ANOTHER TIME, another generation. The year was 1904. The World's Fair was being held in St. Louis, Missouri. Everyone, no matter where they lived, had the desire to see the fair. Stories about the Chicago fair in 1893 created a feeling of longing and visions of what it must be like to just walk along the fairway at the World's Fair. How exciting that would be. News had spread that the exposition at St. Louis would top the events in Chicago and in Paris, France, in 1900.

Back in a small farm community in southwest Virginia, a little gray-haired lady was packing her tapestry bag for a long journey. She was taking the train all the way to St. Louis, Missouri. That sixty-four-year-old lady had never been more than a few miles from home in her life. She raised twenty children, twelve of her own and eight more children of a second husband. Her first husband had disappeared during the Civil War. She was left alone facing enemy soldiers when they ransacked her home, taking all her food and anything of material value. Now, she was living the September years of her life with one of her children on the same farm she had cultivated with her deceased husband. Her name was Sarah but everyone called her Sallie. Today, you can drive through the hills of southwest Virginia, and you might see a grassy sloping hillside called Sal's Ridge. It was part of the farm where my great-grandmother, Sallie, had spent her life.

The entire family was at the train station when the conductor yelled, "All aboard," and helped Grandma Brooks as she lifted her taffeta skirt and took the first step up to the passenger car on the train. She wore her mutton-sleeved jacket and Sunday hat and carried her tapestry bag at her side. The whistle blew and the train began chugging around the bend as the family all waved goodbye. Grandma's son, George, was a supervisor for the railroad company and had sent tickets for Grandma Brooks to come visit him in St. Louis. She was more elated than she had ever been in her life. Grandma's trip to visit her son would also be an adventure to the St. Louis World's Fair.

Nothing could be more exciting than the expectations of a World's Fair. No one in the entire surrounding counties of Virginia and Tennessee had ever experienced such an exciting event. The only thing that could top this for Grandma Brooks was to be able to meet the Queen of England, Queen Victoria, whom she happened to keep a picture of on her bedroom wall.

Brochure from the 1904 World's Fair, St. Louis, MO

Yes, Grandma Brooks finally arrived in St. Louis and her son, George, took her to the 1904 World's Fair. Shuffling along the thoroughfare at the expansive exposition was like nothing she had ever experienced before. People had arrived from European countries speaking foreign languages, none of which she could understand. She was enchanted with their unusual style of dress and the bright, colorful costumes worn by the performers and musical entertainers. Folks in southwest Virginia had never heard of John Philip Sousa, the young and upcoming composer and bandleader, who was a featured attraction at the World's Fair. His musical composition, "Stars and Stripes Forever" would someday be played by nearly every marching band in the country.

The Colombian Exposition had again presented the Ferris Wheel which was first erected at the Chicago World's Fair in 1893. It carried nearly 2,000,000 people at the Chicago Fair. The Ferris Wheel was 264 feet high, and had 36 cars with a capacity of 60 persons per car. Two revolutions which took from 20 to 30 minutes were allowed each passenger. As the mighty wheel rolled each car higher and higher, a grand panoramic view unfolded with an expanse of nearly

50 miles. From there, one could get a far better view of the illuminated grounds with the lagoons, the gondolas, the Pike, and all the movement of happy throngs reflected from the lights. Eye had not seen nor ear heard of a more striking spectacle than the night view of the grand St. Louis Exposition from the top of the Ferris Wheel. It was reported that what could be seen from the Ferris Wheel was worth a trip across the continent. Such a sight was never seen before, and visitors to the Fair would treasure their memories for the rest of their lives.

Grandma Brooks returned home to her family who were anxiously waiting for her at the train station. Her visit to St. Louis was an experience she would relish and share with her grandchildren for months and years to come. She had been to the 1904 St. Louis World's Fair.

YOU CAN READ IT IN THE NEWSPAPER

J ust one of those Mondays when I start pulling out old stuff and sorting through it. This time, it was family history files. And, by chance, I ran across files with newspaper clippings, very interesting articles in my opinion. I found it very entertaining. Just goes to show what they used to print in the news. Everybody learned what went on behind closed doors.

This is in relation to my ancestors, namely Harold Hayes married to Mary Estep.

Articles from the Wilkesboro Chronicle, NC. March 11, 1891: An Aggravating State of Affairs.

"Esquire Harold Hayes of the Brushy Mountain, came in last week and discontinued his paper because of the fact he could never get it until it was a week or ten days old, and that it was ten days old, and generally worn out by someone to [sic] mean and stingy to subscribe to their own county paper. Mr. Hayes would like to take his county paper, but he can't get it on time and in a reasonable condition. Many others came to us with the same complaint, and stopped the paper. We don't blame a man for not taking the paper when he can't get it. Now there is something wrong somewhere. It must be principally with the postmasters and we want a word with them. We send our paper wrapped in bundles to the different offices. The post masters open the bundles, but they have no right to take a paper from the office or read it, and every time they do so they are laying themselves liable to the law, and stealing from the publisher besides. They have no right to give out mail except to the party addressed unless authorized by that party. If the postmasters will properly attend their lawful duties the complaints about the paper not coming regularly and being worn out will all hush. And we propose they shall attend their business, or we will know the reason. Let the postmasters and everybody else who wants to read the Chronicle subscribe and pay for it. If you don't wish to subscribe you needn't do so, but don't steal from the publisher and his supporters by reading their papers. Those who pretend to be citizens and will steal from the publisher and try to rob him of the support of those upon whom he depends for a living, are too contemptible for expression."

March 25, 1891 A Second Article:

"A letter just received from Mr. Oliver Hendren, PM (postmaster) at the Brushy Mountain, one of the best and most honorable citizens of the county, stating he strictly attends to the mail matter at his office and that no delays as those complained of in the former article occurs there. He says that the impressions left by the remarks of Esquire Harold Hayes concerning his paper are entirely at fault and do him an injustice. He says Hayes always got his paper on time when he came after it and that since the election Hayes has not called for his paper regularly from the fact that he didn't want to read Democratic newspapers. He says the reason he didn't get the paper was because he didn't come after it, that the reason he quit the paper was because he turned Republican at the last election.

Esquire Hayes was appointed Justice of the Peace in Wilkes County about 1860... His education was self-taught. Harold Hayes boasted of his record as Justice of the Peace for more than 50 years..."

THE HOUSE IS ON FIRE

This is a story my mother used to tell me. She would get so tickled she had to hold her hand over her mouth to keep from spewing snuff while she talked. It was back in the days when Daddy had bought his first car, a 1923 Chevrolet. You didn't see many cars during those times and the only roads were those cut out for horse and buggy. It was a rough ride trying to follow the ruts in the roads in a car.

Mama and Daddy had spent the day visiting some of her family in Middlesboro and it was starting to get dark when they decided to run by Daddy's sister's house. His sister, Cora, and her husband lived on a farm. Of course, there were no phones to let his sister know they were coming. People didn't give advance notice when they came to visit; they just showed up! If a meal had to be prepared, they went out to the chicken lot and chose a plump hen or chicken and with a bowl of gravy, mashed potatoes which were always handy, and a pan of biscuits, dinner was on the table.

Those were the days when farmers went to bed with the chickens, as soon as it got dark, because they had to be up at early daybreak, eat a big breakfast, and get ready to feed the animals and work the gardens.

Aunt Cora and Uncle Harve were already bedded down for the night with the kids sleeping in another bedroom. Daddy's car went rumbling down the hill, chugging right along with its headlights aimed towards the house and directly at Aunt Cora's bedroom window. The window shades were up and the rumble of the car woke Cora and Harve. They were in such a stupor when they saw the bright light coming through the bedroom window they raised straight up from the bed.

You never saw such confusion and rambling in your life as when Aunt Cora, a right pudgy little woman, jumped out of bed in her nightgown and began yelling at Harve, "Get up, wake the kids, get them outta' bed. The house is on fire!" Harve began rambling around and shuffling in the dark room trying to find his clothes. Where were his trousers? He couldn't find his shirt! Cora had laid her dress and Harve's britches and long-sleeved shirt across the old rocking chair overnight. They finally grabbed the clothes, and rushing to get them on in the dark, ran through the house bellering, "You kids get up. The house is on fire. Get outta' the house as fast as you can."

Meantime, Daddy drove up beside the house with the headlights now facing the front door. He and Mama climbed out of the car, and about that time, the front door of the house flew open and bodies came pourin' out on the porch. Mama and Daddy didn't know what to make of such yellin' and the commotion that went on. Then they saw Aunt Cora and Uncle Harve leap off the high wooden porch. They didn't even take time to go down the steps. A handful of kids dressed in their night shirts, screamin' and hollerin' were right behind them. The family hit the dirt running! The kids were going in circles, not knowing what to do.

Mama and Daddy stood there staring at the commotion and suddenly, Cora and Harve stopped running. They saw my parents. At the same time, they both suddenly realized the house wasn't on fire. What they saw through the bedroom window was the headlights of Daddy's car.

Mama and Daddy began laughing. They were laughing so hard, my aunt and uncle couldn't understand what was so funny until they looked down at themselves. Short, pudgy Cora stood there in the bright light wearing Harve's long plaid workshirt that fell below her knees and sleeves that came down over her hands. Harve had on Cora's dress with his long legs and nubby knees showing beneath the hem of the dress. All of a sudden, everybody was laughing so hard they could hardly control themselves. That was the first time Cora and Harve had ever seen a car.

UNCLE JOHN

It's hard for me to believe I had an uncle who, if living today, would be 148 years old. Uncle John was the firstborn of 11 children and 26 years older than my dad, Hobert, who was the youngest brother.

My Grandpa, Sam, died when my dad was 13. That's when Uncle John became the father figure to my dad. John was an intelligent and ambitious young farmer, living in Frog Level, Virginia. He raised fruits and vegetables and hauled them to Cumberland Gap each week to be sold at an open produce market. Many times my dad joined John on the fifteen-mile journey across the mountain. It took a full day to get there by wagon. They would travel one day, sell their produce the next, and return to Frog Level, near Ewing, Virginia, on the third day.

The Gap was located 2,400 feet below the Pinnacle where Daniel Boone first blazed a trail. Cumberland Gap was a thriving community, growing by leaps and bounds. Families were moving into the town daily. Iron ore was melted at the Iron Furnace located near flowing springs at the foot of the Pinnacle. John and my dad often hauled wagonloads of scrap iron from Ewing to the Iron Furnace.

Cumberland Gap was also a railroad center. The railroad station was near a tunnel built in 1891 that connected the Gap to Middlesboro, Kentucky. In the late 1800's, the valley surrounding Cumberland Gap was known for its mineral waters. An establishment called The Four Seasons Hotel was built near the site where Lincoln Memorial University now stands. On April 12, 1892, the hotel opened for business with a magnificent ball and reception. The owners believed the mineral waters would attract wealthy and notable guests like the Duke of Cumberland and others from around the world. They would come to the area for the water's healing powers. It was a large hotel, built in grandeur style and elegantly decorated with the finest quality furniture. Beautiful chandeliers, sterling silver tableware and the finest quality china were imported from foreign countries. Nearly 125 servants were hired to accommodate the celebrated guests.

Four Seasons Hotel, Harrogate, TN, the largest hotel in the US. 1892

At first, the hotel housed numerous foreign dignitaries, counts, and lords, but as time passed, there were occasions when the servants outnumbered the guests. The hotel soon had to close its doors to the public. It had cost $700,000 to build and sold in 1895 for $28,000. The furnishings were sold for $20,000 and the Chicago Wrecking and Salvage Company bought and disassembled the building and shipped it away.

Shortly after the turn of the century, Uncle John moved his family to the Gap. He had a job working in the rock quarry and at the Iron Furnace which was the Gap's major industry. John and his wife, Minerva, also operated the only hotel in the small community. The hotel provided meals at the cost of thirty-five cents.

John was eager to give his children a good education. They first attended a two-room school called Harrow Hall. Each child had to provide his own sitting bench and desk. After the school building burned, the children went to school at the Congregational Church. They later attended Lincoln Memorial University, which accommodated both high school and college students. The children walked the two miles to school every day.

Cumberland Gap was shaded by the Pinnacle and did not see sunshine until nearly noon each day. By the early 1900's, the small community of the Gap had built four hotels, a bank, two wagon shops, two drug stores, a shoe store, and a millinery shop. Ladies purchased hats at the millinery shop and chose accessories and trims to ornament and individualize the hats. There were two department stores, a weekly newspaper, and several other small businesses.

John's family was the first in the Gap to own a washing machine. The local doctor purchased the first automobile. John's first automobile was a Maxwell. Uncle John's oldest son, Carl, pulled his wagon to the depot near the railroad tunnel each day when the train arrived. He would haul the salesmen's (called drummers) baggage to the hotel, earning five-cents for each trip. When another son later built his home in Cumberland Gap, it was located in the roadbed of the Wilderness Road going up the Gap to Middlesboro, Kentucky. A hundred years later, members of John Estep's family would continue to reside in the small community of Cumberland Gap, Tennessee.

My uncle died two months short of his 100th birthday. He was a sweet old man. I remember when he would board the Greyhound Bus in Middlesboro and come to visit my family for a week or two each summer. Daddy was usually working somewhere in another town or state, but that didn't matter: Uncle John enjoyed my mother's company while Daddy was gone. I can recall thinking how much he looked like Santa Claus with his silvery wavy hair and wire-rimmed glasses lowered across his nose. He loved telling us kids stories of his childhood and then he would laugh with his round belly shaking, just like Santa Claus. We didn't visit my uncle and aunt very often in the old days because the fifty-mile drive around Booger Mountain was a long trip and there was little time for visiting relatives.

When I drive through Cumberland Gap today, my uncle's house still stands beside the little post office and across the street from what used to be Estep's Grocery. The house was last lived in by my uncle's granddaughter. She died recently and the last I heard, the house was for sale. My cousin took me through the house a few years ago and everywhere I looked, I saw the beautiful old furniture and accessories that once belonged to Uncle John and Aunt Minerva. I hope whoever may have bought the house will treat it with the love and care that it deserves.

My Uncle John created more than a hundred years of history for the small town of Cumberland Gap, Tennessee. His son, James Dallard, who was only five years younger than my dad, retired as mayor at the age of 97, the second oldest mayor in the United States. John's daughter, Nola, who had lived her entire life there, had written the accounts of her life growing up in the Gap. She entered a nursing home at the age of 100. Nola told many stories about her life.

Looking out the kitchen window of their house, they could look straight up to the top of the mountain and see the Pinnacle. Nola would tell about the many times she and her friends began their climb up the mountain early in the morning to what was then known as Soldiers Cave, a deep cavern used to hide soldiers during the Civil

War. Nola and her friends would crawl through the cave on their bellies and before long, it was time to make the descent back down the mountain toward home. She had to be home in time for supper.

This family created the history of Cumberland Gap, Tennessee for more than 100 years, beginning 1904 until the death of Ann Estep, about three years ago. Ann never married and was known as Miss Ann, a lady who taught elementary school children until her retirement. She lived with her parents, and died in the old home place which was first owned by her grandfather.

I remember my uncle John with pleasure. His stories have stayed with me all these years. I look across the room and there sits a small cane-bottomed handmade chair that was given to me by my mother. Uncle John had carried it on the bus from Middlesboro to Corbin to give to Mama. He told her it was one of the first things he and Minerva had when they started housekeeping in the late 1890s. He loved my mother as much as he did his youngest brother. Mama was very kind to him in his old age. He hungered for attention and someone to talk to as his years declined. His eyes would sparkle when he threw himself into one of his childhood stories, easily drawing the attention of my sister, Wanda, my brother, Don, and me like a magnet. Every kid should have an Uncle John!

THE DEPRESSION YEARS

Dryland Bridge

The years of the great Depression lasted from the early 1930s until 1942. The whole country was out of work. The economy had reached rock bottom and nobody could find a job anywhere. Franklin D. Roosevelt was president then so he developed a program called the Civil Conservation Corps, (CCC) and another, the Works Project Association (WPA). State parks would be built, bridges, highways, schools and court houses.

Young single men between the ages of 18 and 26 would be hired. They didn't need experience. They would learn as they worked. Lodging would be provided and they would earn a dollar a day. Now, if your math is good, you know that amounts to about $30 a month and $25 of that was to be sent back home to their families.

My Dad had been hired to supervise the construction of a bridge in a state park. He was an experienced bridge builder because he had worked for the L&N Railroad in his early days, building railroad bridges. He was an orphan and only 15 when he started working for the railroad. He had lied about his age in order to get the job.

Everyone today crossing the new bridge leading into the park can see hundreds of acres of forest. You will be standing on what is called Dryland Bridge.

Dupont Lodge, Cumberland Falls State Park, 1930s

When the construction of Dryland Bridge was completed, my dad began work on his next project—Dupont Lodge. The lodge was named for T. Coleman Dupont, a man whose wife purchased the waterfall that provided one of only two moonbows in the world – it and Victoria Falls in Africa. Nearly 600 acres of forest were also purchased after her husband died. The acreage was given to the state of Kentucky to build a state park.

Small cabins were being built in the wooded area around the lodge. Some say there were 15 cabins, but my mother said there were eight, so I'm going to tell her version of the story! As you know, every story has at least three versions—the right—the wrong—and My Version!

Each cabin had two windows and she was hired to make 16 pairs of draperies for the windows. She was paid $7. Seven dollars went a long way during the Depression. It bought a lot of milk, bread and eggs for a family with eight hungry kids to feed. And I believe that was about the time I came along.

Land had been cleared and Dupont Lodge was midway through construction when one of the local businessmen in town approached my dad and said his daughter was getting married soon and he wanted to have her wedding reception in the new lodge.

Well, of course, only part of the lodge was completed; the entrance and lobby were finished, and the large room to the right, with its high ceilings. That room was built with a beautiful stone fireplace, knotty pine walls and huge wagon-wheel light fixtures hanging from the ceiling. According to my mother it was a sight to behold.

I remember Mama describing how big the room was and when I see it today, it doesn't seem very large, but for that time period, it was! There was nothing in the area to compare to the new lodge. On a lower level, a huge restaurant dining room was added, now known as the Riverview Restaurant. The view over the forest and river was spectacular.

Daddy went to the city officials in charge of the project and asked if they would permit this family to hold a wedding reception at the lodge. They gave it much consideration and then said yes! It would be good for the city of Corbin and they couldn't turn down the first request for the use of the lodge.

All of the businessmen, their wives, and the Corbin dignitaries were invited to the wedding reception. My parents were also invited. This was bound to be the biggest affair my mother had ever attended. Actually, that was true for the other people who had been invited. Mama wore her best Sunday dress, her gloves, and her summer hat. Daddy, I'm sure, looked quite handsome in his well-worn Blue Serge suit and brown shoes. Mama polished his shoes every week with a fresh coat of Shinola. My parents looked quite handsome as they entered the lodge that sunny afternoon.

The large room was already filling up with guests and Mama didn't recognize the majority of them. The local dignitaries and their wives were milling around through the crowd. I remember Mama telling me, "I never saw so many strange people. They all talked funny." Everybody we knew had been born and raised in the Appalachian area and they all talked alike. These people were family and friends who had arrived from northern states.

This is the way my mother told the story to me. She said, "I never saw anything like it in my life. Long tables were lined around three walls of the room and all of them were covered in white linen and lace tablecloths." She went on to say, "There were waiters wearing black, short jackets and carrying little white towels over their arms. Each of the waiters carried their arms full of silverware and placed it on the tables then others brought in big silver trays, and bowls." All were piled high with fancy finger foods she'd never seen before. Her eyes were about to bug out of her head. "Big silver pitchers of water were on the table with crystal water glasses lined up beside."

Don't forget —it was the middle of the Great Depression! There were no days of "Wine and Roses" or ballroom dancing! We were Kentucky folks, raised in the hills and on farms; coal miners and railroad employees; families doing their best just to survive during hard times.

Mama said as she continued looking all around the room, most of those out 'a town people appeared to be quite well-to-do. The ladies were dressed in finery like she'd never seen before. Their clothes sure didn't come from the Sears-Roebuck catalog!

Mama's mouth fell open when she noticed a huge barrel in one corner of the room, filled with ice chips and on top of the ice was a big pile of shrimp. I don't know how she knew it was shrimp because my mother had never seen shrimp in her life. She was raised on a farm in the hills of Virginia and Tennessee, and the only fish they caught in the creeks and rivers was catfish and crawfish. They didn't know what shrimp looked like.

Big washtubs, also filled with ice, were scattered around the room.

The ice was probably brought from the ice plant on south Main Street in Corbin. Bottles of pop were embedded in the ice—Coca Cola bottles, big orange drinks, and one tub filled with 7-Ups.

While Daddy talked to the businessmen, Mama noticed some of them appeared to be getting a bit tipsy. There were no alcoholic drinks being served. Those were days of prohibition, and Corbin was definitely a dry county.

She picked up a couple of plates—real china, mind you! They didn't have paper plates in those days. Daddy came over and joined her, taking his plate as they chose several items from the beautiful serving dishes. Mama didn't recognize most of the finger foods, but she was willing to try everything on the tables. At our house, finger foods were biscuits filled with butter and jelly, a fried chicken leg, or anything you could pick up with your fingers.

Daddy took a couple of 7-Up bottles from a tub and suggested they go outside and eat on the steps at the entrance of the lodge. The room was getting overcrowded and it was quite warm that day. They could sit on the steps in the shade of the tall trees where it was cool.

No one was there except them. Daddy opened the 7-Ups then handed one to Mama. She was right thirsty so she turned the bottle up to her mouth, took a big swig of the drink and immediately spewed it clear across the front steps. Her face wrinkled and she blurted out, "This ain't 7-Up!" Daddy reached for his bottle and turned it up to take a sip then he burst out laughing. "Lizzie, I believe this is Champagne."

"Sooooo, that was why the men were getting tipsy!"

It wasn't water or 7-Up in those fancy water glasses they were holding! The champagne had been poured into 7-Up bottles and brought in by family members of the bridal party.

Well, there was one barrel of whiskey that didn't get busted and poured into the streets of Chicago by Elliot Ness! We had bootleggers running moonshine stills throughout the hills of Kentucky, but this champagne certainly didn't come from one of their stills.

Mama loved telling me the story—a day she would always

remember. She had attended the first wedding reception, one of the biggest affairs of the century ever held at Dupont Lodge in Cumberland Falls State Park. It was the talk of the town!

HOME AWAY FROM HOME

The WPA job had taken Daddy to Manchester in Clay County, Kentucky. He was building a court house. Our living quarters were located diagonally across the street from the construction site in a house built like a duplex. It was an old two-story dwelling in dire need of paint, but it was also the Depression years when there was no money even for food, much less painting a house. Nobody had the money for such things as upgrading an old house, especially since it was a rental house. The roofline of the porch held gingerbread trim and a small picket fence surrounded the front yard. A pretty patch of flowers were planted in the corner of the yard next to the sidewalk. We lived in one side of the duplex and the local jailer and his wife lived in the other side with their 'good for nothin' son. The jailer's wife did all the cooking for the inmates at the jail across the street. Three times a day, she and a couple of other women carried a big washtub filled with plates of food to the jail to feed the prisoners. The jailer would get drunk on moonshine whiskey and sometimes sit in a rocking chair in their living room with his shotgun across his lap, waiting for his wife to come home. His wife would be hiding out at our house, scared her husband would shoot her. We already had bullet holes spattered across our front door where someone had shot through the door. The bullet holes were there when we moved into the house and we never learned who put them there! That seemed to be life as usual in the hills of Clay County, Kentucky.

No matter what went on around the house, at least one person was in charge of the upkeep of my three and a half year old sister, Wanda. She never listened to Mama's instructions and a switching of her legs meant nothing to her. She would cry a little while and then turn right back to whatever mischief caught her interest.

Our drinking water came from a well behind the house and Mama spent most of her time chasing my older sister, trying to keep her away from the well. She had already caught Wanda sitting on the side of the well one day, dangling her feet. Mama thought she was going to pass out before she could reach the kid and pull her down off the fifty-foot deep well. Things like this were just daily occurrences for my sister. It took everybody in the house to keep tabs on the unpredictable, small-minded kid that never seemed to stop gambling with her life. She didn't realize how close she was coming to being left on a stranger's doorstep—in another county!

It wasn't the first time Wanda had slipped out of the house and wandered up and down the busy street, but that day, Mama went in search of my sister and she couldn't be found anywhere in the house or the back yard—another situation where Daddy had to be called home from the job to help search for her. There was always the danger of big trucks hauling coal and barreling down the hill. After all, it was coal country and the mines were still in operation even if we were in the middle of a depression.

My sisters, Janette and Bena Mae, ages eight and ten, headed one direction, Mama, with me on her hip, started up the hill, and along came Daddy, looking quite frustrated because he had been called off the job to hunt a little three-year-old who had wandered away from the house. Even the neighbors were alerted to the disappearance of my sister and they were out looking as well.

Finally, the call went out that Wanda had been found dilly-dallying along the sidewalk without a care in the world, picking the neighbors' flowers. Daddy took her by the hand and led her back to the house. She knew she was in trouble. She didn't need to be told; she could tell by the expression on Daddy's face as she skipped down the sidewalk. Just as they reached the gate to the picket fence, Wanda broke loose from Daddy's hand and made a mad dash into the house. There was only one place she could go to hide and that was under the old iron bed with open springs. She crawled up under the middle of the bed and lay quiet as a church mouse, hoping she wouldn't be found and everybody would forget about her running off from home.

Daddy followed her straight to the bedroom, bent down on his knees and sliding the switch back and forth on the floor, said, "Come out from under there little girl." When he reached under the side of the bed for her, she scooted to the back of the bed where Daddy couldn't get to her. He wasn't going to be outdone by a three year old so he pulled the bed out and got down on his knees again and reached for her from the backside. That didn't work either. Wanda scooted to the front side of the bed again.

Daddy's size prevented him from being able to crawl under the bed so he went to the foot of the bed and said, "I'll get you this time," and lifted the bed off the floor. He looked up under the bed and didn't see her on the floor. As gruff as my Daddy could be at times, when he saw Wanda had attached her small hands and feet to the open springs and was moving with the bed, he got so tickled he lowered the bed and said, "I'll get you when you come out from under there young lady. You can't stay there forever!" He didn't have time to play games; he had to get back to his construction job across the street.

Wanda stayed on the cool floor under the bed until she thought Daddy was gone and it was safe to come out.

It was another day when things were a little too quiet. Wanda had managed to slip out of the house again. Everybody was rounded up for the search. Again, Daddy was called home from his job to join Mama and my sisters as they went in pursuit of Wanda. Where could she be this time? About thirty minutes later, she was spotted walking on a sidewalk. Someone had heard a clickety-clack noise and followed the sound. My sister had a long stick and was sliding it along a picket fence. Clickety-clack, clickety-clack! She saw Daddy coming and immediately ran across the road just as a coal truck came rumbling down the hill. The truck couldn't stop and came within a matter of inches of hitting Wanda.

Daddy didn't threaten her with the switch that time because of the dreadful fright of almost seeing his child run down by the coal truck. They walked hand in hand quietly back up the street. As soon as they reached the gate, Wanda again pulled away and ran lickety-split through the house and back under the old iron bed. Daddy followed her into the bedroom and bent down and said, "Come on out young lady." She said, "I will if you'll give me a nickel."

Courthouse, Manchester, Ky. 1938

Daddy had finished the construction of the court house in Manchester, Kentucky, and his next job was building another court house in nearby Stanton. Just another move for Mama and us kids. During the Depression years, he worked wherever there was a job to be done by the Works Project Association. Mama and all of us kids followed him and found a rental house to live in so that Daddy didn't have to drive back and forth home every weekend.

By this time, Mama was pregnant again; just a normal occurrence in our household. She had just lost another blue baby in 1938. The baby died shortly after Grandma Rowlett passed away from cancer. Those were the days when we never heard the word 'cancer'. We didn't know such a condition existed. Mama was just a few weeks from delivery and the doctor advised her not to travel, so she didn't get to attend her own mother's funeral.

I can't describe the house we lived in at Stanton because I was too young to recall. I just know the incident that took place was when my older brother was working in a tin shop at Covington, Kentucky.

The war hadn't started yet. I remember Mama telling me about the weekend my brother, Bug (nickname), had hitchhiked to Stanton from Covington to see our new temporary home. Mama didn't know he was coming so she hadn't given him directions for finding our house. Stanton was a small town and the house Daddy had rented was within city limits, so Bug just started walking up and down the main streets hoping to find the house. It was dusky dark and he did not have any idea which direction to go, but as he walked, he suddenly came to a house and knew he was at the right place. A lamp was burning in the window and when he looked up, he recognized the lace paneled curtains hanging in the living room window. He knew those curtains; they were the same ones that had always hung over the bedroom windows at home.

It was Sunday afternoon. My family, as well as the neighbors, were enjoying the beautiful summer day. They sat in the shade of a huge tree in the front yard, drinking Mama's delicious lemonade and taking in the cool breeze. Mama usually had to do a head count to make sure all of us kids were there. As a rule, we were all good about sticking close to home and she didn't have to worry about what we were doing.

Uh, oh! Things appeared too pleasant and calm. Something had to be wrong with this scene. And something it was! Wanda was missing! Where could she possibly be? Everyone scattered. Time again for the chase! Even the neighbors were on hand to help out. No one had seen her leave the yard. They headed different directions up and down the street. She was nowhere to be seen. Mama was beginning to panic. Mama had lots of reasons to panic!

There was a small field next door where the city's water tower stood. Bug walked toward the field and just happened to look up, and to his amazement, there was Wanda, hanging onto a wooden beam of the water tower. It's a wonder Mama didn't have that baby right then and there. Mama never questioned how the child managed to climb up the water tower. In fact, she never questioned anything Wanda did. Keeping track of the child was a full time job. Bug ran to the water tower and proceeded to climb up the beams below the big tank and bring my sister down. Was she scared? Of course Not! What was everybody so excited about?

GRANDPA'S LAZY SUSAN TABLE

I wish I had stories to tell about my grandmothers, but, I never had a grandmother to tell me about her childhood days, or to teach me her old-fashioned kitchen skills. My paternal grandmother died when my dad was eighteen months old and my grandfather died when my dad was thirteen. My maternal grandmother, Grandma Rowlett, died when I was a baby. From the stories I have been told, I truly wish I could have known her. I did, however, have a mother who repeated the old time stories and who also had gained enough kitchen experience to pass on her skills to all of her seven daughters.

   This story is about one of the family's Sunday ventures to Middlesboro, Kentucky, to visit aunts, uncles and lots of cousins. It was 1941, a few weeks before Thanksgiving and prior to the bombing of Pearl Harbor. Daddy drove the fifty-mile journey across Booger Mountain where the road twisted and turned until you could see the tail end of your car coming around the next bend. Coney Island had its roller coaster. We had our Booger Mountain! I, of course, always got car sick before we were twenty miles into the trip. I got to sit by the window in the front seat of the car where I could get plenty of air. My sister and brother, of course, sat in the backseat squawking and complaining that I was freezing them to death with the car window wide open. "Daddy, stop the car. I'm gonna throw up!"

You don't tell a five-year-old, "Can't you wait'll we get there?" when she's holding her hand to her mouth with a brown paper grocery bag under her chin. I carried the washrag, the crackers, and every remedy from the old wives' tales, in my lap. The two lane road had hairpin curves all the way with absolutely no place to pull off for emergencies. There was a mountain on one side of the road and the river a hundred feet below on the other side.

I remember thinking I was going to die of motion sickness when we would finally reach the end of the road and pull up in front of the small white frame house with a long front porch. A creek ran alongside the house and a big barn stood a short distance away in the back yard. This was where my Uncle Paris and Aunt Bertha lived. Uncle Paris was Mama's younger brother. His wife, Bertha, was one of the sweetest aunts a kid could have. She was quiet and soft-spoken and always smiling. The place was already bouncing with kids. Mama headed straight to the kitchen where Aunt Bertha, Cousin Gladys, and my Aunt Renie were busy preparing Sunday dinner. They had been given advanced notice that we were coming. Daddy joined Grandpa Rowlett, Uncle Paris, and Uncle Lon in the front yard where it was shady.

It was a small house and I've sometimes wondered where all the kids slept at night. I could easily say the same thing about my own family dwelling since we only had three bedrooms and a drove of kids to bed down at night. Grandpa Rowlett's bed sat in the parlor. It was common practice to have a bed in the parlor in those days. I remember following Mama through the parlor and dining room and on into the kitchen. My memory sometimes fails me when trying to recall childhood events, but I believe there was a fireplace with a large oak mantle in one of the rooms.

Going to visit my aunt and uncle was such a treat after the older siblings had married and moved out of the house. It was like being in the country. I loved playing in their big barn behind the house and climbing the ladder to the hayloft. We didn't have anything like that at home. Their hayloft was like a secret hiding place where you weren't disturbed by the grownups. We could laugh and talk while listening to the rippling water from the creek beside the barn.

Aunt Bertha raised chickens in a lot behind the house. When company came, she had her pick of stewing hens and chickens to fry. Mama and other aunts contributed their dishes to the Sunday dinner as well. The smell of fresh green beans cooking and the bread baking in the oven made your stomach begin to roll from hunger. Of course, there would be mashed potatoes, gravy, and dumplings; they were part of every big dinner.

It wouldn't be long until we all gathered around the big oak table in the dining room. There was room for everybody. Grandpa Rowlett sat at the head of the table in a black wrought iron chair that sat above the other chairs. His feet barely touched the floor. I was afraid of Grandpa. I was very shy and at the age of five, I hadn't been around him enough to get to know the man.

Everybody knows the term 'lazy susan' but have you ever seen a real Lazy Susan table? In my lifetime I have seen only two, and the first one was the big round oak table in my Uncle Paris's dining room. The second was in a museum at Norris Dam State Park in Tennessee.

From where I sat, I could see the large round Lazy Susan that had been built in the center of the table and sat up six or eight inches above the main table. The Lazy Susan was big enough to hold all of the vegetable dishes and the chicken platter. I could barely see to the top of the flat round surface. Grandpa was the first to serve himself and then he turned the Lazy Susan to the left where he could take a helping from the next vegetable dish. I watched Grandpa take a drink from his glass which left a white film on his handlebar mustache. Mama said he always drank buttermilk with his meals.

Each person at the table took servings from the dishes as the Lazy Susan slowly moved around. I couldn't reach the food so Mama filled my plate for me. I was in awe as I watched the Lazy Susan slowly turn until it had made a complete circle. I could hear a strange grinding noise from inside the table. I couldn't understand why it was making the almost haunting-like sounds.

After dinner, all of the kids headed outside to play. The women ambled back to the kitchen to wash dishes and talk. Grandpa Rowlett was seated in the parlor and as I scampered through the room, he called me over to his chair where he took me on his lap and gave me a hug. I was quite uncomfortable with this beady-eyed elderly man and his handlebar mustache. I was too young to remember him from previous visits to Middlesboro. He talked to me for a couple of minutes and seeing my discomfort, he took me off his knee and told me to go outside and play with the other children.

That Sunday afternoon is the only recollection I have of my Grandpa Rowlett. My grandfather died shortly thereafter on Valentine's Day, 1942. The only experience I ever had with a grandparent was that one day, sitting on Grandpa Rowlett's knee. He was the only grandparent I ever knew. Mama often talked about Grandma Rowlett and you could feel the warmth of her love being communicated through her words. I believe it when she and my Aunt Renie, at different times, both said, "If there is an angel in Heaven, it is your Grandma Rowlett."

I never forgot the unique dining room table that sat in my aunt and uncle's house. When I was older, my mother and I were talking about that visit to Middlesboro in 1941. She told me that Grandpa Rowlett built the oak Lazy Susan table. He was quite the craftsman. The strange grinding noise I remembered hearing while we ate our dinner was created by a huge bolt in the center of the table that made the Lazy Susan rotate. Oh, how I loved that table and the memories of sitting with my grandfather, aunts and uncles who have now been gone many years! Sometimes, when I think about it, I can almost smell the fried chicken, biscuits and gravy that were served that day and wish I could sit at that table one more time. I never saw Grandpa's lazy susan table again.

"MAMA, TELL ME ABOUT THE WAR"

The Civil War was a hundred years behind us and none of us kids were interested in digging up old roots about our ancestors—none, except me! "Mama, tell me about Great-grandma Brooks in the Civil War," I would ask. It pleased my mother that I would show interest in her family background. All she needed was a nudge and she was into tales about our family history. Grandma Brooks was her maternal grandmother. She was Sarah "Sallie" Campbell when she married Enoch Carmack, the youngest of 13 siblings. Abraham was their first child. They called him "Abram." In 1862 when Abram was two, Sallie gave birth to a baby girl and named her Amanda. Amanda was my grandmother.

The war had already started and my Great-grandpa, Enoch, had been taken away from their home in the Virginia mountains and became a member of the Tennessee Cavalry. Great-grandma Brooks, then still married to Enoch Carmack, was left alone to run the farm with a two year old and a newborn baby. She didn't know where her husband had been taken or if he would ever return.

Both Union and Confederate soldiers tramped across farmland taking anything and everything of worth, including all available food products. From day to day, Sallie, as she was then called, constantly watched and worried that the soldiers would come. One day they appeared at her door and began ransacking the little log cabin. They soon discovered there wasn't anything of value to be found. The Carmacks were a poor farm family.

Sallie stood aside with Abram and Amanda twisting her skirttail and trembling in fear. Amanda was a toddler by this time. A cellar lay beneath the floorboards of the cabin with a trap door hidden under a large handmade braided rug. All of Grandma's canned goods and winter turnips, potatoes, and onions were stored in the cellar. Amanda's handmade doll cradle was also used to hide small hams. They were covered with the child's doll blankets and then her rag doll was laid on top of the cradle. The soldiers never touched any of the children's playthings. A young soldier had given up his search when he lifted the lid to a wooden meat box and pulled out a large piece of bacon, the last of the family's meat supply. He started for the door and Sallie lifted her fists to her hips and turned to the young soldier and said, "Go ahead! Take it, and I pray that every night when you go to sleep, you hear the cries of these hungry children and they lead you straight into hell." The soldier turned and lifted the lid to the meat box and carefully put the bacon back in its place then turned and walked out the door.

My Great-Grandpa Carmack never returned from the war. Believing he was dead, Grandma Carmack remarried. That's when her name became Brooks. She married John H. Brooks, a widower with eight children. Together they had ten more children, raising a total of 20 in one household.

My mother could get caught up in her storytelling when she had an audience, and I was her audience. She said that Pap, also my grandfather Floyd Rowlett, was a young boy during the Civil War. The farm, where he was raised the oldest of 13 siblings, was large. His uncles helped work the farm after his father, Luther, joined the Confederacy. Luther's brother, Jesse Ben, had already pledged his allegiance to the Confederacy as well. It wasn't easy deciding which side of the war to serve but Luther made his choice one day when a Union Colonel and his troop rode up to Jesse Ben's blacksmith shop and ordered all of the horses to be shoed while the soldiers waited. Luther didn't like the attitude of the Union colonel so he announced to his brother that he was joining the Confederacy. The territory where they lived was much divided between the north and the south, even among family members.

Young Floyd was sent out to the entrance to the farm at early daybreak each morning to watch for soldiers coming up the hills and across the farm. It didn't matter which uniform they wore because to farmers, both sides were the enemy. They raided the farms and often killed the men working in the fields. The uncle would set the boy up on the stone gatepost where he could see far out over the fields. The child sat there waiting, hour after hour, and when he saw signs of life coming up the hills he jumped down from the stone post and ran, yelling "the soldiers are coming, the soldiers are coming," and the men would escape to the woods. His uncle Jesse Ben was later killed at the battle of Gettysburg.

Mama enjoyed telling me the old family stories partly because I was the only one willing to listen. She would describe the layout of the farmhouse and the adjoining three rooms where Grandma Brooks resided. Pap had built an additional bedroom upstairs for the girls. Pap was quite the craftsman and had constructed a large open fireplace in the dining room with the backside facing the parlor where there was a small fireplace. Pap had bought Grandma the finest kitchen cookstove being sold. It was a Kalamazoo with the name in large chrome letters across the front. It had warming ovens and a three-gallon water tank at one end. No one else in the community had anything that nice.

Mama would talk about the winter nights when she was a child and the family gathered around the open stone fireplace with the kids dressed in their warm flannel nightclothes, ready to eat roasted chestnuts and baked eggs. The eggs were the ones that had cracked in the nest from the winter freeze and couldn't be sold at Pap's general store. She would wrap them in cheesecloth and then place them in the coals of the fire. Sometimes the eggs would slip out of their wrappings and explode then spatter everywhere. This caused a burst of laughter.

It was storytelling time. Pap was expected to tell about the war. He told about another uncle also named Jesse who was a civilian pilot for the Federal army. He knew the mountainous territory well and would guide families out of Tennessee and Virginia through the narrow trail at Cumberland Gap then into Kentucky for safety. My mother said she and her two younger brothers and two sisters never tired of Pap's war stories. He told them about the time Uncle Jesse rode through the gap to safety on a wagonload of dead horses. His life and the lives of his entire family were always in jeopardy. He had been arrested a couple of times and placed in prison at Rose Hill, Virginia. On one occasion he was being led to Rose Hill by a soldier when they stopped at a creek for drinking water. The soldier wasn't paying close attention when Jesse bent down, cupping his hands for a drink of water and came up with a large rock in his hand. He whirled around and hit the soldier in the side of the head, knocking him out. Jesse was only about 15 miles from his own home when he made his escape. He soon found himself having to lead his own family through the gap and into Kentucky. They made their home in Owsley County where he ran a retail store and preached the gospel.

Pap knew many stories like these and the kids never grew tired of hearing them. When he finished, then it was time for Grandma Brooks to relive her life as a young mother during the days of the Civil War. When she finished her story, the kids were shuffled off to bed. The three girls slept huddled together in a large bed. Their only warmth came from the heat in the open fireplace below and the goose down featherbeds. Grandma Brooks' favorite resting place was the swing occupying the breezeway between her living quarters and the rest of the house. That's where she would sit and while away the hours in summer months, watching the evening sun go down. The house was on the twilight side of the hill and the orchards and gardens at the top of the hill got the advantage of the full day's sun.

Great-Grandma Brooks had been living with my mother's family 35 years, since her husband John died in 1896. He was the first to be buried in the Brooks Family Cemetery on the side of the hill. Great-grandma Brooks lived to be 90.

My mother would continue her story. It was two days after Christmas when two granddaughters rode to the farm and asked Grandma if she would like to go home with them for a few days. It was a warm sunny day, so she said yes. She packed her tapestry bag and came out of her bedroom wearing her bonnet. The girls had cranked up the old grammaphone and Grandma lifted the sides of her skirt and began waltzing around the room.

The girls helped Grandma to the buggy and they were soon home where they took her to the parlor to rest while they went to look for their mother, Minnie. A few minutes passed and one of the boys entered the house and saw Grandma Brooks sitting very quietly in a chair. He spoke to her but she didn't respond. He walked over to her and touched her on the shoulder. She must have fallen asleep because her head was lying forward on her chest in an awkward position. Her grandson ran to the door and called for his mother and sisters to hurry to the house. "I think something is wrong with Grandma." Minnie took her mother's hand and lifted her head. Grandma Brooks was dead.

There are no photographs or memorabilia from my great-grandmother's life, but I can now drive down a winding dirt road through the hills of southwest Virginia and pass an infinite hillside of grass that glows in the afternoon sun. It draws my attention and a road sign reads, "Sal's Ridge," commemorating my great-grandmother and the place where she lived and raised 20 children.

DAMMIT, IT'S MY TURN!

"Two kids, two adults, and only one bathroom!" When I hear this, I want to respond with, "Try nine kids, two adults, and only one bathroom." You haven't lived until you go through that experience on Sunday morning in a good Baptist home where everybody is getting ready for Sunday school at the same time. There was no cussin' in our house, especially when Daddy was around, but fortunately, Daddy was hard of hearing and wasn't around a whole lot! Mama just rung her hands and shamed us.

Seven girls, two boys! Naturally, we had all taken our Saturday night baths and our hair was washed with Prell Shampoo and shining like Sparkle Plenty. But on Sunday morning all of us had to have a turn in the bathroom to brush our teeth, and whatever else we found necessary to do. There was a small hallway outside the bathroom. Sometimes one or two of us waited at the bathroom door and the minute we stepped away, the door would open and a sister or brother would fly from the other end of the house, run in, and slam the door. That's when the fussin' and cussin' really began, the fussin' and cussin' that Daddy didn't allow: "Dammit, it's my turn," along with a bit of hair-pulling and fingernail scratching. When it was Daddy's turn to occupy the bathroom we all stood aside, quiet as church mice, and let his Lordship enter.

Nine Estep Children, ca. 1941

Mama was always the last to make use of the small room with its claw foot tub and the tiny mirror on the medicine cabinet above the sink because she was too busy in the kitchen fixing biscuits, ham and eggs for breakfast. She believed everybody should have a good breakfast to start off their day. Of course, there was always that pan of oatmeal every morning of the world that she also believed kept us healthy. Another good reason to cuss because one of us girls had to wash the oat pan! Oatmeal didn't slide out of the pan with ease in those days. Teflon hadn't become a household word.

I don't know about other homes, but ours had a front bedroom, a

WAIT 'TIL YOU HEAR THIS ONE!

middle bedroom, and a back bedroom. The back bedroom was added on later when I was about eight years old. Daddy enclosed part of the back porch.

It was difficult and painstaking for one dresser in the front bedroom to accommodate all of us girls. A big round mirror was used for applying cosmetics and seeing that every hair on every girl's head was in perfect place. I really didn't need the dresser mirror for the first few years since I was the youngest and was concerned with building my vocabulary by listening to my older sisters cuss. The sisters were good at cussin' under their breath when Daddy was close by. They couldn't risk having him hear the filth that came out of their mouths, especially on Sunday morning. We grew up in pairs. That way, we could wear the same size clothes which meant another fight over who was going to wear the freshly washed blouse or sweater. You had better not reach for the clean slip that a sister had washed the night before if you didn't want to lose a hand.

Daddy was the first to leave the house in his blue serge suit and Panama hat. When he climbed into the driver's seat of our car, everybody had better be there and ready to go to Sunday school and church, or else! We didn't know what the "or else" was but we sure weren't going to test it. Daddy was a church deacon and an adult Sunday school teacher. We didn't dare upset him before we entered the church doors. That would call for a lesson on fire and brimstone.

By the time he bought the 1950 turquoise Hudson Commodore, I was a teenager. There were just three of us kids left at home by then, Wanda, Don, and me. We still fought over who was first in the bathroom on Sunday morning. Sometimes, if you didn't get into the bathroom fast enough, you were in danger of the door closing on your arm!

We had our Easter outfits and corsages each year but working with Mama on getting the clothes was hardly worth the effort. We begged and finagled with her because she budgeted every nickel and dime that Daddy made, but we finally got what we wanted. Sometimes our dresses were handmade. She continually said, "Don't tell your daddy you are wearing a new dress, new shoes, or hat and purse." We never could figure out why we weren't supposed to tell Daddy. He never interfered with the household budget and buying for us kids anyway. He never noticed what we wore, or asked, "Where'd ya' get that new dress?" And besides, did he think those new clothes were manna from Heaven?

There were often snowy days with eight or ten inches of snow on the ground on Sunday morning, but that didn't keep us from going to church. Although Daddy couldn't drive the car, we could still wrap up in warm coats and galoshes and walk to church. The church was several blocks from where we lived. Daddy would lead the way and each of us kids would follow him, walking single file in his foot prints. I can remember when I was older and most of my sisters had gotten married and left home. That was after we got rid of the warm morning heater in the living room and had a floor furnace. It would be so cold that the heat would go off and we had to get ready for Sunday school in a freezing cold house with not even hot water to wash our faces. We were anxious to enter the church house doors then because it was the only place we could keep warm. Every weekend we went through the same process in preparation for the Lord's Day. During the church service we prayed for forgiveness for fightin' and cussin' every Sunday morning. That freed us of sin for another whole week.

THE PUSH MOWER

If you are looking through the eyes of a nine-year-old, our yard was the size of half a football field. In the upper corner of the yard stood a black walnut tree and a clump of grapevines just below it that harvested the best Concord grapes you ever ate. Down by the branch were two apple trees and a cherry tree. Two plum trees with juicy red plums grew at the back of the house. In the middle of the back yard was a big Poplar tree where all the neighborhood kids climbed and played Tarzan and Jane. It had huge limbs and we could climb clear to the top. Mama spent half her time calling us down out of the tree. The shallow branch ran down through the edge of our yard with a foot bridge crossing over to a small patch of ground Mama used to put out a garden every summer. Her gardening skills were taken from her younger days on the farm when she and her sisters worked in the huge gardens alongside their brothers, planting and hoeing fields of corn. She liked to tell me stories about when they would get so hot from the lack of air between the rows of corn, they would faint and Pap would have to ride the mule to fetch the local doctor. They planted everything that would grow in the rich soil on their 300-acre farm. Mama knew all of the astrological signs for gardening.

My eleven-year-old sister and I were playing in the lower side of the yard one day and she happened to spot the old push mower sitting in the shade near the branch. I could tell by the look on her face her wheels were spinning and she had come up with an idea. When she came up with ideas of things for us to do, that meant trouble. Every time!

She headed for the push mower, "I think I'd like to ride the lawn mower. You get behind the mower and I'll sit on that bar across the top and you can push me." Something about that suggestion just didn't ring clear to me. I knew it wasn't a good idea. Her ideas were never good! Above the blades of the push mower was a steel bar that went across between the two wheels. My sister positioned her bare feet on the middle of that bar and held on with her hands on either side of her feet. When she was in position, she hollered, "Now push me!"

As usual, I did whatever she said do, and began pushing the mower across the yard. I didn't get more than five feet when, suddenly, my sister jumped off the mower, screaming bloody murder. She took off up the hill toward the back of the house and all I could see was her hand stuck out in front of her with blood streaming down her arm and leaving droppings behind on the grass.

"Oh, Lordy! I cut off my sister's finger!" Naturally, it was my fault because I was the one pushing the mower. While my sister flew up the steps to the back porch, still screaming, a little more than necessary if you had asked me, I ran to the door below the porch and into our dirt-floor basement, pulling the door closed behind me. I headed for the big pile of coal Mama kept in the basement for our warm morning heater in the wintertime then curled up on top of the coal pile like a mealy bug to await my fate. There was a small window at the side of the house that created enough light to see around me. And, all I could see was the sun shining on spider webs attached to the brick walls in each corner of the basement. It looked like I might be hiding there a long time and without a bite of food to eat because I knew when Mama found me, she would kill me. That's all there was to it—she would kill me! I had cut off my sister's finger. I could either stay hidden in that dirt floor basement until I starved to death or the spiders decided to devour me. Or I had the choice of waiting to see what Mama was going to do to me for cutting off my sister's finger. Some choices, huh! I could also run away from home, but where would I go? Who would take in a distressed little girl with coal dust covering her from head to toe? This wasn't a movie; it was real life, and in real life nobody wants another kid taking up space at night in an already overcrowded bed.

As you well know, when you are living in fear, and your life is at risk, five minutes can seem like an hour and spine-chilling thoughts tend to fill your mind. I kept watching the spiders, hoping they would stay in their webs where they belonged, but I knew when it got dark and I couldn't see my hand in front of me, those eggs would burst open and hundreds of hungry baby spiders would come crawling straight towards me with eyes bigger than their bodies.

I was frightened out of my wits and too numb to cry. Was it fear of the spiders or the fear of Mama when she got her hands on me? She couldn't possibly care more about my sister, Wanda, than she did me! After all, 'trouble' was Wanda's middle name.

The longer I stayed curled up on that coal pile the bigger the punishment became and the larger the spiders in the corners of the basement seemed to be. I could see them actually staring at me and thinking how good I would taste.

It wasn't long before I heard the screeching of the basement door —that Inner Sanctum screech. It was too late to pray, and besides, it wouldn't do me any good anyway. The Lord couldn't help me. My fate was between the spiders and Mama and the time had come! I looked up and there stood Mama, calm and cool.

"You can come on out now. Everything is alright." Standing behind her was my frizzy-haired sister with jelly on her face (she always had jelly on her face), holding her hand in the air with her middle finger wrapped in a big white bandage like it was a trophy or something. She wasn't screaming anymore. In fact, she didn't even look like she was in pain! I looked at her and all I could think was, "Did you have to scream loud enough to make people think you were dyin'?" She didn't even have any traces of blood running down her arm.

I soon discovered I hadn't really cut off my sister's finger. A blade on the push mower caught the end of the finger and sliced it off at the tip. One thing I discovered was that my sister sure had a lot of blood. And she was a convincing screamer. I was too young to realize that Mama was a lot smarter than my sister, or me, and she knew that whatever daring act performed by this now disowned sister, or attempt to get attention, would fall short of its mark. That girl would make a good actress some day and I was hoping she would play the role of the girl captured by King Kong because she was such a terrific screamer, or the criminal who got caught and had to sit in a nasty old jail cell filled with spiders the rest of her life.

At that moment, I managed a sigh of relief. I knew I was set free from my guilt and pain, free to live another day when this same sister would undoubtedly come up with a new idea and a new game for us to play.

Wanda Estep

I didn't have to wait long. The very next day we were jumping rope on the old wooden bridge that crossed over the branch. I was swinging the rope and took a step backwards to take up slack in the rope and my foot went over the edge of the bridge. I found myself lying on my back on a huge flat rock in the middle of the branch. I was so numb I couldn't move a muscle. The breath had been knocked out of me. My sister, looking down at me, very cool and composed from the edge of the bridge, jelly sandwich in hand, and jelly smeared across her mouth, calmly said, "Are ya' hurt?"

NORGE FRIGIDAIRE

You probably won't believe there was a time when a car dealership sold not only cars and trucks, but kitchen appliances such as refrigerators, stoves, and washing machines.

It was the mid-1940s, the beginning of modern times. The war had ended and my family had just moved back from Tennessee. Sitting on the back porch was the old icebox that had kept our food cold and fresh for many years. Electricity had come to the cities and was also being provided in the rural areas. Mama had seen the electric refrigerators and decided it was time we owned one. She and Daddy went down to Anderson Motor Company at 705-707 Main Street in Corbin, whose phone number was (#85), to look at their refrigerators. They found a nice one that had been repossessed and Mama felt it would meet the needs of our family, so Daddy told the salesman to deliver it to our house. It was a Norge Frigidaire, the kind that had a small compartment at the top that held two aluminum ice-trays. We could now have ice in our tea and lemonade drinks anytime we wished and not have to chip off a big hunk from the ice delivered by Mr. Lee, the ice man from the local ice plant at the south end of town. Mama no longer had to place her ice card outside the front door showing how many pounds of ice she wanted delivered each week. With electricity in the house and an electric refrigerator, we were moving into modern times. The old icebox that often leaked water all over the back porch was hauled out the back door.

Daddy paid the salesman $12.40 down-payment, for which he was given a receipt. The total cost of the Frigidaire was $194.00. Monthly payments would be made on the appliance. The salesman said he would send a payment book in the mail for Mama to use when making her payments.

I remember when the Frigidaire was installed and it had a light inside that came on every time we opened the door. Also included with the Frigidaire were clear glass dishes with fruit and vegetable designs on the lids. A covered water bottle was added. This was the most exciting day of our lives!

The first month passed and Mama had watched for the postman every day, expecting to see her monthly payment book in the mail. When it went past a month, she called Anderson Motor Company and asked about it. My mother was a person who was never late with a payment of any kind and she certainly would not be pleased if she were to receive a Dun in the mail for an overdue payment. That's when you would hear the wrath of a woman's scorn!

She waited a couple more weeks—still no payment book. Almost two months had passed so Daddy drove down to the car dealership thinking maybe he could pick up the book. When he arrived, the place was nearly empty. The company had gone bankrupt and was moving out. They had no records of the purchase of the Norge Frigidaire.

My mother never received a statement from the company and she never made another payment on the Norge Frigidaire. The receipt showed the first and only payment made on our electric refrigerator...$12.40.

PATRICIA ESTEP O'NEAL

CURSING THE THRUSH

"The Legend states the 'Seventh Son of a Seventh Son' is the unborn one in the poetic sense, 'He' being preordained by his birthright to be a 'Maker of Things' endowed with gifts of 'second sight' 'predicting the future' 'healer' 'lucky' and a 'devil may care attitude' being referred to as the 'Divine One' or the 'Chosen One.'"

There is much more to this person's description but this gives you an idea of the supposed powers of a seventh son.

My mother was talking to a neighbor one day whose little three-year old son had a condition called the "thrush." I'm sure most of you remember the "thrush," a yeast infection that occurs in the mouth and throat, creating blisters and sores and oftentimes referred to as 'Hoof and Mouth Disease.' It was not that uncommon and you readily recognized when a person had the infection because it was treated with an ugly purple medicine coating the inside and outside of the mouth. There was nothing more embarrassing to a kid than having their friends point at them when they had the "thrush."

Obviously, this neighbor believed in old fashioned ways and miracle cures and when she learned that I, the twelve-year-old child, who was also known as the "seventh daughter," must have the miraculous powers known to the seventh son. If a seventh son could be a healer, why couldn't the seventh daughter have those same powers?

You know what happened then! The neighbor insisted I come to her house and "heal" her child. Mama, of course, was in agreement if the lady thought I could cure her son of the "thrush." Now, keep in mind—I was twelve years old. I couldn't heal myself of a stumped toe, how was I going to heal the thrush? Mama pushed me out the door and sent me in the direction of the neighbor's house. I kicked rocks all the way and mumbled words I wasn't aware I knew until I arrived at the neighbor's house one street over from where we lived. Mama was looking out the kitchen window to make sure I went to the right house. "How could my mother do this to me, her seventh and youngest daughter?"

Now, the procedure for the cure was that I must breathe so many times into the little boy's mouth all covered in purple medicine, and the cure would begin to take place. If I didn't believe in my special powers, how in the world was I going to cure that kid? Do you know what that is like for a shy, self-conscious little girl, and how embarrassed and humiliated she would be when her friends discovered what she had done? I would become the laugh of the neighborhood.

I performed my duties, left the little boy's house and ran all the way home. To this day, I never learned if the little boy was cured of the "thrush." I took the long way round the block everywhere I went for months after that, in order to avoid facing that family. I don't remember the little boy's name, and hopefully, he was too young to remember the girl who was prodded into performing her miracle powers to heal him of the "hoof and mouth disease." To this day, I feel a wave of embarrassment come over my face when I tell this story.

A DOSE OF SULPHUR AND MOLASSES

I was driving along US 25 because it was the scenic route back home. Fields were beginning to glisten with fresh green grasses and some of them were glowing with color. Wildflowers covered the acreage; some in bright golden yellow, others in little white violets and here and there were signs of lavender and purple blossoms. Could the little yellow flowers have been Sweet Grass? I remember tasting the tiny blossoms as a kid to see if they tasted sweet. The redbuds were in full blossom. I didn't know what any of the wildflowers were called but I knew if Mama was with me, she could have named all of them. Mama had a broad knowledge of flowers and wild plants.

Sometimes I get to thinking, if I don't write it down, the future generations will have no knowledge of their family history, of the way their grandparents and ancestors lived, and where they lived. Documenting names, dates of births, deaths, and marriages doesn't tell the story. The stories come from Family! The young people of today are more interested in electronic technology and the world as it is now. None of these things seem to include family. There is no time for family. They aren't interested in what Grandma does, paying her a visit and hearing what she thinks, and stories of her own past history. I am disturbed by this. So, like many of you, I am writing down all that I can remember and all that my mother left for me to tell. Unlike my mother, my knowledge is very limited, but it reveals the upbringing of a girl from a large family who was born and raised in a small community. There were no journals kept in the old days, so word of mouth was my source of information in documenting my family history. You don't need to derive from a family of prominence or wealth to provide a great history. No lords, counts, authors, inventors (and the list goes on) were in my ancestral lines, but their simple lives are as interesting and worthy of record as those who made great discoveries. What would history be without the simple man and his contributions, his discoveries, his inventions?

I tell stories about my mother and the stories she told me about her mother. They were the most important people in my family history. They were the glue to holding a family together. They are the ones who gave us life and nurtured us.

I still have my handwritten notes from 1992 when Mama was telling me about home remedies. I remembered one of our neighbors who kept a small tin of Ex-Lax in her medicine cabinet in the bathroom. It looked like chocolate candy and was taken for constipation. One day her daughter told me to never touch the Ex-Lax. It wasn't for eating. Mama and I began laughing when she told me about the same neighbor talking about her Ex-Lax. She ate a small square of the chocolate once a week. She told Mama that "everybody needs a good cleaning out at least once a week." Mama and I couldn't stop laughing. Mama then continued describing her home remedies, saying to cure a cold she picked a weed called Boneset then boiled it to make a bitter tea. The patient then sweated it out. A bad cough called for Mullen, wild cherry tree bark, boiled and strained, added brown sugar to form a syrup. She said Grandma Rowlett would mix yarrow with cornmeal and white plantain placed in cabbage leaves and wrap around the heel with gauze to make a poultice for stone bruises. Some of these things I had never heard of, but she could describe all of the plants. Mama knew the signs for planting crops.

She could tell you the remedy for anything that ailed you, from toothache to corns and bunions on your feet.

In the old days, kids would get worms. Mama's remedy for that was boiling vermafuze weed in molasses. Every spring the kids were lined up and given a dose of sulfur and molasses. A spoonful of sugar soaked in kerosene helped cure a cough. A poultice of onions fried in lard was used for pneumonia; vinegar for burns. Spider webs stopped bleeding and willow leaf brought down a fever. Ginger tea was for upset stomach and I remember when Mama dissolved rock candy in whiskey for chest congestion. All of these cures had a scientific basis. She named several more mixtures for various conditions. How she could remember all those things, I will never know. After all, she was ninety-five years old by then.

You would have thought green striped marbles were growing on thorny bushes at the back corner of the house. There were only two or three of the bushes and as the berries ripened, they turned to a light shade of burgundy. These were the gooseberries that Mama picked to make a few jars of jelly each summer. The blackberries growing at the edge of the branch were picked and turned into blackberry jam and one or two cobblers. The two apple trees in the back yard weren't good for much and we usually just threw the apples in the branch. But there was nothing more beautiful than the two large plum trees when they were in bloom with their tiny white blossoms covering the trees in clusters and when the wind blew, the petals flew across the yard and covered the ground like snow.

The days seem so long ago when every spring and summer Mama would plant a new patch of zinnias out by the edge of the road where the long row of hedge ended. They grew tall to perfection. On the upper side of the house Mama planted dahlias and gladiolas. There was a long fence covered in wild roses and she would take some of her old nylon stockings that had runs in them and use them to tie the long stemmed flowers to the fence because they grew so tall they would fall to the ground if they weren't stabilized with a stake or tied to the fence. I can remember us kids fuming and fussing because Mama used her old stockings to tie the flowers and the big knotted stocking was noticed more than the flowers. But that didn't bother Mama. All she noticed was the beautiful flower!

Along the side of the house was a row of large purple irises with thick golden beards. Several of the same irises also grew along the banks of the branch down below the house. Nearly all of Mama's flowers were perennials except for her petunias, geraniums, and impatiens. Daddy brought a small lilac bush from the woods down on his little twenty-acre farm and planted it at the back corner of the house. At the front corner next to the bedroom window was a pink dogwood tree and lots of the sweetest scented honeysuckle you ever smelled. There was nothing like waking up in the mornings to the smell of those honeysuckle vines and lilacs coming through the open windows.

I remember waking up on summer mornings to the sound of birds singing. I crept up to the edge of the window and just a few feet below was a cardinal's nest filled with baby birds. I could stand back in the middle of my bedroom and watch as the mother flew in and out of the nest.

It wouldn't be long before I looked out and saw the elderly ladies of the neighborhood passing through our yard, headed for the holler across the road. The names, Adams, Parks, Lay, Eagle, and Sears come to mind. These are the ones I recall and I have long forgotten their first names. I am sure there were others headed up the holler in their stiffened bonnets made from feed sacks and carrying a large brown grocery sack, or as they were called back then, "paper pokes," in one hand and their handy butcher knife in the other. They were going hunting for poke while the plants were still young and tender. The ladies knew the wild plants well because they had all been raised on farms. It wouldn't be long until I saw them passing through the yard again, on their way home with the brown paper sacks filled with poke. I can see my mother now, preparing poke sallet and frying it in bacon grease on the old gas stove.

Just below the front bedroom window was a large rose bush that grew with pink clusters of blossoms. That rose bush must have been there at least seventy-five years. It was the one my sister, Velma, found in a pile of rubble and drug home for Mama to plant. The rose bush was beyond saving, but Mama planted it anyway. Who would have believed it could be brought back to life and become one of the prettiest blossoming bushes in our yard. Wisteria vines grew along a trellis above the porch swing. They were pretty but messy. Mama hated the smell so one day she decided it was time for the Wisteria to go.

When I didn't recognize a flower, I would ask Mama what it was and without hesitation, she could tell me. As long as I can remember, a small spirea bush stood at the edge of our front porch and had tiny clusters of rose-colored blossoms. It bloomed all summer. As soon as the weather was warm enough to open the windows for fresh air, the lace curtains were taken off the windows and washed. Out came the curtain stretchers—the dread of the summer. My sister and I set up the stretchers above the spirea bush and started pinning on the curtains. There must have been two hundred pins, sharp as the tip of a razor blade. At the end of the day, the curtains were removed and placed back on the rods over the windows. This treatment was performed once each year.

I don't think I ever realized how smart my mother was in those days, considering she only had a sixth grade education. Pap didn't see the need for girls getting an education since everything they needed to know about being a farmer's wife, they had learned from experience on the farms.

Mama could tell you about anything you wanted to know when it came to medicines and home remedies, having babies, cooking, sewing, housekeeping, planting gardens, and flowers. She could identify any flower. She also knew a little bit about raising kids the right way. "Spare the rod and spoil the child" must have been invented by her because she certainly didn't believe in spoiling us kids. That long switch from the hedge was always handy, and she used it when need be.

This appears to be one of my tales that can go on and on. I suppose I should just say: "To be continued!"

SISTERLY LOVE

Did you grow up with a sister where every chore you were given you had to share with her? Things like washing and drying the dishes, ironing, making the beds on Saturday morning, dusting, and mopping the floors? Mama was an immaculate housekeeper but she made sure we girls shared in the chores every Saturday when we were going to school. Thank goodness it was just once a week or I would have drowned myself in the branch from having to work with my sister, Wanda, who was two years older than I.

We had to do the supper dishes every night and you wouldn't believe how easily she got out of that. Wanda had a beautiful singing voice and sang in the church choir, often singing solos. Just as we were all finishing our supper, Wanda would appear in the kitchen and say, "I gotta' go to choir practice." If they had had as many church choir practices as Wanda said she had to go to, they'd have had to add extra days to the week. Mama never called her back as she shimmied out the back door and down the path, heading for town. I knew she wasn't going to choir practice but I couldn't tattle tale on her if I wanted to stay alive. Of course, that left me doing the supper dishes. I don't think Mama minded when Wanda pulled one of such tricks because she was the worst dishwasher in the world. And besides, Mama didn't object because she was proud to have a soloist in the family. Also, what mother would prevent her daughter from going to "church"?

Did you ever know anyone who would put a bowl of scraps left from supper in the Frigidaire to keep from washing the bowl? And save the sticky oatmeal pan on the stove from breakfast until it was my turn to do the supper dishes? Well, now you do! If it was her turn to wash the dishes, she would slap the dish through the soapy water and half rinse it then stick it in the dish drainer for me to dry. She dipped the silverware and each time I picked up a piece, usually still covered with gravy or potatoes, I'd stick it up in front of her face and say, "You didn't even wash this one." She would answer, "Ah, just wipe it off!" Mama knew she was slaphappy when it came to doing the dishes but she made her do them anyway. Her kids were not going to go through life without learning household responsibilities. Mama might as well have done the dishes herself in the first place, because with the mess Wanda left, she had to re-clean the kitchen. I was very particular about how I performed my chores and working with Wanda was a real pain in the neck. She never did anything right, and didn't care if she did it right or not.

I will never forget the evening I was standing on the front porch where I could see all the way through the house to the kitchen. I just happened to look through the window in time to see a plate go sailing across the kitchen. Of all things, Mama, a woman with the patience of Job, was the one throwing the plate! I didn't hear it crash but I knew Wanda must have really gotten Mama's dander up this time in order to provoke her enough to throw a dish across the room at her. That was definitely not the time for me to go in the house.

We fought more over sharing household chores than anything else. On Saturday we changed the sheets on our bed and made it up. In those days, we had chenille bedspreads. They weren't easy to spread over the bed. You had to pull and tug and straighten the covering until it was just right. If I worked on the backside of the bed, I couldn't see if Wanda was positioning the bedspread so that it was even in front. I would walk around the bed and lo' and behold the spread would be on the floor at the foot of the bed and gradually slant upwards until it barely covered the edge of the pillow. A fight would follow which usually only amounted to mouthing off to each other, and Mama would have to break us up.

Wanda and I were responsible for ironing our own clothes and my younger brother, Don's, jeans, which were the most dreaded of all the laundry. Wanda and I always shared a wardrobe because we could wear the same clothes. I didn't dare let her iron my blouses or ruffled skirts. I was ashamed to be seen in anything she had ironed. We wore white bobbysocks and when they got a hole in the heel, we had to darn them with needle and thread. You talk about cursing—I could whisper more foul language even if I had to make up words when Wanda put her skills to work. I wanted to choke her when I picked up a pair of white socks that had been darned with red or black thread. No way, was I going to wear those socks.

If I'd had to go to confession every time I told a lie when trying to alibi for my sister when she was late coming home at night, I'd have had to park my pillow and blanket in the confessional. Whatever activity we were attending, we had to go together and come home together. Well, we left home together, but when we were out of sight of the house, Wanda met up with her boyfriend. She went one way and I went another with the plan of meeting at that spot at a specific time when we came home. I would stand on the street corner wringing my hands and pacing because she hadn't shown up on time. If Mama didn't kill her for missing the curfew, I would. I always had to make up a story when I showed up at the front door without Wanda.

THE LUMBERYARD

No matter where we kids went, whether it was a school function, church, ballgames, or downtown shopping, we had to pass the lumberyard to get there. All of the family activities took place on one end of town. The lumberyard covered a whole city block between Main and Kentucky Streets. There was no way to get anywhere unless we passed the lumberyard. It was like a pain from a thorn in the side that would never go away. Day or night, the huge stacks of lumber piled ten and twelve feet high were always there. Street lights hadn't been added to that part of town so nighttime activities at school and church presented a big problem when we kids wanted to attend any of them. The pathways between the stacks of lumber were very dark and spooky. You couldn't see your hand before you. And, to make matters worse, they stood tall beside Moore's branch. Well, hustling across the bridge at Moore's Branch would have us in fear of some big ugly creature bounding up the bank and onto the bridge just as we got there. I lived with the fear that one of those nights Big Foot or some eerie, seven-foot tall hairy, bearded creature was going to jump out from between the lumber stacks and swallow me up. I wasn't the only one who had those feelings. All of my older sisters had the same fears.

Mama wouldn't let any of us girls go to our social activities without another sister tagging along, whether it was a date or something that didn't even interest the other sister, sisters went in pairs. That was a house rule! We had a lot of house rules and quite often we broke them, especially the ones about a sister tagging along on a date. One thing I can say is that my sisters never tattled when one of us changed the rules and did things our own way. We were basically good kids. All we wanted was the privilege of doing things our friends were allowed to do. And if we had to lie and fabricate our stories a bit, that's just what we did. What was it going to hurt? Mama wouldn't know the difference and we would get to join our friends downtown somewhere for a good time.

Of course, we always paid for our sins because we could never enjoy whatever we were doing for fear of getting caught. Or, for fear of a big hairy creature jumping out from behind one of those stacks of lumber and swallowing us up whole. Our fun activities always carried a lump of bittersweet with them—would we get caught?

I was just a small kid when one of our neighbors who was the same age as my two older sisters, Bena Mae and Janette, would spend the nights at our house. Mama paid him a quarter a week. Since Daddy's jobs took him out of town during the weeks, Mama was afraid at night without a male figure in the house. So that male figure was Harold, a neighbor's teenage son who went to school with my sisters. The neighbor had a hard time making ends meet and she took in washings and ironings for a living. There was an advantage to letting her son stay at our house on week nights. It gave extra bed space for her other kids and Harold ate some of his meals with us. Harold had auburn red hair and a trickling of freckles across his nose. He was a quite handsome boy with a practical sense of humor and was always playing pranks on the girls. He kept us laughing all the time. He could turn the tables on my sisters at any time and scare the living daylights out of them. They would tear into him like fighting a rattle snake. It wasn't long until he had them laughing again at one of his practical jokes or stories. They were never really mad at the things he did. He was like a pussycat but Mama considered him their protector when they went places after dark. Harold was expected to accompany them.

Janette and Harold ca. 1940

Mama would give my sisters and Harold enough money for a late afternoon movie at the downtown Hippodrome Theater. It would be dark when the movie ended and they had to pass the dreaded lumberyard on their way home. But, never fear, Harold was with them! Just as they reached the corner where they were ready to cross the street and had to walk past the lumberyard and over the bridge at Moore's Branch, Harold would stop, dead still, and say, "You girls can go the rest of the way by yourselves. I want to go back up town and meet my buddies for awhile." Janette would begin to fidget. Bena Mae would get the look of daggers in her eyes. Harold would take a few steps backward, and say, "You'll be alright. There's nothing to be afraid of."

Bena Mae ca. 1940

The two girls would look towards the dark lumberyard and then back at Harold. He was smiling and prancing around like he was ready to leave them alone to go the rest of the way home. At that point, Janette would start the tears streaming down her face. She couldn't take another step, but she was above begging! The girls picked up their feet to take a few more steps, going forward while Harold took a few steps backwards. When he saw he had them afraid to continue on, he would hesitate and say, "Ahh, I changed my mind. I don't think I want to go back to town. Let's go!"

By the time the three of them got home, my sisters were ready to smother Harold in his sleep. Harold remained their faithful friend, whether in fun or sly scheming pranks. My sisters had a different set of friends at school, but around home, Harold was their constant companion except when he was helping his mother deliver loads of laundry up and down the hill to their house.

Elsie's Store was located down the path behind our house on the next street. The pop man who sold cases of soft drinks to Elsie would be inside the store making his delivery. That was when you could get a two-cent deposit back if you returned empty pop bottles to the store. Harold would climb into the back of the pop truck while my sisters stood guard, hand a couple of empty bottles to each of the girls and take a couple for himself then jump down out of the truck. They slithered into the store and waited for the pop man to leave then handed Elsie their bottles. She gave each of them their two-cents for the bottles. They turned around and bought Baby Ruth candy bars and scampered out of the store. Ah, yes, a bit deceitful, but that was the only way they could have store-bought candy and nobody ever caught on to their little scheme.

By the time my sister, Wanda, and I became teenagers, we rambled the streets together. The house rule still dominated our lives. Even when Wanda had a date, I had to tag along with her, and Wanda had boyfriends from the eighth grade until she graduated high school. It was as irritating for me as it was her, having to follow behind her and the ever-present boyfriend to every ballgame on Friday night. We had a pact that when we reached the corner of Ninth and Kentucky Streets, we would separate then join up again in time to meet our curfew at home. There was just one little problem with that pact— that was the corner where we had to pass the lumberyard. It meant that when the ballgame was over, I was alone passing the lumberyard then waiting on the corner for Wanda to show up. Mama was a stickler about us arriving home at the curfew hour, and we had better be together when we got there! Or Else!

I could never count on my sister to follow the rules and keep me from dying of fear because we weren't going to get home by the designated time Mama had expressed. We were never allowed extra fun time after the games like other kids. We had to go straight home. Wanda didn't seem to take the house rules very seriously. She would amble along with her boyfriend while I stood on the street corner glaring at my wristwatch over and over. "She's late, she's late. I'm gonna strangle her when she gets here. And then Mama's gonna ground us both for being late."

Week after week, I stood on that street corner after hustling past the monstrous dark lumberyard in fear of my life, and waited for my sister and her boyfriend to arrive. Already fifteen minutes past our curfew, here she came, not a worry in the world while I paced back and forth, waiting, and ready to cry! What kind of punishment would Mama render? She never did such things like sending us to bed without our supper, but she had other ways. Extra housework and grounding from other activities was the worst for us.

Wanda was the talented sister in the family. She had a beautiful voice and was the soloist for the high school chorus. She and I sang in the junior choir and sometimes the church choir. Choir practice was after Wednesday night prayer meeting services. It was nearing Halloween and one of my classmates was going to have a party. The party was planned for the same night as prayer meeting. I knew Mama would never allow me to go to the party with it being the same night as a church service, but I just had to go to that party. There were no ifs, ands, or buts about it, I had to go. I had learned that the young man I had a mad crush on was invited. I began planning and scheming how I could go to the party without Mama knowing. Since Wanda and I always stayed for choir practice after prayer meeting on Wednesday night, I had figured a way to attend the Halloween party. Instead of going to church and choir practice, I would go to the party which was right up the street from the church. Then I would leave early and meet Wanda outside the church doors and we could walk home together. Mama would never know the difference. Even though I wouldn't be able to dress in costume for the party, I could still go, and hopefully, the boy of my dreams would also be there.

Before I got a chance to tell Wanda my plan, she had already left the house that night. That was okay; as long as I arrived at the church when choir practice was over, my sister and I could walk home together and Mama would never know where I had been. I walked up Kentucky Street, passed the lumberyard, shuffling my feet as fast as possible then passed the church which was about to start services, and ran on up to the end of Kentucky Street to the hill where the water tower stood. It was a small party, with bobbing of apples, and the usual games, and I watched and waited for the love of my life to appear. I kept one eye on the hands of my watch the entire time, making sure I wasn't late in leaving the party. I couldn't take a chance on missing Wanda outside the church since I wasn't able to tell her my original plans. The young man never showed up at the party. I was devastated and ready for tears. I quickly made my exit from my friend's home and started down the hill towards the church. I was completely out of breath when I got there. Not a single soul was to be seen leaving the church. There weren't even any lights on inside the church. How could I have missed my sister? And, how could I have known they wouldn't have choir practice that night and she would be leaving early? I was doomed! Wanda was already on her way home. Maybe I could catch up to her if I hurried.

I couldn't walk any faster. You could hear the patter of my penny loafers hitting the sidewalk. And then I came to the corner where I had to pass the lumberyard. It was Halloween! Who knew what pranks could be played that night. I could hear my heart beating. My imagination was playing tricks on me. I had to pass the lumberyard. There was no other way to get home. The wind was blowing and the trees on my side of the street were swaying and creating shadows. My eyes were shifting from left to right. A big tall wooly creature was there somewhere; I just knew it! He was hiding in the shadows between the tall stacks of lumber. I picked up my feet and ran with all the fervor I could muster up. I was afraid to look behind me.

That fear was bad enough, but even worse was the fear of my fate when I arrived home alone and Wanda couldn't tell Mama where I was. I was certain I couldn't count on Wanda giving me a good made-up alibi. She wouldn't do that for me as I had done for her hundreds of times.

It was obvious I wouldn't get by with my deceitful plan. I never could get by with lying to Mama like Wanda could. Mama believed anything Wanda told her. She could look into my eyes and know when I was lying, so I just quit trying.

It was bad enough that after I got by the lumberyard without the threat of terror, I still yet had to pass the old house that we all referred to as the "house of the wicked old witch." It sat on the corner just a few feet from the road and a thick row of hedge at the edge of the road, perfect for someone to hide behind! I stuck to the middle of the road as I hustled along, thinking of all the rumors and tales of a stillborn baby being buried in the chimney beside the road. Year by year, more tales were conjured up about the old lady in the weathered brown siding house.

By this time, I had conquered the first few fears, but the most dreaded was still ahead of me. What was I going to tell Mama when she met me at the front door? I couldn't lie to her this time! What kind of punishment was in store for me? All I could think was, Mama didn't have to punish me. I had already been through enough torment that Halloween night to last a lifetime. I bounced onto the front porch and Mama was opening the front door! That was a Halloween night that would live with me a lifetime. The young man for whom I had the mad crush, travels from California to attend all of my class reunions. The minute I see him, thoughts recur of a long ago Halloween night.

To my knowledge, nothing mysterious ever happened in the vicinity of the old lumberyard, except the fear created in a kid's mind. After I graduated from high school, the lumberyard had been removed and a motel stood in its place. The many tales fabricated around this one square block of town where the local lumberyard once stood were then erased forever!

THE PAPER BOY

Patricia Estep

Being the last in line in a set of seven sisters wasn't such a great thing when it came to wearing hand-me-downs. I hated them, all my sisters hated them, even the older ones who had to share the same wardrobe had hated them. You haven't seen World

War 3 until you see two sisters fighting over who was going to wear the clean sweater when the one who had washed it was about to be on the losing end. That's when having a neighbor like Long John Smith came in handy. He was the local police officer that everybody in town knew. He, too, had a family of eight children and five of them were girls, so he understood the circumstances when he heard squealing from our bedroom window. No reason to get alarmed! Mama came in as referee on occasion with her long switch. And then, there was the drawer of white socks we had to share, especially when Wanda had darned the hole in the heel of the socks with black or red sewing thread. Not only that, but she would sew little knots so that when you wore the socks with your penny loafers, they caused blisters on your heels.

I have to admit, in my case the hand-me-downs weren't such a bad idea because my older sisters all had jobs and bought their own clothes and I thought they had very stylish taste. They had outgrown J.C. Penney's and were doing their shopping in small boutique shops. It's fortunate that we could nearly all wear the same size by the time I was in high school. When a dress was handed down to me it was like getting a new one. Wanda and I were still sharing the same wardrobe and I sometimes wonder how both of us managed to reach adulthood without battle scars because she always grabbed the freshly washed sweater or dress first. I don't think she ever put anything on a hanger when she finished wearing it, and I had to iron it again before I could wear it. There again, was the battle of words. I suppose that's why my family wasn't Catholic. We'd have spent half our lives in a confessional trying to get atonement for cussin' each other.

I was a freshman in high school, and of all things, I had a crush on the most popular boy in my class. What made me even think I had a chance with him when the pickin's in my class were so slim and in my opinion, the good ones were already taken. They all had steady girlfriends. I didn't know the first thing about flirting and if a boy looked me in the eye, I turned blood red in the face. Every morning at six o'clock I was lying at the foot of my bed, looking out the window toward the street and waiting for the paper boy to pass our house. Of course, I had a mad crush on the paper boy. I didn't dare let him know it though.

It was time for the athletic banquet to be held at school and that year the banquet would be at the Wilber Hotel. To this day, everybody remembers the grand hotel with the beautiful crystal chandelier hanging in the lobby. The hotel was the only place in town that had chandeliers. Football and basketball players from all four high school classes would be inviting girls to the banquet. All I could do was dream about being one of those girls. But that would never happen. I wasn't that popular. And I was too shy.

Wilber Hotel, Corbin, KY, ca. 1950

The Wilber Hotel was located all the way across town. I had never been inside the two-story brick building, but I could see through the windows in passing on the sidewalk going to and from football games each week. I loved looking at the huge chandelier glittering brightly and casting its shadows around the lobby. The door man lived several miles up the road and he was a familiar sight standing outside the door of the hotel greeting people. Everyone in town knew him. He always waved and spoke to folks driving by.

The school year was coming to an end and I came running home from school as fast as my legs would carry me. I couldn't wait to tell Mama! I hurried through the door and stammered with my words.

"Mama, I've been invited to the athletic banquet at school!" Naturally, any other mother would have been so excited she would have paid to have her daughter attend such a delightful affair, but not my mother! She was from the old school, so to speak. The first words out of her mouth were, "If it means you have to buy a new dress, you will have to tell him you can't go." You talk about deflating your ego…all I could think was 'my mother must have been born an old woman. Doesn't she remember what it was like to be young?' She could never see the joy of her pretty daughters involved in school activities and being voted the most glamorous girl in school, or the most popular girl in the school superlatives; one was selected for the Mountain Laurel Festival, and another was the school choir soloist. Everything for Mama had a price tag attached to it. If it was going to cost money, the answer was No. She had had to pinch pennies all her life. Naturally, it was difficult sticking to a budget and seeing that all the bills were paid each month, but on special occasions, there had to be a way! What Mama didn't understand was what an honor it was to be popular in school and get an invitation to the athletic banquet. I was fifteen years old and only two girls in my class had been invited to the banquet, and I was one of them. I was walking on cloud nine. And better still, the invitation came from the boy I had been gazing at every morning through my bedroom window—the paper boy!

There was no way I was going to turn down my invitation. I just couldn't! I'd rather die! My oldest sister, who was married, was always on my side in these issues. She said, "Don't worry, we'll find a way." Most of my clothes were handmade. I wanted a new dress this time and to pick it out myself, but it was obvious that wasn't going to happen. By chance, my sister from Tennessee came home that weekend. When I told her my dilemma, she assured me I would be going to that banquet. She had a new flowered red silk dress that would be perfect for me to wear and as soon as she got back home, she would mail it to me. I could always count on one of my older sisters to come to my rescue. They had gone through the same ordeals year after year. Why couldn't Mama get pleasure from our experiences and enjoy our teenage years? We had to beg, plead, and finagle to get what we wanted and sometimes just plain lie but we usually won out.

I spent the next few days on pins and needles. I had never had a date before. My shyness was a drawback; what would I talk about? Would there be any girls at the banquet I knew? Instead of getting to go downtown to Maggie J's or Murphy's and buy a pretty dress, I would have to wear one of my sister's hand-me-downs.

The mailman delivered my package. Much to my surprise, it was just as my sister described, red silk, short puff sleeves, fitted to the waist and a gored skirt that swished when I walked. If I stood up straight and held my shoulders back like a young girl should, the extra looseness in the bodice wasn't too obvious. Of course, a padded bra would have helped take up the bustline!

My date had to walk from the area by the football field all the way across town to pick me up, which was at least a mile. High school kids, especially an underage freshman, rarely had access to Dad's car, if Dad had a car. I was a nervous wreck. Two of my sisters prepped me in good table manners – which fork, how to cut the meat, which side the salad was on, lay your napkin in your lap, etc., etc. The drink sits on the right—but I was lefthanded!

My date arrived looking quite dapper. We had to walk all the way back through downtown to the Wilber Hotel, a mile. The weather was perfect for the long walk. The room for the banquet looked beautiful, and I looked quite pretty in my sister's red silk dress. I wore my white Sunday gloves and black patent shoes. I had never been to anything this formal and I wanted everything to be perfect. I breathed a sigh of relief when I saw the other girl from my class. We sat together at the same table. She had been invited by the boy just up the street from where I lived. I was the lucky one that night. Everything went well throughout the evening; I never spilled my iced tea, and I discovered my red silk dress was one of the prettiest at the banquet.

It was another mile's walk to take me home that evening. Near the hotel was a small building with a rustic front door. From the sounds we heard something bazaar was going on inside the building. The large hole in the door allowed each of us kids who had gathered on the sidewalk a chance to peek inside the building and see what was happening. It was something I had never seen before—a religious gathering by what we called a bunch of holy rollers. I had attended many religious revivals, but none like this! The people were singing, shouting to the top of their voices in what was called unknown tongues. It certainly was a new experience for me.

By the time my date left me at my doorstep and returned to his own home that night, he had walked four miles. That was my very first high school date...and it was my last date with the paper boy. He wasn't about to trek four miles every time we had a date! Michael was such a fun-loving person, intelligent, and he was a favorite with the teachers. He was one of those kids who could get by with pranks in the classroom, and I'll never forget the added stunts he pulled during our senior play. He made the play a big hit! After graduation, he attended every class reunion that was held. He died suddenly the week of our 40th high school class reunion. I still remember lying in wait by my bedroom window to see the paper boy pass my house, the young man who was my first high school date.

JUICY RED PLUMS

When I watch the pear trees, redbuds, dogwoods and other trees spread their blossoms, I remember how blessed we are and what a beautiful gift spring has brought us. I recall the two plum trees that grew in our backyard when I was a kid. They opened up with snowy white blooms and when the wind blew, the petals fell to the ground like a blanket of snowflakes. I looked forward to seeing summer come and the budding of the two plum trees.

Money was tight in our home and bikes, skates, sleds, and other popular toys were only dreams. My younger brother was the only one to own a bicycle. My first wristwatch came when I was in the eighth grade of school. Oh, how proud I was of my 21 jewel Bulova with a black band. I still have that watch.

It was late spring when I watched the little pods appear on the two plum trees, waiting for them to swell into large juicy red plums and fall into the thick grass. Mama kept her large apple basket hanging on the back porch. When the plums were ripe, she said if I picked them up and filled the basket, I could sell them to the ladies in the neighborhood for making plum jelly. The basket held about two gallons of plums and I could sell them for twenty-five cents a gallon. I double-dared my brother and sister to even think of picking up any of the plums. They were Mine!

Each morning when I got out of bed, I hurried to the back porch to see how many plums had fallen during the night. Would there be enough shiny red fruit to fill my basket? I couldn't wait to get dressed and head for the back yard. Sometimes I would shake the limbs of the trees and a few more plums would fall to the ground. I was certain to fill my basket each day.

My shy manner made it hard for me to knock on the neighbors' doors and ask if they would like to buy my plums. What I didn't know was that they were already prepared because Mama had called them and told them I would be coming to sell my plums. When the ladies answered the door, they were always smiling and pleased to see me. Each day I was able to fill my basket and each day I earned a quarter or fifty-cents. I felt rich. My bounty only lasted a few days and then the trees were bare of fruit and the green leaves on the tree had taken the place of the juicy red plums.

The next time I went to the Hippodrome Theater to see a double-feature show, I not only bought a bag of popcorn, I enjoyed a fountain coke, something I was not able to do any other time. And on my way home from the movie, I stopped at Cottongim's Drug Store and bought a movie magazine for ten cents. That was living! My scrapbook of movie stars was waiting for the addition of a few more pictures—John Payne, June Havor, or Lana Turner. I saved the remaining handful of quarters for buying Christmas gifts for my family.

When I walk through the grocery store each week and I see the fresh fruit piled high in a bin, I can't help but remember the summer days when I collected my juicy red plums in Mama's apple basket and earned all those quarters. Those were good days!

The trees are long gone now and it hurts when I go back home and the back yard is bare. Even the huge poplar tree where I played each summer day is no longer there. They were as much a part of my childhood as the people around me.

HEADLESS HORSEMAN

It was the night of a high school basketball game. The gymnasium was only a short distance from home so we walked together out the road with my older sister trailing behind us clinging to her boyfriend's arm. My sister always had a boyfriend to take her to school activities and parties.

It was a very dark night and there were no streetlights on the backstreets of town, which was where we lived. The three of us had rounded the bend at the end of the road and turned onto the very narrow part where tall hedges grew on one side of a deep ditch. The other side of the road had bushes as tall as trees. One could walk down the middle of the dark road and almost reach both sides, so there really wasn't any safe haven along the way. It was a stormy looking night with black clouds rolling, and occasionally we could see a glimpse of the moon as the clouds cast shadows across the road in front of us. Every shadow looked like something real and very scary. Our shoes crunched on the gravel as we hurried along. We had reached the part of the journey that could cause a kid's imagination to go completely helter-skelter.

My friend, Bobbie Jean, my brother, Don, and I were approaching the old Perkins house where many stories had been conjured up about ghosts and haints, and for us it was like walking by the house next door in *To Kill A Mockingbird* where Atticus Finch and his children lived. When we had to take this trail after dark, it was always with a big lump in our throats. There was no other way to get to the school gymnasium.

The bushes swept back and forth and we just knew that any minute the headless horseman would leap out at us. Our footsteps got slower as the three of us came to the corner of the old house where it had been rumored that a stillborn baby was buried in the chimney beside the house. There was thick hedge along the edge of the yard, no more than four feet from where we had to pass, and yet, close enough for something or someone to jump out and attack us. We may not have been very smart but we sure had vivid imaginations. Suddenly, we noticed the strangest noise, one we had never heard before. Stopping dead still in the middle of the road we turned and looked at each other. Don was clinging to my left arm and Bobbie Jean was pinching my right arm. There was no doubt I was as scared as they were but, being the oldest, I pretended I wasn't afraid. I said, "Ah, it's nothin'! Let's go on."

We took several more steps and the cry came out again, stronger than before. I swallowed hard and said, "It's nothin' to be afraid of. Come on." We were almost to the chimney and the long cries of a baby came out so loud that we nearly turned to stone. I took a deep breath, turned to my left and my little brother was gone. Oh, Lordy! He had been grabbed up by the headless horseman, just like in "The Legend of Sleepy Hollow." Then I turned to my right and Bobbie was not there either. She, too, had disappeared into the dark shadows. At that point there was no more reasoning and no waiting to see what was going to happen next. I made a 180 degree turn and headed back up the road and around the bend with my feet hardly touching the ground.

Coming towards me were my sister, Wanda, and her boyfriend sauntering along. They had yet to reach the bend of the road. They were baffled by our actions as Bobbie Jean lifted her feet off the ground and grabbed my sister around the neck. She was still in motion like she was riding a bicycle. Wanda couldn't imagine what had happened. We were white as ghosts and completely out of breath. It was then my sister said, "Where's Don?" He was nowhere to be seen. We yelled for him. He didn't answer. I was right; the headless horseman had definitely reached out into the black of night and taken my little brother.

Nevertheless, we were going to a ballgame so we continued walking to the end of the road and around the bend. Although the cries in the night had ceased, I was shaking. But, where was Don? The four of us finally arrived at Edwards Gymnasium and when we got inside the door, there stood my little brother, red faced with grass stains on his trousers, dirt on his school jacket, and he was breathing heavily. How in the world did he get to the gym ahead of us? And why did he look such a mess?

There was a field behind the bushes at the bend of the road that led to our cousin's backyard. We often took that path as a shortcut to school. Right behind the house was a brick wall about six feet high. We could jump the wall to the ground below and continue on our way to school. When I discovered Don missing that night, it never occurred to me that in his attempt to escape the frightful scene, he had cut through the bushes then across the field toward the brick wall. He later admitted he was so scared that when he came to the edge of the field, he forgot about the brick wall and ran straight over it, landing flat on his face in my cousin's yard. He didn't have time to see if he was hurt and it was too dark to tell. He knew something was right behind him and he had to keep running. Pounding footsteps were closing in on him. There was no time to look back.

We were too young to have learned the mating habits of the animal world, but that night was our first lesson concerning the mating habits of cats. The cries we heard that dark gloomy night came from a couple of stray cats. They sounded exactly like babies crying.

To this day, when my family begins the storytelling sessions about our childhood, this one always brings a ton of laughter. I can visualize my young friend's legs still moving as she had her arms wrapped around my sister's neck. Tears stream down my face as I remember and treasure the fun and laughter I shared with my playmate and best friend, Bobbie Jean.

GOING TO AKRON

George worked for the railroad company. He could get free passes for him and his wife to travel on the train. Her name was Fanny. If you can picture Mutt and Jeff, that's what you had in husband and wife. George was a tall, rather handsome man. Fanny was short, more the Aunt Bea type with a touch of redneck style. Her hair was fixed in a short perm and she wore wire rimmed glasses low on her nose. She also had a high pitched whiney voice that could grate on the nerves at times.

Fanny's family was from a small community near us called Rockhold. She called it "Rock-oat." She dipped snuff and cleared her throat a lot, and I do mean 'a lot'. Every day, she would come to our house while we kids ate dinner and then hurried back to school. Mama cooked a hot meal each day at noon and we ate the leftovers for supper that night. Fanny sat at the corner of our kitchen table while we ate, dipping her snuff and clearing her throat. If she told a story once, she told it a hundred times, day after day and week after week. She had a niece named Harriet Ellen and over and over we heard the same tale about "Haar-dellon." My younger brother, who was about 12 at the time, had a very weak stomach. Every time Fanny cleared her throat and spit into her little tin can, my brother's face would turn a shade whiter and then blue around the mouth. He would push the kitchen chair back and make a mad dash to the bathroom. For his benefit, sometimes Mama would catch Fanny at the front door and suggest they sit on the porch swing while we kids ate our dinner.

One day George came home from work and told Fanny he had train passes for them to go to Akron, Ohio, to visit her brother, Archie. Well, day by day, she told us she was going to "A-kern, Ohowee" to see Archie. The day came, she packed a small suitcase for both her and George; they walked downtown to the depot station and boarded the train to Akron. This was to be Fanny's first train ride.

It was about ten o'clock at night when the train pulled into the station at Akron. George spotted a taxi cab and motioned to the driver to pick them up. While the driver loaded the suitcases in the trunk of the taxi, George and Fanny climbed in the backseat. Fanny was pretty ill at ease because, first, this was her first train ride, second, she was in a strange town, and third, she didn't like the looks of the taxi driver. He wore his cap pulled down where she couldn't get a good look at his eyes. She wasn't real sure he could be trusted. However, since George was by her side and he was larger than the taxi driver, she felt somewhat secure.

While riding along George was looking out the window at the night lights. Fanny had her eyes glued to the back of the taxi driver's head. She thought she could hear him talking to somebody. He held a little black thing up to his mouth when he talked. Then she could hear another voice talking back but she couldn't figure where the voice was coming from or understand what he was saying. She began to get nervous. She started elbowing George who just ignored her and kept looking out the window. Then Fanny heard the driver say something else. What did he say? She still couldn't understand him and when she heard that other person talking back to him, she got more scared. She nudged George; he still paid no attention to her.

Fanny began thinking, "That driver's talkin' to somebody on that little black box and he's plannin' on takin' us out 'n the country somewhars' and he's gonna rob us 'n kill us." She couldn't get that thought out of her head. Fanny was about to wet her pants. She twisted and turned and kept leaning forward and listening every time the driver said something in that little black thing he held up to his mouth. "Oh, Lord 'a mercy in Heaven! We're gonna die!" she thought.

She still couldn't get George's attention. She was trying to tell him, "That driver's gonna take us out 'n the country somewhars' and he's gonna rob us 'n kill us." It took about thirty minutes to get to Archie's house and by then Fanny was so distraught she was weak and in a nervous tizzy.

Week after week, Fanny sat at the corner of our kitchen table and we heard that same story about her trip to Akern, Ohowee, while we ate dinner, with her honkin', coughin', spittin' her snuff, clearing her throat and saying, "He wuz gonna take us out 'n the country somewhars' 'n rob us 'n kill us." And my white-faced little brother was making a mad dash every time to the bathroom. When Fanny joined us each day at the kitchen table, my sister and I watched and grinned as the kid's face went from gray to white and he jumped from the table, making his mad dash to the bathroom.

THROUGH THE EYES OF A CHILD

When I came upon a group of vintage photographs, I was so struck with emotion I just sat back and cried. The photographs show the small town where my family lived during World War II, a time in history that will live forever.

In the spring of 1943, my family moved from our home in southeastern Kentucky to Clinton, Tennessee, a small town located about eleven miles east of Oak Ridge. My dad was hired as a foreman supervising the building of houses and dormitories. He had been out of work for several months when he heard about the need for experienced carpenters and builders in Oak Ridge. There was no time limit on how long the job would last.

During the months following Japan's attack on Pearl Harbor, the Federal government purchased approximately 55,000 acres of farmland in Anderson County and Roane County, Tennessee, and much to the surprise of the farmers who had owned that land, a city would be built. The Tennessee Valley Authority (TVA) power that had been developed by the building of Norris Dam in the mid-1930s, and the seclusion of the surrounding mountains, made the farmland an ideal location for the government project. The secret operation would become known as the "Manhattan Project" and in time, the city called Oak Ridge would be labeled "the city behind the fence."

Ten thousand houses would be built, even more dormitory units, 16,000 barrack units, and three defense plants. Two-hundred miles of streets would be constructed. Forty-two thousand construction workers and 40,000 defense project workers were being hired. Although a house would be completed on the average of every thirty minutes, living accommodations would still be in demand. Houses were identified by letters of the alphabet, numbering from A through F. The houses were assigned according to size and status of the occupants. Engineers and scientists had first preference. Families arrived daily, some pulling small trailers behind their cars. Many people made temporary homes in army tents. Men who could not find living quarters were known to take shelter in old railroad boxcars.

My two oldest sisters had married and my older brother was in the Army Air Corps, leaving six of us kids at home. My dad found housing early that spring, just before thousands of families relocated to the area. A wood frame structure, recently used as a café on Cullom Street in Clinton, Tennessee, had been vacated. It was built like a regular house with seven rooms and a large screened back porch. Mama did not see the house until the day we moved in. Daddy drove the moving truck the seventy miles over the mountain with my little brother and me occupying the cab of the truck with him and Mama. Our burgundy mohair sofa had been placed across the back of the paneled truck so that my two older sisters could be comfortable during the trip. Only enough furniture to meet our needs was packed in the truck. Daddy had been careful to place the furniture in secure positions for the safety of my sisters.

I remember the sallow expression on my mother's face when she climbed out of the big truck and had her first look at our new home. It sat flush against the sidewalk. The tears streamed down her cheeks as she looked at the house. She would be spending weeks cleaning and scrubbing every room. Rubble and paper trash was spread throughout the front rooms. The kitchen held a large wood-burning stove and deep double sinks, the restaurant style. Two bedrooms and the living room had small grates for heating the house. We also had a dining room. Two rooms at the back of the house were rented to a couple from Corbin who had come to work at Oak Ridge. After Mama was able to see how other families were living, she then realized how fortunate we were to have suitable accommodations. Once the house was scrubbed down, curtains on the windows, and furniture in place, it would look like a decent home.

A creek ran behind the house and the Clinch River was behind the Magnet Knitting Mills located directly across the street from us. The Mill had manufactured nylon hosiery and immediately went into production of parachutes when the war began, employing women to replace the men who had left their jobs to enlist in the military. Due to the rationing of automobile tires and gasoline, workers carpooled or walked to work, leaving the Mill parking lot nearly empty. Before long, the parking lot became home to families who were living in tents. I remember a small army tent set up in our back yard. Two men working in Oak Ridge had left their families behind in their home towns and they were using the army tents for living quarters. I can visualize the two cots now, placed on either side of the tent and a portable propane heater between the cots for warmth on cold nights. Their lighting was created with oil lanterns. One day, a man knocked on our door and asked my mother if he could use our dirt floor basement for shelter at night. A pile of coal was stored in the basement for use in our grates.

Mama began to realize how fortunate we were to find a rental house even if she had rubbed her fingers to the bone to improve the living conditions. Living space and lodging had been difficult to find. Times were very hard. Many men had come to the area to find work, leaving their families back home, wherever back home might be. It could be anywhere from Texas to the east coast.

Before leaving for work each morning, men would stop at Denney's Cafe, two doors up the street from our house, and have breakfast. My two older sisters were sophomore and junior in high school. They worked at Denney's Café after school and every evening before coming home from work, they prepared dozens of sack lunches to be ready the next morning for men to carry with them to Oak Ridge. So many food products had been rationed and the men were lucky if their little lunch bags held as much as a cheese sandwich and a boiled egg. They never complained. The daily lifestyle for kids living in the communities surrounding Oak Ridge was in no way like it might have been in any other small town. It was just a matter of days before my sister, Wanda, and I met the neighborhood kids. Linda and Patsy lived a few doors up the street in a huge, two-story white house that looked like a mansion to us. It stood on a large sloping piece of ground and the front of the house was augmented by tall white columns. It was like nothing we had ever seen before.

Every room on the second floor was empty except for clothing and household items being stored there. It was the ideal place for us to play on cold or rainy days. We could play 'Let's Pretend' to our hearts' content. I thought Heaven had opened its gates when I entered the sunroom and spotted a grand piano in the center of the marble floor. Windows surrounded three sides of the room. Just outside the sunroom was a path leading to the steep riverbank where we spent hours on end sliding down the bank to the edge of the Clinch River. Sliding down that bank on large sheets of cardboard was the delight of many days. Of course, Mama never knew her six- and eight-year-old girls were playing on the riverbank.

The city of Oak Ridge would soon be known as the nation's number one enemy target and every child was being conditioned to the fears of war. Blackout drills were conducted on a regular basis. During late nights, the sirens alerted residents to take cover. The alarm came from the Magnet Knitting Mills across the street. The sirens could be heard throughout the small town and were deafening in our household. Local police cars patrolled the dark streets. Dark green window shades were pulled and curtains drawn in every home to prevent even a spark of light in open fireplaces from reflecting into the night. In the event of an enemy air attack the area was to appear as if there was no sign of life. As a seven-year-old, I remember sitting before the open grate in wintertime hugging my sister and trembling until the siren ceased and all was quiet.

The constant threat of war connected the people to one another like nothing else could. Half of the community was now occupied by new residents. Churches were filled every week by families seeking hope, comfort, support and a place to worship and pray. Windows in nearly every house had a banner revealing a blue star, indicating someone in the family was overseas fighting for our country. On occasion, a banner bearing a gold star could be seen. This meant a member of the family had been killed in battle. It was a fearful time for all.

My small body shook with fear when we drove through the Elza Security Gates at the edge of the city of Oak Ridge on Sunday afternoons to visit my oldest sister. Her husband worked in a chemical lab and they lived in one of the newly built Alphabet houses. Daddy wore his identification badge and the rest of the family carried passes which allowed us entry into the city of Oak Ridge. Even passenger trains arriving at Oak Ridge were not allowed past the gates. People disembarked beyond the fence and revealed identification before they could enter the city. I would slide down in the backseat of the car hoping to hide from the security guards. They wore guns strapped to their sides as they made routine inspection of all automobiles. Every vehicle entering Oak Ridge was under scrutiny. Now and then I would peek through the bottom of the window, watching as the guards opened suitcases and bags, searching for weapons and questionable items.

WAIT 'TIL YOU HEAR THIS ONE!

Elza Gates entering Oak Ridge, TN, WWII

Amid the fear of war and the dangers of enemy attack, Oak Ridge had become the country's number one enemy target. At the same time, my parents had their own inner fears. My brother, Howard, was a corporal in the Army Air Corps and was awaiting orders to be sent overseas to join in the battle against the Japanese. He had been in the Air Corps exactly nine months and was training to be a B-17F bomber pilot. It was June 1943, shortly after midnight. Everyone was sleeping soundly when there was a loud knock at the front door. Daddy opened the door to find our next door neighbor standing in the dim light. She revealed a troubled expression as she told him he had a long distance telephone call. Since we did not have a telephone, Mrs. Scaggs's telephone number had been given for necessary calls. But who would be calling in the middle of the night?

My dad followed the lady back to her house. When he answered the phone, a deep somber voice responded. A commanding officer at the U.S. Army Air Base at Rapid City, South Dakota, was calling to report the tragic news that my brother, Howard (nicknamed "Bug"), had been killed in a plane crash at the Army Air Base. A crew of ten was on board the plane. My brother and five other airmen were killed when the plane crashed into a bank beyond the airfield. The B-17 was loaded with fuel tanks and 25,000 rounds of ammunition. The plane was too heavy to make the lift from the runway. Bullets were like fireworks exploding in the air.

Howard (Bug) Estep, 1943

The next day, we returned to our home in Kentucky where funeral arrangements were in process. Neighbors and friends overflowed our house when the news was spread throughout the town. Events in days that followed are sketchy in my memory. I remember a large casket draped with an American flag sitting in the living room of our home. Life for me as a seven-year-old soon returned to normal, but for my mother, her grief would never cease.

Don Estep, age 4

The summer ended and it was time for my three sisters and me to enroll in the local school system. My younger brother, Don, had just turned four. My sister, Wanda, was in the fourth grade. I was entering the second grade. Wanda was responsible for my safety crossing the main street on our way to school. The town had doubled in size with the influx of people coming from all across the country. The conditions brought about by the war would create a bond between the students that would last a lifetime.

Week after week, and at any unexpected moment, blackout drills would be carried out. Fear never lessened. Each time the piercing sound of sirens penetrated the silence of the night, residents hovered in their homes, and waited. Mama pulled the dark shades on the windows and closed the draperies to ward out any spark of light inside the house. My sister and I would cling to each other with our small bodies quivering from fear. We never whispered a word. The sirens came from the Magnet Knitting Mills. The whistle blew loud enough to be heard throughout the entire town and on into the rural communities. At any unexpected time the nights would be filled with the sound of the sirens.

It had been a year since my sister, Velma, had graduated from high school. During that year, she lived with Inez. Our first grade teacher had promised Velma that if she would save her earnings from the local bank in Corbin, she would take her to California for several weeks to visit her family. It was early summer when they left on a Greyhound bus together. While moving from one town to another, Velma left her friend and took a bus down along the coastline to visit our Uncle Wiley, Daddy's older brother, who was living at Dos Palos. It wasn't long until Velma grew homesick, so she and our uncle boarded a bus back to Kentucky. My sister, Inez, and her husband were now living in Oak Ridge in one of the C houses, a two-bedroom, one bath unit. Her husband was working in a chemical lab for the Federal government. Velma moved to Oak Ridge to work for Eastman Company. She took up residence in one of the newly built dormitories.

Velma Estep in California, 1944

A year had passed since our arrival in the small town of Clinton.

It was nearing bedtime on the evening of July 6, 1944. Families never got used to the loud cry of the sirens, and that night the sounds were again as frightening as before. It was another blackout! But this time, the sirens didn't stop after twenty or thirty minutes; they continued, hour after hour, all night long. Huge lights began flashing across the sky. Back and forth, back and forth! They, too, went all night long.

Communication wasn't the same as we know it today. You couldn't turn on your TV and get an instant replay. There were no televisions or radio communication. People stayed in their homes. No one was allowed on the streets. So, all that night they sat in fear waiting to learn what was taking place. Not a single resident entered the dark streets. We had become familiar with blackouts, but had never experienced the flashing lights before. Was there going to be an enemy air attack as we had been warned about so many times?

No bomb shelters had been built or facilities established for the townspeople. There was no place for people to take shelter if they heard the sounds of planes approaching the community. About half a block down the street from us, near the end of the Magnet Knitting Mills, was an old bridge that crossed the Clinch River. The bridge had been closed to traffic several years earlier. The abutments below the bridge on each side of the river were the only possible means of shelter for our neighborhood, an area where vagrants and hobos found shelter at night when they were passing through town.

About forty miles north of Clinton, a troop train carrying more than 1,200 soldiers had left Louisville, Kentucky, and was headed toward South Carolina. The train was 30 minutes behind schedule and the engineer needed to make up the time. The train approached the mountains of Jellico, Tennessee. The tracks wound through the mountain bordering a 50-foot gorge and river below. If a train traveled more than 35 mph it stood the chance of never making the sharp curve at a place called The Narrows. The train traveled at a high rate of speed and when it reached The Narrows, jumped the tracks. Five cars went into the river gorge. Bodies were scattered everywhere. Thirty-six soldiers and the engineer and fireman were killed. Some were trapped in the water below the train cars. As many as two hundred soldiers were injured. Ambulances from towns all around arrived on the scene to transport bodies to hospitals. The townspeople of Jellico came out in swarms to assist the wounded. Since the soldiers were not fully dressed because they were preparing for bed when the trained plunged into the gorge, they were in need of clothing and shoes. Residents of Jellico brought blankets and began preparing food. The shelves at the local stores were depleted of milk, bread, and canned products. Sandwiches and soup were made by all the ladies. Some soldiers were transported to homes to spend the remainder of the night. A second train was called to transport the ambulatory soldiers on into Knoxville, Tennessee.

Not a person in the small town of Clinton slept during the swell of loud sirens and flashing lights that broke through the silence of the night. Everyone sat in wait of an enemy air attack. You could almost hear a person's breathing. The following morning news of the train wreck spread rapidly throughout the town. The derailment of a troop train at the Narrows on Jellico Mountain was the second worst train accident during World War II.

Blackouts continued and the secrecy of the Manhattan Project stretched on in the city behind the fence. President Roosevelt had passed away and Vice President Harry Truman was now in command of the country. Truman had had no knowledge of atomic bombs being built that would end the war. The bombs were dropped on Hiroshima and Nagasaki, Japan, in 1945, thus ending the war between the United States and Japan.

After two years, there were no more blackouts, no more sirens blaring in the middle of the night. My dad's job had ended. He, like thousands of workers in Oak Ridge, Tennessee, returned to his home state. The war was over. The little house on Whitley Avenue was waiting for my family, but there would be one less member coming home. A banner bearing a gold star now hung in our window.

WAIT 'TIL YOU HEAR THIS ONE!

IN RESPONSE to recently discovering the old photographs on Facebook, I wrote this story. A dear friend and past co-worker of mine before my retirement from the State of Tennessee read my story and called me immediately. We had worked together for fifteen years and kept in contact after I moved back to Kentucky.

Magnet Knitting Mills, Clinton, TN during WW II

I was taken aback by the story my friend, Edna, told me. Her father and grandfather were farmers back in the early 1940s and owned farms in the Oak Ridge, Tennessee area, which at that time was not even called Oak Ridge. When the Federal government came in and bought up all the farm land, her family had to give up their homes and farms and move away. They found housing in the small town of Clinton.

Every morning when I left home with my sister, Wanda, and walked to the elementary school, another little girl was crossing the old bridge that spanned the Clinch River just a number of yards from our house, on her way to the same school. She, too, was in the second grade and the school was also new to her. It wasn't until my friend read my story about life during World War II in Clinton, Tennessee, that I learned the little girl crossing the old wooden bridge had been my friend and co-worker, Edna. I was almost speechless. I could hardly believe we had been friends for thirty-four years and never realized she and I were those two little girls walking from Cullom Street to the local elementary school every morning during two years of World War II. I was amazed at how much we had in common during our childhood and were just now discovering our past history together. The bridge in the attached photograph was a stone's throw from my house and was Edna's path to school each day.

The Magnet Knitting Mills are gone now and all that remains are the memories of a long ago time when they played a vital role in the lives of American soldiers during a perilous war.

It had been at least a year and a half since my family had moved back home from Tennessee after Daddy completed his job with the government, building houses and dormitories in Oak Ridge for the Federal government's Manhattan Project. My sister, Velma, had married a young man she met while working in Oak Ridge during the war and they were living in Tennessee. Janette had married her high school sweetheart who was in the army, and Bena Mae had graduated from high school and returned home to Kentucky with the rest of the family. She was working at the Grapette Company after completing a business course with Coldiron Business School. Now and then she brought home a case of those little Grapettes, and we kids thought we had died and gone to Heaven when we saw her walk through the front door with the little six-ounce bottles of that purple drink, a soft drink that was better than anything we had ever swigged down our throats.

I was in the fifth grade of school when one afternoon, there was a knock at our classroom door. My teacher opened the door and after speaking to a young man a couple of minutes the two of them entered the room. The young man was very pleasant and he began introducing himself to the classroom. He said he was a "magician." Well, I can tell you, now, that created a bit of excitement among my classmates. On rare occasions we had the privilege of being entertained by a variety show in the school auditorium but we had never seen anything like a magic show arrive in town. We only saw magicians when a carnival came to town once a year.

The most exciting thing that we could ever experience was when the carnival arrived in town, staying a full week, and every kid in the neighborhood was begging his parents for a dime to go to the carnival. The boys who didn't have a dime to get into the carnival rigged up a way of helping each other crawl under the back of the tents without being caught. We didn't care if we had money for rides and cotton candy as long as we were privileged to be under the hot lights and in the atmosphere of all the music, entertainment, and rides at the carnival. But, of course, having a few nickels for the rides would be the icing on the cake. There was nothing like being on a Ferris Wheel and riding to the top in one of the cars where we could look out over the entire town and see all of the lights in the houses at night. I was the one kid who always got sick from riding any of the rides, including the Merry-go-round. That didn't matter to me as long as I could sit on a bench and watch my friends yelling and laughing with excitement on the rides.

But on this special day at school, it wasn't anything like a carnival coming to town. We were being introduced to a program that would be held in the school auditorium, a magic act by real magicians. There were two brothers who would perform. The young man standing before us began working his hands back and forth, performing a magic act with coins. The classroom became very excited as they watched him make the quarter in his hand disappear. I was getting a bit fidgety while I watched the magician work. There was something familiar about him and I just couldn't figure it out. What was there about him that drew my attention? I continued to watch him perform his magic and then he finished his introduction and invited us all to attend the show. He turned and walked out the door. That's when it hit me like a bolt of lightning. "I knew him!"

I was a very shy little girl but at that moment, my shyness left me and I ran to the front of the classroom and spoke to the teacher. I told her I knew the magician and could I leave the classroom and find him. I needed to talk to him. She gave me permission. I could feel the perspiration on my face. Would he still be where I could see him in the hallway? I rushed out the door and immediately spotted the tall lanky young man as he was climbing the stairs to the second floor level. I called to him in my soft meek childlike voice, "Steve." He stopped and turned. I ran up to him and said, "My name is Pat Estep. I used to live in Clinton during the war when you and Benny worked at Denney's Café. You knew my sisters." I didn't have to say another word. Steve smiled real big. He remembered me! He remembered my sisters. He remembered my family!

Steve looked at me as though I was his long lost little sister. He recognized me even though I had grown a few inches! He was suddenly as excited as I was.

Steve and Benny had worked as magicians, taking their show on the road. And then war was declared. My family didn't know why the two young men were never drafted into the army, but when the war started, they had to discontinue their travels from town to town because gasoline and automobile tires had been rationed, therefore, they could not continue their magic acts. Employment was difficult to find and then the two brothers ended up in Clinton, Tennessee, where they had taken jobs working at Denney's Café until the war ended. Denney's Café was two doors up the street from where my family lived. It was a busy little place, due mainly to the Magnet Knitting Mills just across the street that employed several hundred people. They were manufacturing parachutes for the war effort. Men working in Oak Ridge would stop by every morning for breakfast and my sisters, Janette and Bena Mae, who worked as waitresses in the café after school and on Saturdays would have sack lunches prepared for the men when they arrived. Wanda, Don, and I, would often play outside the café and when Steve and Benny took their afternoon breaks, they would entertain us with their magic, showing us how to make a quarter disappear and working their magic with playing cards. We had never seen a magician in our lives and there was nothing like watching the simple tricks become an illusion. We were true believers of their talents. They told us about their travels and how they could pull a person through the keyhole of a door. That kept our little minds baffled. Every day, during the summer months, we kids trotted up to Denney's and were there on the wooden benches when Steve and

Benny came through the door to take their breaks. Not only had they become very close friends to my older sisters but they always greeted us and treated us kids as though we were very special. A strong bond had been created between strangers during a traumatic time in history, a bond that could never be broken. This was true throughout the entire community. Nearly everyone living there was from somewhere else and was seeking something to make their temporary living quarters seem like home.

In my excitement at seeing Steve at school, I told him that my sister, Bena Mae, was living at home. He appeared to be thrilled to learn this. He told me that the magic show cost a quarter but not to worry; there would be tickets at the door for all of my family to see the performance which would be held during school hours and also in the evenings. I returned to the classroom and explained to my teacher why I knew the magician. I had just become the classroom celebrity!

My feet didn't touch the ground as I ran home from school that day. I couldn't wait to tell Mama and Bena Mae about meeting Steve, of the Steve and Benny duo. As you can well guess, Wanda, Don, and I attended the performance of the magic act and that evening, Bena Mae was there to see her old friends again. It was as exciting as if we were meeting movie stars. This was a once in a lifetime experience. During the show, Steve and Benny performed the magic act of pulling a person through the keyhole of a door, the act he had told us about but we could never quite imagine such a thing happening in real life. During the performance, they needed a volunteer to help them perform the act, and as you can probably guess, they called my sister up on the stage to help them. She was totally embarrassed, but she could not say No. They pulled my sister through the keyhole of a door. Don't ask me how it happened because I never knew, but it was the best thing this ten-year-old had ever seen.

Steve and Benny were back on the road again after the war had ended. We never saw them after that, but that one greeting was so special, we would always remember them as a very important part of our lives and the experiences we shared during the war. When I see the famous artists like David Copperfield and others perform on television today, I always remember the best of them all, two young men who put a little joy into the lives of a few small children, day after day. These were two unknown young men who made a few lives happy while the rest of the country was experiencing hardships and suffering from the war. I'll always remember two very special souls – Steve and Benny. God bless you both!

BLUE HORSE WRAPPERS

Do you remember the day when kids collected anything and everything by sending in box tops, labels, and coupons? The best example for this is *The Christmas Story* when Ralphie ordered his Dick Tracy secret code book for a dime and four box tops. And there was the Red Ryder BB gun. Every kid wanted one of those. My sister still has my nephew's little wooden gun with Red Ryder written on the side. What a treasure that is today.

But this story is about collecting Blue Horse Wrappers. At the beginning of every school year, kids went shopping with their mothers to buy their new school supplies, pencils, notebooks, erasers, rulers, and of course the notebook paper that came with a loose leaf filler wrapper around the paper. A small package came with about 25 sheets of paper for a nickel. A picture of a horse's head was printed in the center of the wrapper. If you sent in a certain number of wrappers to the company, you could win a prize. There was a long list of prizes and all were very nice. The prize you would receive depended on the number of wrappers sent to the company and you never knew what your prize would be.

Now, just think of this. If you could collect enough blue horse wrappers you could receive a new bicycle. Not many kids in my neighborhood owned a bicycle. There wasn't a set number of wrappers required for the bicycle but I decided to go for it. I started saving blue horse wrappers. I asked every classmate to save their wrappers for me. I knew another girl who was saving them and I asked if she would sell hers to me. Of course, I had to beg Mama to give me the money. I finally succeeded and found myself paying $2.00 for 200 wrappers.

Little by little, my collection began to build. After a while Mama started fussing about so many little piles all over the house. She was getting tired of looking at them. Month after month, I added a few more wrappers to my collection. It was beginning to be difficult to find friends who had bought notebook paper.

Every few days I would count my wrappers. The numbers were adding up. I had finally saved 5,000 blue horse wrappers. By this time, Mama wasn't only tired of looking at them all over the house, she was beginning to yell, "Get those things out of this house and out of my sight!"

I checked the list of prizes and every item looked very inviting. Five thousand wrappers should reward me with something really nice. I read the instructions for sending the wrappers to the company, thinking I would need a large box for mailing. Well, I discovered I had to cut out the picture of the horse and that was the only part of the wrapper they wanted. The horse's head was featured in the center of the paper band. I had to cut out 5,000 horses' heads.

I sat at the kitchen table for hours at a time, cutting, cutting, cutting. When Mama saw the mess in the kitchen floor, I was getting really close to becoming a child up for adoption. I very neatly cut out every horse and when I finished, they were stacked and packaged, ready for mailing. A few days after sending my package in the mail, I met the postman every day before he reached our house, hoping he had a delivery for me.

About two weeks later, there it was – my prize, all wrapped up in a box about 10 x 12 inches and covered in brown paper! My hands shook as I removed the wrappings. And then I opened the box to discover five thousand Blue Horse wrappers had earned me a tabletop Magnavox radio. It was the first time I had ever saved items to win a prize.

For years the little radio sat on Mama's Hoosier cabinet in the kitchen where we got to listen every night at suppertime to Gabriel Heater as he broadcast, "Aahhh, there's good news tonight," or Fulton Lewis, Jr. Daddy insisted on listening to the latest news and we kids were not to interrupt the broadcast for any reason. It is peculiar how no one in the family can remember whatever happened to that little radio. Oh, how I would love to have it today. So many memories are connected to the Magnavox radio purchased with 5,000 Blue Horse Wrappers.

DADDY'S CLASSIC CAR

We kids were in the front yard when we saw a car coming down the road, shining bright as a new penny. It looked like something a movie star would drive. We watched as a cream colored convertible pulled up in front of our house. It had wooden side panels and enough chrome on the front and back ends to light up the whole town on Saturday night. Our mouths dropped when the door opened and who should get out of the car, but my Daddy. He was driving a 1948 Towne and Country Chrysler convertible, a car like nobody in our town had ever seen the likes of and probably never would again.

Chrysler Town and Country Car, 1948

The Chrysler had a special feature about it that you didn't ordinarily see on other cars. On each side of the hood was a long brass fog horn, the kind that only big tractor-trailer trucks used. I'm sure you remember those. The truck would pull up to the rear of your car and blow those fog horns loud enough to scare you through the roof of your car. It might also put you in mind of the big car driven by the handsome movie star, Dale Robertson. You should remember him in "The Tales of Wells Fargo." He had that swaggering southwestern accent, and everyone recognized him when he drove down the street in his long white customized Buick convertible. Yes, Dale had his longhorn steer head horns for a hood ornament and my Daddy had his long brass fog horns.

Most of Daddy's jobs were miles from home so he left each Monday morning, somewhere between 3:00 a.m. and 6:00 a.m. for work and returned on Friday evening to spend the weekend with the family. I can't remember the car Daddy drove at the time, but on Saturday morning he made his usual run to the bank downtown and then drove his car to Morgan Motor Company to get his regular oil check and change of spark plugs. One thing Daddy had bigger than a bank account was his ego. While he stood around waiting for the car to be serviced he looked over the cars in the car lot and talked to the salesmen at the dealership. Before the conversations ended, the owner of the dealership had convinced Daddy what an important man around town he was and a person of his status should be driving a nice new car. By the time Daddy left the car lot, instead of coming home in his old car, he was driving a spanking bright new one. The 1949 movie, *The Sun Comes Up* with Jeanette MacDonald driving one of the classiest automobiles ever made, was released the same year my daddy bought his new car.

Daddy wasn't always one who could use good business sense when somebody was boosting his ego, and this time, they went overboard. Mama took one look at the beautiful Chrysler and nearly fainted. It didn't take much for Mama to reach for her smelling salts. "We can't afford a car like that, and besides, it's not the kind of car a family man drives. What'll people think when we drive up in front of the church on Sunday in a thing like that? They'll think you've lost your mind, and as far as I'm concerned, you have!" As for us kids, it was definitely the kind of car for a family man. We couldn't wait to hop in the back seat and go through town with the top down where all of our friends could see us. Daddy would look just like Dale Robertson.

Daddy bought the convertible in early October. People may have called it a case of male menopause, and even though we kids didn't know what male menopause was, we didn't really care. We had the fanciest car in town. That was the fall we took a trip around Booger Mountain to Tennessee for a family reunion. As we drove along a winding dirt road to the church, a couple of teenage girls were walking along the edge of the road. Without warning, Daddy took advantage of the situation and blew his fog horns. The girls jumped so high they nearly fell into a ditch. Yes, I suppose Daddy was suffering from male menopause, but we kids thought it was the funniest thing we'd ever seen our Daddy do. Mama just slid down in the front seat turning red from embarrassment.

We kept the Town and Country Chrysler convertible exactly two months and never once got to ride in it with the top down. Daddy took it back to Morgan Motor Company and traded it for a 1950 turquoise Hudson Commodore with big whitewall tires. That car stayed in the family until the 1980s. Both cars were considered 'classics'.

I'd give my eye teeth to ride in the beautiful Chrysler convertible again—and hear Daddy blow those fog horns.

FATHER'S DAY

If any of us kids said we were sick on Sunday morning and didn't feel like going to church, we had better have a fever because when Daddy said, "You're going to church," he meant it. Daddy sang in the church choir and he sat on the back row on the very end where there was no one seated in front of him. Now, Daddy was a large man and when the choir stood to sing, he was the last one to stand. When the song ended, Daddy was also the last one to be seated. He had to tug at one pant leg and then the other before he could sit down. We kids knew everybody in the congregation was staring at our daddy, and there was nothing more embarrassing to us.

Not only that, but during the sermon I just knew Daddy was staring at me with that expression on his face like Moses on the Mountain, and that told me I'd better not wiggle or talk to my little chatty friend sitting next to me. Daddy would twist in his seat and all I could think was, "He's coming down here. He's coming down and gonna sit right beside me. Oh, Lord, what did I do to deserve this?" While I thought Daddy had his eye on me, my other sisters were thinking the same thoughts, "Oh, Lord, he's getting up. He's gonna come down here. He'll embarrass me to death! I know all my friends are watching!"

We never missed a church service, even when the snow was above our ankles and we had to walk the half-mile distance. There was one Sunday of the year when Daddy didn't sing in the choir and it was on Father's Day; he sat in the congregation with Mama, right in the center of the middle section of the auditorium. All of us kids were required to be in church that Sunday—all eight of us! It was a very special occasion. That was the day the pastor recognized the youngest father, the oldest father, and the father with the most children present. They received token gifts. Of course, we knew we were the largest family, except for one other who always showed up together on Father's Day. That was the John Smith family, also with eight kids. Five of them were girls.

There's nothing more embarrassing to a bunch of kids than to have attention called to them in church. We had to go through the ordeal once a year every year! The pastor had already recognized the oldest and youngest fathers, and then asked the fathers with the most children present to please stand. He began the countdown with the reasonable number of 10. No one stood. When he got to the number 8, Mr. Smith and my dad both stood. Mr. Smith was called Long John by all of the local people. He was our faithful police officer on the street, protecting the citizens. "Alright, let's start with Mr. Estep. Would the children please stand." We kids were scattered throughout the congregation and the pastor started the count. "…4, 5, 6, 7!" He counted only seven. Okay, "Hmmm! Let's count them again. I must have missed one." Something wasn't right and both Wanda and I knew what the problem was. With a second count of seven, we were asked to sit and the pastor called on the Smith family to stand, "…5, 6, 7, 8."

That wasn't good! All eight of us were there on Father's Day every year. The pastor said, "We need to count the Estep children again. "Would you please stand?"

My sister, Wanda, was sitting beside me and we were both twisting our church bulletins and whispering under our breath. I won't say what we were whispering but the expressions on our faces were quite revealing. There was a little brother out there somewhere and his life wasn't going to be worth a plug nickel when we got our hands on him.

He was causing us embarrassment. Wanda and I knew why the pastor only counted seven of us in the congregation. Every Sunday Daddy gave us each ten cents for the Sunday school offering envelope. If he happened to give us two nickels, we pocketed one of them and as soon as Sunday school was over, we slipped out the side door of the church and made a mad dash to the Milk Dairy for the biggest and best ice cream cone in town. Wanda and I knew our brother was somewhere walking down the street licking on an ice cream cone. He had forgotten it was Father's Day.

The seven sisters stood again. And again, we heard, "…4, 5, 6, 7!" There should have been 8! That's when the pastor said, "I think a couple of you deacons had better go home with Brother Estep. There's a young boy that may need your protection. HaHaHa," everybody laughed except seven sisters. As far as we were concerned, our little brother didn't need protection from Daddy. It was his sisters he had better be hiding from.

John Smith received the Father's Day recognition that year.

A DRESS WITH COVERED BUTTONS

By this time, I was in high school. All the rest of my sisters were either married or planning to get married. I guess you could call it luck when all of us could wear the same size clothes. It came in handy when you needed a new or different dress for an occasion and you could borrow one from a sister knowing that none of your friends had ever seen the dress before and as far as they were concerned, it was a new dress. Now and then, one of my sisters would have a dress they didn't particularly like and they would give it to me. That's just what happened in this case. My sister, Bena Mae had taken a business course at Coldiron's Business School and was a bookkeeper at the Grapette Company and working on her Hope Chest for when and if she got married. She was already 23 and considered to be 'an old maid!' She had given me a pretty chambray dress of soft pink and milk chocolate brown. It was a quite classy summer dress with tiny covered buttons all the way down from the neckline to the waist. Little tabs at the shoulders and neck were also held back by the tiny covered buttons. The dress had an eight-gore skirt which accented the figure and I loved wearing it. After awhile a few of the little covered buttons came off and couldn't be replaced so I went to town and bought several cards of baby pearl buttons to replace them. I spent hours sewing those buttons on the dress.

No two sisters have ever given their mother a better reason to turn to hysteria than Bena Mae and me the night we got into a fight. I can't begin to tell you why my sister and I were fighting, but we rarely needed a reason. We were good at calling each other names and locking the other out of the bathroom, sitting on the toilet reading a book for what seemed like ages, just for spite.

It was a night when Daddy was home. Daddy's job kept him away during the week and he came home on weekends. One rule we always followed was never to let Daddy know we were arguing or as Mama would say, "He'll take his belt to you!" He never had before and we had no reason to believe he would actually "take his belt to us!" However, we didn't chance it! That was one of Mama's ways of keeping us in tow. Daddy would twist in his chair, clear his throat and wrinkle his brow then start rubbing his fists together. He kinda reminded you of a wrestler getting ready to climb into the ring. Next, he would unbuckle his belt. That was a sure sign that one of us kids had done something wrong and Daddy was going to "take his belt to us." We would look at each other and then scramble. You can't imagine how fast a bunch of kids could crawl under the bed—waiting to hear a name called, hoping it wasn't theirs; when actually, Daddy had had a little too much to eat for supper and was just loosening his belt.

Anyway, my sister and I were in the middle bedroom which didn't have a door we could close to act as a sound barrier for keeping Daddy from hearing us 'scream' at each other. We were in each other's faces clawing and scratching. My sister had long fingernails which were to her advantage, and she knew how to use them. We weren't being kind about it and at the same time, we knew we couldn't let Daddy hear us from the living room where he was reading the newspaper. So we had to whisper. Yes, "whisper"! It would have helped tune out our argument somewhat if the radio had been on. I believe we were the only siblings who could have a knock-down, drag-out squabble, scratch and pull hair, and never attract Daddy's attention in the next room. Don't ask me why we were arguing because I can't begin to tell you. By the time we were finished, we had no idea what the argument was about anyway. After several minutes of breathing fire in each other's face, Mama began wringing her hands and begging us not to fight. She was just about ready for her Geritol but she wouldn't leave us alone long enough to go to the kitchen to take a dose.

Somehow, in the course of our heated argument, the subject of the chambray dress came up. Whatever I had just said, Bena Mae responded, "If that's the way you want to be about it, I'll just take my dress back." I answered, "If you take your dress, I'll take my buttons." I reached for the scissors which just happened to be lying on Mama's treadle sewing machine. I began cutting off the buttons — whack, whack, whack — taking no care to prevent damage to the dress itself. For every button removed, at least 20 buttons, I cut a hole in the fabric. Bena Mae grabbed the dress, and with fire in her eyes said, "Now, nobody will wear it!" *R-i-i-p-p.* She tore every seam from the hem to the waistline of the eight-gored skirt. All the while, Mama was still wringing her hands and pleading, "Girls, please don't destroy a perfectly good dress." Meanwhile, Daddy had no idea anything out of the ordinary was taking place. He continued reading his newspaper.

Rather than see the garment end up as cleaning rags, the next day Mama repaired the skirt of the dress by sewing the seams together again and adding a waistband from what was left of the bodice. The bodice itself was beyond repair. I had done a good scissors act on it, but all in all, I still had a pretty pink and brown summer skirt to wear.

Ah, Yes! Life was somewhat insufferable and yet amusing at times around our house. Nobody suffered serious harm from our week to week scuffles over whose turn it was to wash the supper dishes; why Wanda left the oatmeal pan for somebody else to wash; hogging the whole bed at night; who used the last of the shampoo; who used all the hot water; "it's my turn in the bathroom"; being locked out of the house on purpose; "I ironed that blouse and you're not going to wear it first"; and last but not least, "I'll kill you if you tell." A little Mercurochrome or Iodine took care of the bruises and scratches and Mama just took a dose of Geritol now and then to calm her nerves.

Daddy was so oblivious to it all, thinking our household was peaceful and quiet—well, in a way it was—when Daddy was home!

The pickup truck could be heard scuddling out the gravel road and the two in the middle of a fight, stopped immediately, wiped their tears and cleaned their faces. The ones in the top of the tree could scuttle down faster than a squirrel. The girls in shorts and halters were in the house changing to a skirt and blouse in the blink of an eye, and somebody else was hiding the playing cards. Another grabbed a book and started reading. All was peace and quiet. "Daddy's Home."

THE DOOR TO DOOR SALESMEN

"Mama, there's a man at the door. He wants to see you!" Oh, goodness gracious, why did she have to open the door? It's another salesman. This time it was the Fuller Brush man. The Fuller Brush Company was quite popular and Mama had bought many of their products over the years. She had their cleaning products, shoe polish for all our shoes, especially Daddy's, and household brushes. I still have the old clothes brush that had a ribbon tied to the handle and it hung on the back of my parents' bedroom door. Every Sunday morning after Daddy was dressed and ready to go to church, Mama brushed his suit jacket down so there wasn't any hair or lint on his clothes. The clothes brush hangs on my bedroom door handle today but it is never used. It looks as good as new.

Another door-to-door salesman who frequented our door was a neighbor, John Adams. He didn't come very often because he sold men's custom-made suits. Every two or three years, Daddy would be measured for a new Sunday suit. Daddy was a large man, hard to fit, so Mr. Adams would come to the house and take Daddy's measurements for his new suit.

About once a month, the Jewel Tea man would arrive and Mama

would find herself purchasing another piece of the Jewel Tea dishes and some of the flavorings and baking products. She never bought the plates, cups and saucers for the dishes, but she had collected the serving pieces. I remember the teapot, a coffee dispenser that hung on the wall, a pie plate and a large platter.

If it hadn't been for the door-to-door salesmen, I doubt that there would be a single photograph of the kids in my family. The man would be standing on our front porch with his big camera on a long-legged tripod. Mama was always guaranteed she didn't have to buy the pictures after they were developed if she didn't like them.

We were living in Manchester, Kentucky, when the photographer knocked on the door. I was eighteen months old and Wanda was three and a half. We were both wearing our little feedsack dresses with rickrack trim Mama had made for our everyday wear. I had on black hightop shoes with long stockings that pinned to the undershirt I always wore under my dresses. We weren't exactly prepared for picture-taking that day, so Mama washed our faces, wet my hair on top and twisted a curl around her finger then she folded down my long stocking over the top of my black shoes. As the man said, if Mama didn't like the pictures, she didn't have to buy them. She was told the pictures might be entered in a baby beauty contest. The photographer sat us up on an oval table in front of the living room window. Mama's Sears 'n Robuck paneled lace curtains hung as a backdrop for our picture-taking. There was little doubt that either my sister or I would win the contest.

Several days later, Mama was shopping on the Main Street of town a couple of blocks from where we lived. She passed a store window and noticed a group of framed pictures in the window. Taking a closer look, she saw that they were all pictures of babies and much to her surprise, she was staring at an 8 x 10 colored photograph of the contest winner. It was me! I had won the beauty contest. The prize for the contest was free pictures of both Wanda and me.

1937

Among the sales people who knocked at our door month by month, one special person was a sales lady named Aunt Lizzie Redmond. If we were sitting on our front porch, we could see the elderly lady coming down the hill towards our house. The little old lady always leaned forward to keep her balance. She wore a long black dress and in winter time she wore a black cape and bonnet and carried her black bag of merchandise in one hand and a walking cane in the other. All the neighbors knew her. She was about ninety-percent blind. Selling her medicinal products and salves was her only means of income. Her young granddaughter came with her, holding her arm and guiding her path as she went door-to-door making sales calls.

We heard the tap, tap, tap, of her cane as she slowly crossed the front porch. We knew who was there before opening the door. Aunt Lizzie was one sales person with whom Mama couldn't say No. She would sit patiently while Aunt Lizzie removed her products from the black bag, one by one.

My sister, Bena Mae had been infected by insect bites above her ankles on both her legs. Large sores had formed. Mama believed she had been bitten by mosquitoes. The doctor couldn't identify the infections and couldn't come up with a remedy. The sores grew larger and larger. When Aunt Lizzie offered a salve that might cure the condition, Mama decided to give it a try. So far, nothing else had worked and scars were beginning to form on my sister's legs. Mama bought the salve and a few days later the sores on Bena Mae's legs improved, but they left deep concave scars. The doctor told Mama to continue using the salve until the infections had healed.

When Mama handed Aunt Lizzie coins for payment, she would rub the coins between her fingers then hold them close to her eye to identify them. I can remember watching her place dollar bills up under one eye to see the numbers on them. Month after month, Aunt Lizzie Redmond hobbled down the gravel road to our house, and each month, Mama bought her products.

THE BLUE SERGE SUIT

About every two years, Mama had a new suit custom made for Daddy. John Adams, one of the door-to-door salesmen would come by the house to get Daddy's measurements and Mama would pick out the suiting fabric for his next Sunday wardrobe. Mr. Adams had lots of six-inch suiting samples and he often gave a batch of discontinued fabrics to Mama for making tack quilts.

All of us kids had married and left home and Mama and Daddy were alone in the six-room house to live out their old age. It was very quiet on Sunday mornings getting ready for Sunday school and church since all of the kids were gone. There was no more fighting over who was next in the bathroom, or the weekly fussin' and cussin' under our breaths where Daddy couldn't hear us.

After breakfast was over, Daddy went to the back bedroom to get dressed while Mama occupied the front bedroom alone. What a blessing it was for her to finally get the use of the dresser mirror without three or four girls scrounging in front of her to brush their hair and apply their makeup.

Mama usually laid out Daddy's suit, shirt, and tie that he was to wear to church that day. She had forgotten that morning, and was in the front bedroom getting dressed. Daddy walked into the room and said, "Are you about ready to go?" Mama made a quick swivel turn and said, "Surely to goodness you're not wearing that old suit! It's as old as Methuselah. You haven't worn that suit in twenty years and it's way too tight on you. Go change that tie, too! It's got gravy stains down the front, and is the ugliest tie you own." Daddy had a collection of ties given to him for Christmas and Father's Day. One of my sisters had a knack for picking out ugly ties, and this was one of them.

It was almost time to leave for church and Daddy decided there was nothing wrong with his suit. He wasn't going to take time to change into one of his good suits, but he took the time to grab another tie from the hook on the back of the bedroom door. His ties always had the knots tied securely and ready to pull over his head. The light blue serge suit was so old it still had a button placket in the trousers and was also so tight on Daddy that the seams would probably rip when he sat down.

There wasn't time for changing, so out the door he went and waited in the car for Mama. When she climbed in and closed the car door, she knew it was too late to argue over his clothes. They would be late for Sunday school and since Daddy was the Bible teacher, he couldn't afford to arrive late at the church.

Park Hill Church was small and Daddy taught the adult Sunday school lesson in the main auditorium. Mama chose a pew about three rows from the front and was getting settled in her seat while Daddy spread out his quarterly and Bible on the podium. Daddy was about six feet tall and weighed no less than 200 pounds. He unbuttoned the jacket to his suit and began teaching the lesson he had prepared. He wasn't a person to stand still when he was talking. He paced back and forth across the pulpit and talked with his hands a great deal.

Mama looked up and noticed the button placket in his trousers and then she saw that Daddy forgot to put on a belt that morning. Oh, Lord in Heaven! The way Daddy was pacing and waving his arms up and down, Mama knew the buttons on the tight trousers were going to pop any minute and his pants would fall to the floor.

Daddy was absorbed in delivering the lesson and it sounded more like he was preaching than teaching. At the same time, Mama wasn't hearing a word he said. She started to perspire and was even beginning to feel a bit dizzy. How could he have forgotten his belt that morning? If she didn't oversee everything he did, Daddy could never get himself properly dressed to go anywhere.

Did he have to present such a long lesson that morning? She didn't think she could suffer through to the end. Her eyes were fixed on those buttons; waiting for the first one to pop and a seam to rip and everyone in the auditorium to see a performance they would never forget. She'd never be able to face those people again for the rest of her life, and when she got home, she was going to see to it that Daddy paid for her misery.

They both made it through the church service and on the way home, Mama didn't speak a word, she was so upset. She and Daddy changed clothes, and when Daddy took off his blue serge suit, she grabbed it, headed straight for the front door and down to the side yard. In those days, residents used large oil drums for burning their trash. The tall oil drum stood at the edge of the branch. Mama threw the blue serge suit and the gravy-stained tie, all into the oil drum then she added a little fuel and lit a couple of kitchen matches, setting the suit and tie afire. That was the end of the blue serge suit. Daddy would never embarrass her and make her suffer again like he did that Sunday morning.

A PLACE CALLED FROG LEVEL

"Frog Level! Who ever heard of a place called Frog Level?" my daughter said. "Well, you have, now! Your Pappaw Estep was born and raised there." She looked at me in disbelief as I continued, "and we're going to find it today, the Lord willing."

Talk about stopping on a dime, that, she did. My daughter, Jan, was driving when suddenly, she saw the signpost reading "Estep Lane" and it pointed to a narrow winding lane leading to the top of a hill. Hmmmm, only one house sat at the top of that hill and a few young calves were scattered over the hillside. Could it be possible that an Estep family lived in the house?

We had no sense of direction but we had been given instructions on how to get to the old family cemetery and from there, we would use the Daniel Boone method and wander through until we found what we were looking for, hopefully, without getting completely lost! Since our first mission that day was to find the cemetery, we drove on around the main road until we found the fenced-in graveyard on the side of a hill, located right in front of a large barn. It was one of the prettiest graveyards I had ever seen. What was once called the Estep Cemetery had been renamed and was being called the Jones

Cemetery. There were many Estep gravestones, including my grandparents, Samuel and Matilda Nevils Estep, and great-grandparents, William and Elizabeth Eastridge Estep who had journeyed from Wilkesboro, North Carolina, to southwest Virginia in the mid-1800s.

I think we read every epitaph in the graveyard wondering which of the deceased had been related to us. At the bottom of the hill stood a renovated two-story house I had seen years before on another trip to Virginia with my parents. My great-grandparents had once lived there. My heartfelt desire had always been to take a tour of the house, believing the spirits of my great-grandparents were still there. They were the immigrants who had come by wagon on their way west. My grandpa, Sam, was the youngest of four children and a newborn infant at the time. I had been told the family was headed west and it wasn't an easy journey when the wagon broke down. They were on a sojourn and realized with four small children, they could go no farther, so their journey ended in the hills of southwest Virginia.

Leaving the cemetery and turning back to the main road, Jan and I came to the road sign again that said "Estep Lane." Debating whether or not we should take a chance on driving up the lane, we decided, "What's the worst that can happen to us?" Well, maybe nothing unless we were met at the top of the hill by someone holding a shotgun and pointing it in our faces! We hadn't spotted any trespassing signs posted anywhere, so, up the hill we went!

The events of the day became an expedition I never thought would occur in my lifetime. As could be expected, Jan turned onto the long narrow drive knowing we had no place to turn around if we changed our minds. I could see the big sad eyes of cows gazing at us. I kept saying, "We have no way of knowing if an Estep family lives in that house."

My daughter's brilliant reply was, "If they have cows, they have to be named Estep." If that wasn't some rationale! I just shook my head! Daddy had left the farm when he was thirteen and hadn't seen a cow since, except for the one blocking the two-lane road around Booger Mountain on one of our trips to Middlesboro, Kentucky, to visit relatives, and he had to stop the car to pull the cow off to the side of the road while other cars drove around us. We kids slid down in the backseat of the car, knowing what the other people were thinking: "Look at that crazy man leading a cow down the middle of the road!" And, years later, Daddy bought a little 20-acre farm with about twenty cows on it. Each cow had a pet name. Figure that! I kept shaking my head at my daughter's comment, "If they have cows, they have to be named Estep!"

We reached the top of the hill behind the house and parked in the driveway. Jan was the gutsy one so she knocked on the front door of the beautiful two-story dwelling. Down the valley and looking over to another mountain was a breathtaking view of the Sand Caves, a trail blazed by Daniel Boone in the 1700s when he journeyed across the mountain finding his way into Kentucky.

A lady answered the door and to my surprise, identified herself by the name, "Estep." Who would have believed it? She welcomed us into her home when we identified ourselves, and in a matter of minutes we were discussing family history. We were deep in discussion when the lady's husband entered through the kitchen door. I stood and introduced myself and the man immediately said, "I know you! I wrote you a letter one time." How true!

"And I remember the letter!" I was amazed that he and I could recall a letter written fifteen years earlier. The letter he had written was in my genealogy files and dated 1999. This was the first time for us to meet. As soon as Jan was introduced to my newfound cousin, she said, "Mom was hoping we could find the farm where my grandfather was raised, and she is also wondering if it is possible that the little log cabin where he was born in 1896 is still there!"

My cousin's response left us speechless when he said, "Yes, I know where the farm is, and yes, the log cabin is still there. It's for sale."

I could hardly speak. I grew weak in the knees. This was a day I never dreamed I would experience. I was taken back to a time in history I had only heard about from my mother's family stories. This was a day never to be forgotten.

I knew Jan and I could never follow my cousin's driving directions since we were not familiar with the territory. Terry's wife spoke up and said, "Instead of giving them the directions, why don't you just take them?" The next thing I knew, we were piling into an SUV and heading back down the narrow lane towards a place called Frog Level, hidden back in the Virginia hills. We could never have found Grandpa Estep's farm on our own. The SUV wound around the dirt roads and through the hills of southwest Virginia covering three counties, Lee County, Virginia, then Claiborne County and Hancock County, Tennessee. Terry pointed to a large expanse of hills where the grass was so green and glistened so bright in the sunlight, I had to squint my eyes. Its beauty was beyond belief.

"See that hillside over there?" Terry said, pointing to the area I had been observing. "That's called Sal's Ridge". I immediately squealed, "You mean my great-grandmother owned all of that land?" Terry gave me a big grin. Sal was my great-grandmother's nickname. To my family, she was Great-grandma Brooks. She was the lady who went by train to the St. Louis World's Fair in 1904.

Terry had driven a few miles when we came to a signpost reading VA/TN State Line. Standing before us was a large gray barn. Oh my goodness, we had come to Grandpa Rowlett's farm, the place where my mother was born and raised. The barn stood in Virginia and we traveled on past, crossing the state line into Tennessee where the house once stood. Up to our right was the Brooks family cemetery on the side of a hill. Driving on down the dirt road, and taking a wide turn, there in the valley in the coolest part of the countryside was my dad's birthplace.

The road sign read, "Estep Hollow." A rippling creek with water flowing from a mountain spring ran alongside the cabin. The unoccupied log cabin had seen many years of use and abuse. It had been enlarged at one time and covered in batten board siding. There was a small front and back porch. We could see large logs peering through from the rafters and behind the batten board siding stood the original three-room log cabin. The ancient little cabin was surrounded by weeds and Jan couldn't wait to wade in the creek and gather rocks to take home. The creek was so cold and clear you could count every rock lining the bottom. All I could think was, "If only Mama could be here with us today."

Birthplace of Hobert Estep, Frog Level, VA. Born 1896

The cabin had stood empty since Grandpa Estep died in 1910, until my parents moved into the house about 1918 while Daddy worked for the Railroad. Mama bought only the necessities in furniture and then she made curtains for the windows. They made their home in Daddy's birthplace for a short period of time during the years of the Influenza Epidemic. Mama had given birth to my now 98-year-old sister in the little log house.

I could hardly wait to get home and tell my sisters of our discovery. The Lord provided his blessings that day. Jan and I drove out of Virginia so filled with joy we could hardly control our emotions. We were two very happy ladies. With tears brimming our eyes, we drove into the sunset, sharing our joy on that beautiful summer day in June. We couldn't stop talking. It was a day to be remembered. We had traveled to a place called Frog Level, Virginia, and found the little log cabin where my father was born.

BEFORE THE DIXIE

Every small town is remembered for something or someone special. My hometown is known mainly for Colonel Harland Sanders of KFC, but what I remember it for is the best chili in the world! In my hometown it was called the Chili Bun. No, there wasn't a wiener on it...that came later and was called a chili dog. Most people from other towns didn't know what you were talking about, and still don't, when you mentioned eating a chili bun. "A chili bun! What's that?" we often heard. Chili buns were always the family favorite, besides soup beans and cornbread.

My niece recently bought a book at Barnes and Nobles that featured foods of Kentucky and where they originated. I don't know the writer's name but in her book she told about the chili bun, which seems to have originated in London/Corbin vicinity of Kentucky, and was very well known. She gave the recipe and credited a small restaurant called Weaver's in London for their Chili Bun in the 1950s.

My niece was a bit curious about the writer's information and did a little research. She discovered the Chili Bun was being sold in Corbin years earlier by someone named Madison. She had never heard of an eating place called Madison's. To her surprise, I informed her that my brother-in-law, Talmage, (her uncle) and his older brother had a stand on Main Street in Corbin in the early 1930s where they made chili every day and sold Chili Buns to customers passing by on the street. The brother's name was "Madison."

I don't know when the Dixie first opened for business, but this story dates back even farther than the Dixie. I doubt that any of you have ever heard the story. I am guessing at dates, so bear with me. It was around the early 1930s when a couple of brothers opened a little chili stand on the southwest corner of Fifth and Main Streets. The two brothers were Madison and Talmage Young. Their parents had moved to Corbin from Georgia back around 1920. Mr. Young had transferred with the Railroad Company. Before opening the small business to sell chili buns, Talmage, the younger brother, had a job on the Island Queen Ferry at Cincinnati, Ohio. Making chili was one of his jobs on the ferry.

Madison and Talmage set up a stand on Main Street and sold hot dogs and chili buns to the passing patrons walking to and from downtown Corbin. I don't know which came first, the job on the Island Queen or the chili bun stand in Corbin; nevertheless, Talmage also made his own potato chips to go with the chili buns. According to my sister, the huge potato chip vat looked like one of the old wringer-style washing machines. Most of the residents walked everywhere they went in those days. There were very few automobile owners, so people could stop at the chili bun stand on their way home and pick up enough buns for the family supper.

Talmage Young was the husband of my sister, Inez. He made the best chili I have ever eaten. About once a month, Talmage would make a big pot of chili and divide half of it with my family. I remember the night we were eating his chili and my first bite nearly set my mouth on fire. Talmage had spilled the chili powder in the pot, an excessive amount, and didn't tell us about it. You didn't throw it out just because it was a little "hot"; you ate it anyway! His recipe was simple but he was very particular about the process he used in making it. The hot dog stand did a good business for two young men during Depression years just trying to make a few bucks.

By the time I was in high school during the early '50s, every Friday was football game night for the Redhounds. I believe the concession stand at the games was operated by the band mothers or Boosters Club, or possibly one of the other clubs, but they prepared the chili every week for the games. I remember my sister, Inez, carrying her big kettle of chili to the ball park, chili made by my brother-in-law, Talmage. You couldn't go to a football game without munching on a chili bun and everybody there knew they were the best chili buns ever made. I was one of those kids that barely had enough money to pay for my ticket and it was seldom that I could purchase a chili bun during halftime of the game. My mouth watered at the smell of the delicious chili buns.

My hometown is still known for its appetizing and tempting chili buns. People drive for miles to munch on them. Several locations sell the delicious meal and each has its own individual method of preparing the chili.

Talmage and Inez Estep Young, ca. 1941

A PIECE OF HISTORY

This story developed from the discovery of a 75-year-old small, blurry, black and white photograph. It's amazing what I see in this photograph that no one else can visualize. This is a piece of his life. It is also a piece of history!

Hobert Estep, building river bridge. 1930s

Except for the times my dad worked for the Works Project Association in the late thirties building court houses, schools, churches, and park facilities, until we moved to Tennessee in 1943 where he supervised the construction of houses and dormitories in Oak Ridge, I never knew where he worked. I had been told he once worked in North Carolina during those early years but I never questioned his job and where it was located.

Not until today, this very day, when I happened across a photograph I had never seen before, did I learn about my Dad's job between 1939 and the spring of 1943, the years when I was just a little girl and Daddy was always away from home. The photograph I was staring at showed a river bridge in the process of being built. Although the picture had to be at least 75 years old, I recognized one of the men standing on the edge of the incomplete bridge. The men had their backs to the camera but I immediately knew one of them was my dad. I recognized the clothes he wore, his belted khaki pants, the long sleeved, button-down-the-front shirt to protect his arms from sunburn, and the Panama hat he always wore in the summer to shade his face. None of those things had changed as he grew older. The photograph showed him with both his hands in his pockets. I had seen that many times. I recognized his stance. It was like opening the door again and seeing my dad standing there. Where has that picture been all these years?

I had to call my sister and tell her about the photograph. That's when she told me that before we moved to Tennessee during the war, Daddy had worked on the Fontana Dam in North Carolina. I had never heard this before. I didn't even know there was a Fontana Dam. How could I have gone so many years never knowing these things? I had never done a lot of traveling during my lifetime, so there were many geological and historic sites I hadn't seen.

I did not realize how skilled my father was in his trade. He was a man who had supported himself from the age of thirteen, had built bridges, highways, buildings, and even worked on the Fontana Dam in North Carolina which is the largest dam in the eastern part of the country and was built to aid in the war effort, just as Norris Dam in Tennessee was built for its electric power to Oak Ridge. Daddy never spent much time at home and talking about his work was not something he did at home, therefore, I didn't learn about his trade. He was just Daddy, the man of the house who brought home the paycheck every week, and we kids dotted our I's and crossed our T's when he was home. We were polite at the dinner table and we didn't interrupt the evening news broadcast by Gabriel Heater when he announced at the beginning of every program, "Ahh, There's good news tonight!" We were careful about slamming the screen door each time we went in or out of the house.

I don't know what part Daddy played in building the huge dam. He could have been a carpenter, a blueprint reader, one who dug dirt with a long-handled shovel, or he could have played a supervisory role. It really didn't matter; he helped build that dam!

After talking to my sister, I researched Fontana Dam and read the history of its construction. Oh, what a massive project! But it was built for the war effort and the people of North Carolina were willing to give up their homes, their farms, and their properties to help keep America safe. That is what you call "sacrifice"!

DON'T TELL MAMA!

Mama kept a bottle of Castor Oil in the kitchen cabinet and it didn't matter what the ailment, every kid got a dose of the Castor Oil, undoubtedly the worst tasting medicine in the world. Nothing was disguised with a cherry flavor or tasted like Teaberry Chewing Gum. We wouldn't tell Mama when we were sick because we knew she would force the Castor Oil down our throats and we would rather just die than take that stuff. She also had her liniments that smelled to high Heaven and they were often used for any ailments. I remember the time I got hit in the back of the head with a baseball. I didn't dare tell Mama because, first, I knew I would get a lecture for being where I was and doing what she didn't think I should be doing, and to top that, if there was an accident or someone got hurt, she always said, "I told you so!" It didn't matter that I had a knot on the back side of my head the size of a baseball and I couldn't move my head right or left.

I had hiked to Laurel River that day with a church group. Mama tried every way she could to keep me from going. She had all sorts of superstitions about a girl's monthly cycle. There were all kinds of precautions a young lady must take during the 'changing of the moon'. One thing she wouldn't let us do was wash our hair. We would get sick! And that day, if I went with my friends hiking to Laurel River, she was sure something would happen to where she could say, "I told you so." She seemed to like saying those words to us kids when she was against whatever activities we were anticipating.

Wouldn't you know, while I was sitting on the ground eating my picnic lunch, several of my friends were playing a game of softball. My friend, Ruth Ola was up to bat. She was a pretty good athlete and when she hit the ball, it might have been a home run if it hadn't sidetracked and slammed into the back of my head, knocking me out. I came to very quickly but I wasn't able to move my head the rest of the afternoon. The knot on the back of my head kept increasing in size but I wouldn't admit to the pain and swelling, even when we all climbed the three sisters, the huge rocks slanting toward the river. You didn't go to the river without climbing the rocks.

I managed to survive the climb up the huge rocks and when we made the descent to the picnic grounds, it was a three-mile walk back home. It was all I could do to keep up with my friends. After I arrived home, I swore my sisters to secrecy when I told them the story. "Whatever you do, don't tell Mama!" We all knew she would give me the usual lecture—wrong place, wrong time and you had no business going.

During the night, I woke up to the awful smell of Mama's liniment or camphorated oil. She was applying the medication to my neck and chest. One of my ill-fated sisters had told! Mama was placing the hot piece of flannel over the liniment and when I opened my eyes she said, "You could have been killed."

As the years went by, I could remember lying on the living room sofa and smelling her concoctions simmering on the kitchen stove. Sometimes I wish I had taken note of her home remedies used for years in healing us kids. I could smell the sweet onion, the rock candy, and whatever else she used. It always smelled good, but I can guarantee, it didn't taste good. A bottle containing a couple ounces of whiskey sat at the back of the cabinet. It was used for toothaches. Sweet oil was kept on hand for every earache. I made use of the oil winter after winter as my hearing began to diminish, little by little. I missed many days of school due to ear infections.

In later years, when I would visit Mama and sometimes came down with a virus or wasn't feeling well, I would lie on her sofa and nap. On the average of every fifteen minutes, I could feel Mama's hand on my forehead, checking to see if I had a fever. She would be making soup and preparing foods that she thought would be soothing and healthful. My naps didn't last long because she was constantly quizzing me about my condition. On one occasion I had a flu bug and I spent most of the day on my couch. My sisters and Mama averaged calling me every ten or fifteen minutes. Just as I would fall asleep again, they would call to see how I felt. Finally, one of them said, "What you need to do is lie down and get some sleep." I answered, "I would if I didn't have to get up every ten minutes to answer the phone." My phone never rang again that whole day!

CISSY GREGG'S COOKBOOK

You have your Betty Crocker cookbooks, Martha Stewart, Paula Deen, etc., but none can compare with Natalie Dupree or Cissy Gregg from the 1940s and 50s.

How many of you are old enough to remember Cissy Gregg who wrote for the Louisville Courier Journal newspaper in the 1950s? Not many, I'm sure, but if your mother lived in Kentucky, she remembers! My mother swore by recipes in Cissy Gregg's monthly cooking section of the newspaper. I have two copies of her magazine section; one dated 1953 and the other dated 1959. Each copy has as many as 150 pages. The latter copy is very well worn and pages are missing. It belonged to Mama. The notation in the middle where it says "Old fashion Jam Cake recipe inside" was written on the cover by Mama. Every Thanksgiving, Christmas, or other holiday, she made the jam cake. Hers had caramel icing. I can truly say, although I was not a jam cake lover, I certainly liked this recipe. There are so many interesting articles and recipes to read. I felt like I had fallen into a gold mine when I ran across the 1953 copy of Cissy Gregg's magazine in an antique shop about twenty years ago.

There was another Cissy Gregg favorite Mama baked during the holiday season—a nutmeg feather cake that almost melted in your mouth. It was made in a tall tube pan and topped with a coconut, pecan bubbly icing. Mama was the only person I ever knew who made this cake.

While I worked in Tennessee during the 1980s-90s, we often had luncheons and receptions for dignitaries and other state officials visiting our office. The office staff always provided the hors d'oeuvres and refreshments. I introduced them to a recipe they had never eaten before: "Benedictine." Yes, you can find it in the larger grocery stores now, but I guarantee, it isn't the same recipe. The recipe appeared in Cissy Gregg's magazine in 1959. It was created by a Louisville resident named Mrs. Benedict. I have made the party sandwiches many times for receptions and everyone loves them. I plan to read through the two magazines again. Although Mama's copy is very fragile, I'm sure I will discover information I have long forgotten. If an article has notations written on it, I know Mama used the recipe.

THE DAYS OF COMIC BOOKS

I don't know why I thought of my special friend today, but a story came to mind about her that made me laugh. It takes me back to my teenage years when we had such fun times and didn't even know it.

I'm not here to bring the skeletons out of the closets, but there were some good stories to tell if you grew up during the same time period I did. I keep telling myself to be careful what I say because somebody might be offended!

There were neighbors like the Smith family who had moved from house to house in our neighborhood and had lived in two houses on my street. They had recently moved to another house down the path on the street behind us. You may ask, "Which Smith family?" Well, in this particular Smith family, everybody in town knew at least one of them and they also knew the head of the household, "Long John," our local friendly police officer who kept the streets safe. John Smith was well over six feet tall and walked the beat on Main Street.

I was the youngest of the seven girls in my family and Ruth Ola was the youngest in the Smith family. She was a year ahead of me in high school and several inches taller than I was. She taught me how to jitterbug on the linoleum rug in our dining room. It had been turned into our sitting room after my sisters had married and left home. Of course, playing cards and dancing were against the Godly rules of our household, but I would look around and see Daddy peeking over the top of his newspaper while we promenaded around the room and I could see the twinkle of a grin on his face. I knew then I didn't have to worry about the wrath of God coming down on me for sinning.

The Smiths were a musical family with four of the sisters forming a quartet. They were good and I remember listening to Ruth yodel like some of the country music singers on the Grand Ole Opry! I must admit that as much as I liked Ruth Ola, she was the one who scared me out of five inches of my growth I should have had – a situation one never forgets. It was the middle of summer. I had just come from my girlfriend, Julie's house where her two brothers had stacks of comic books that lay piled behind the warm morning heater in their living room. Their mother paid no attention to me squatted down against the wall for hours, reading those comic books. It didn't matter whether or not Julie was around, I was perfectly satisfied to sit behind the stove and read her brothers' comic books. Along about supper time, I knew it was time for me to skedaddle home. I would get up and ask if I could borrow a half-dozen comic books to take home and read. The next day, I would return them and borrow six more. I never had to spend a dime of my own money on the comic books.

I had just brought home a new batch of comic books, and although we called them 'funny books' the stack I had were anything but funny. Actually, they were those horror mysteries, my favorites! I entered the house and went straight to the old davonette in the dining room that sat under the double windows. The sun had gone down and it was beginning to get dusky dark. I could hardly see the pictures on the pages, but I wouldn't stop long enough to turn on a lamp. I can hear Mama now, saying, "You're gonna go blind trying to read in the dark." But, I kept on reading. The story was getting intense and I was beginning to get a little tense myself. I could feel that imaginary knife in my back and occasionally I looked over my shoulder to see if someone was there.

About the time I was absorbed in the chilling part of a murder mystery, Ruth Ola came up the path beside our house. I wasn't expecting her and couldn't hear her through the window screen. Just as she walked right past the dining room windows, she could see the top of my head above the window sill but she couldn't see what I was doing. She was tall enough to reach up and touch the window screen, so she decided to rake her fingernails down the screen, still not aware that I was right in the middle of reading a gross, gory, horror story.

When I heard that low, slow screeching sound behind me, the funny book went flying across the room, and I leaped off the davonette screaming bloody murder. Ruth fell backwards onto the ground. Mama came rushing from the kitchen while I was still screaming and my head flopping back and forth. I couldn't stop! By then, Ruth was coming through the screen door. Lordy, Lord! What had happened? Surely, she wasn't responsible for this! All she did was rake her fingers down the window screen. She slowly crept into the dining room where Mama was trying to figure out what caused such an outlandish display of emotion and at the same time, she tried to calm me down. Did a spider bite me? Or maybe I saw a mouse, but a mouse wouldn't call for that kind of action. I would have just climbed up on the davonette and yelled for Mama to get the broom. Ruth didn't know what to do except just stand and stare at me. Why was I throwing such a conniption fit? All she did was rake her fingernails down the window screen!

Once I was able to control my shaking and screaming, and Mama and Ruth Ola realized what triggered my panic attack, we spent the next thirty minutes in laughter. We couldn't stop laughing.

Strange, the silly little things in life we remember! Many years passed when Ruth and I didn't see or talk to each other and then one day, we met up again on a bus tour to Nova Scotia. We had a lot of catching up and laughing to do.

My friend passed away about 16 years ago and now and then I think of her and the fun we had together as young girls.

SADIE HAWKINS DAY

We fought over the newspaper comic strips on Sunday mornings because the page was in color. I had a few favorites, one of them being Rex Morgan, the doctor whose nurse assistant was secretly in love with him. And then there was Mary Worth who was always solving peoples' problems. That lady really got around. She knew the private lives of nearly everyone in town, especially if they had romantic problems. And of course, "Li'l Abner and Daisy Mae." Everybody loved them. That comic strip ran for 43 years. The comic strip had the hillbilly theme and took place in Dogpatch, America. There were Mammy and Pappy Yokum and who could pass up an episode of Joe Btfsplk, the world's worst jinx who continually carried the dark rain cloud over his head.

There was a multitude of characters in the Li'l Abner comic strip and one just as entertaining as the next. And then there was Wolf Gal, an Amazonian beauty who was raised by wolves and preferred to live among them. All of this reminds me of high school when we had time away from our book studies for Sadie Hawkins Day in November of every year. Sadie was the homeliest gal in them thar' hills. All of the students were required to dress like a Dogpatch character, and it was easy to make a choice because there were dozens of them in the Dogpatch hills.

I was a sophomore and my sister, Wanda, was a senior. She was very pretty and quite popular. Her popularity came in part because she appeared in all the variety shows at school. It was Sadie Hawkins Day at school. Wanda came dressed as Sadie, the Wolf Gal. The portrayal suited her perfectly. The skirt of her black dress hit just above the knees revealing her pretty legs; she was barefoot, and had teased her long curly hair to the point it looked like a rat's nest. A few swipes of dirt on her face and arms completed the image.

Wanda's friend and classmate dressed as Daisy Mae. There was no doubt she would win the Daisy Mae contest. She was barefoot, wearing a short black skirt and white blouse covered in large red polka dots. Her long, wavy, almost-blonde hair bounced when she walked and she was as pretty as a doll. There couldn't be a better representation of Daisy Mae.

Sadie Hawkins Day was probably the most fun day all year at school. And, as expected, Wanda's friend, Pat, would win the Daisy Mae contest. After awarding prizes in the school gymnasium to all the favorite characters, a variety show followed in the auditorium on the second floor of the high school. As usual, the headliner for the program was my sister, flaunting her Wolf Gal style. She was chosen to sing a solo on stage with her friend, Pat, backing her up on the old upright piano.

To describe Wanda as shy and bashful would be a complete misrepresentation. She was anything but that! My sister entered center-stage with all the ease in the world. Ordinarily, I was always glad to watch her perform because she was a very good soloist and I was confident she would be the best in any program. She had perfect pitch and could hit the high notes causing the crystal glass to break. But that day, I was stymied by her choice of songs to sing.

Wanda had a lot more confidence in her ability to perform than I did. Pat began to play the piano and Wanda opened her mouth to sing. I am not sure if I can honestly say what she did was singing, because what came out of her mouth nearly had me sinking to the floor and wishing it would open up and let me fall through to the basement of the building.

Sitting beside me were several of her male friends and when Wanda started warbling, they started whistling and yelling. I was never so embarrassed in my life. The more the guys whistled and hollered, the louder Wanda sang and the more she twisted her hips. She had chosen the Homer and Jethro version of "Temptation, and I was Yorn" which, to her, seemed quite appropriate for a Dogpatch hillbilly show.

But did my sister need to put her entire body into the song? "You came, I wuz alone, I shoulda know'd—you wuz temptation. It would be thrillin' if you wuz willin' if it can't nevar be, pity me for you wuz temp-taa-shun and I wuz yorn…" She not only sang the full song once, she was so revved up, she began a second time and as you would guess, the boys kept whistling. By then, I was almost under the school desk, mortified and hoping nobody knew she was my sister. I was making a mental list of the things I was going to do to her when we got home that afternoon, the first being, cut her vocal cords. I wasn't even sure if I could attend school the next day. Everybody would be staring at me and whispering, "That's her sister!" I was sure! To this day, when anyone says the words "Sadie Hawkins Day," I melt and my face turns red.

LOVE LETTERS

There was a time in history when writing love letters was the only means of communication between couples living apart. The war separated husbands and wives from each other for long periods of time so they kept in close touch and sent the family news each week through affectionate letters. Letters were also written by many soldiers and their sweethearts during war time. The ones that come to mind are those tattered love letters that were treasured and hidden away in a special place by many mothers and grandmothers and all tied together neatly with ribbons to keep them safe.

I remember when a friend gave me a bundle of letters that had been written by her grandfather during his early years of college to his girlfriend who later became his wife. She asked me to type them up and make a file of them for her computer. Her grandfather, though a young man at the time, was a very interesting writer. I looked forward to reading the next letter as I typed. Oh, what a wonderful story was contained in his letters.

Those days are gone now. We don't have those keepsake memories anymore; maybe a nice greeting card now and then with a sweet note in it, but no love letters between a girl and her young man, expressing their feelings of affection and their longings to be together. I remember writing love letters when my boyfriend was in the Coast Guard. He was stationed too far away for frequent visits and getting leave for several days wasn't easy to come by. We couldn't afford phone calls so we wrote letters. I spent my weekly allowance on five-cent postage stamps.

My mother told me a story about my sister, Velma. It was during the early years of World War II. She had just graduated high school and her boyfriend was in the Navy. They corresponded frequently and Velma kept her letters hidden in a small cedar chest, the kind that came as a gift filled with stationary and matching envelopes. The pretty chest was later used for storing jewelry, and in her case, it protected her love letters. The cedar chest with its little lock was placed in the bottom drawer of the dresser in our front bedroom. She may have thought the letters were safely hidden but in our house, nothing was safely hidden!

One day, my sisters, Bena Mae and Janette, decided to do a little exploring. Well, actually, they were looking for Velma's love letters. Their friend, Harold, was usually involved in whatever mischief or trickery they could drum up and they regularly turned to him for protection whenever needed.

Oh, what fun they were having reading the young sailor's letters. His spelling was rather lacking and after they replaced the letters in the dresser drawer, they waited for Velma to come home. They were laughing when she walked in the front door then they began singing, "I'm T-I-R-D and I think I'll go to sleep." Well, how much more obvious could it be to Velma that they had been prowling through the dresser and reading her letters. She began yelling, "You've been reading my letters! I'm gonna kill you!" Those were the 'famous last words' in our household.

About three years later we were living in Tennessee and Bena Mae and Janette were junior and senior in high school by then. Both of the girls had boyfriends, and in Janette's case, the relationship was getting quite serious. Although her boyfriend was still in high school, he had been inducted into the army and was serving his basic training in

New Jersey. I recall the night of the big fight. Oh yes! It was one of those times when the average individual would have called in the National Guard if there had been a National Guard in those days. Wanda and I were sleeping on an army cot while my two older sisters slept in the double bed. Wanda was awakened suddenly by the growling and hissing sounds from the big bed. Bena Mae and Janette were arguing. Because Bena Mae's boyfriend had not received his draft orders, Janette called him a "draft dodger." That was about as bad as it could get when one sister blurted out such an insult to another sister. Everything was done under the covers and in whispers. They couldn't let Daddy hear them arguing and fighting in bed. He would have been in our bedroom at the flip of a lightswitch. Bena Mae was angry! Nobody was going to call her boyfriend, Smitty, a draft-dodger. She squealed, "I'm gonna choke you to death!" About that time, Janette began coughing. Wanda was wide awake and listening to every whisper. When she heard Janette cough, she just knew Bena Mae had her hands around Janette's throat. She flew off her end of the cot, grabbed the string to the ceiling light and yelled, "I'm gonna tell Daddy. I'm gonna tell Daddy."

Both my sisters were out of their bed, one grabbing Wanda and placing her hands over Wanda's mouth and the other grabbing the light string before the light woke Daddy. They were holding Wanda down and struggling with her until they had her quieted and convinced Janette was not being choked to death.

The love letters between Janette and her boyfriend went back and forth quite frequently and she kept them hidden in a shoe box. Again, trying to hide something in our house was futile! One of us kids would find it.

Sure enough, one day Wanda found the shoe box of letters and she and I crawled behind the sofa in the living room and started reading them. Actually, Wanda read the letters to me because I was too young to read script. We were having so much fun. The letters were lined up on the floor around us and Wanda was in the process of reading another letter to me when suddenly, the front door opened and who should walk in, but Janette. You've heard those stories about the fur flying, well, in this case, the love letters were flying and Wanda and I were running for our lives. The fire in Janette's eyes meant she was serious when she said, "I'm gonna kill you!" If Mama hadn't intervened that time, I think we would have been digging our own graves. You can't imagine how angry a girl can get over a little thing like someone reading her love letters, even if the culprits were only seven and nine years old. It was days later before Wanda and I even offered to come within ten feet of our sister. We made sure Mama was always there to protect us. Let me tell you in case you've never had the experience, Love Letters was a serious matter and could be life threatening!

The war had ended and years passed and then Wanda and I were in high school. Wanda always had a steady boyfriend and this time, her boyfriend had already graduated high school and went to Ohio to get a job. Most of the graduates who didn't enter college went north to Ohio or Detroit, Michigan where they could find employment in the auto industry. This time, it was Wanda who was writing the love letters. I knew that she, too, was hiding her letters in the bottom dresser drawer in the front bedroom, but I didn't offer to sneak and read any of them. I valued my life too much for that and you might say, I was chicken! Wanda was the last person in the family you wanted to challenge when she was angry!

One day, she had received a letter from her boyfriend and when she came out of the bedroom her face was red and there was fire in her eyes. Her expression told me not to ask any questions. She nearly tore the screen door off its hinges as she left the house. Something was wrong, really wrong. Uh oh! Her boyfriend must have said something that went against the grain. Now, how was I going to find out what he said or did? Since I knew Wanda wasn't going to tell me, there was only one way for me to find out. I waited until she left the house and I went plundering through the dresser drawer where her letters were kept in the same little cedar chest that Velma had used years earlier. The most recent letter from the boyfriend was right on top. I pulled out the envelope and was very careful about retrieving the letter. In the letter was a photograph.

Wanda's boyfriend loved cars. He was always working on them. I pulled out the photograph first before reading the letter and realized it was a picture of his new car. He must have been doing well in his new job. The photograph revealed a beautiful, shiny red convertible, very eye-catching. Also, stretched out on the hood of his car was a beautiful, eye-catching girl with long dark hair wearing a two-pieced white bathing suit.

I placed the photo and letter back inside the envelope. I never let Wanda know I had seen the picture. That young man was very stupid, and at the same time, very lucky he wasn't anywhere near my sister. To my knowledge, that love affair ended immediately. We never saw hide nor hair of that young man in town again. I have often wondered what was said in that final letter!

I was the last to hide love letters but I wasn't foolish enough to store them in the little cedar chest in the dresser. Mine went into a drawer in a tall chest in another bedroom. The only household members around to sneak and read them were my younger brother and Mama. Hopefully, they weren't interested. Just to play safe, I gathered up the letters from my boyfriend who was serving in the Coast Guard, carried them to the big oil drum by the branch and burned them.

THE MODEL T FORD

Yesterday was my sister, Wanda's birthday. We had just been to Cracker Barrel for a late lunch and were driving home by way of the back roads, crossing Laurel River Bridge and on to Gordon Hill. As we crossed over the bridge, Wanda looked back and said, "Do you remember when we used to climb the Three Sisters as kids," and pointed back towards the river. I said, "Wanda, don't you remember they were covered by water years ago when the dam was built at Laurel Lake?"

She laughed, and then I said, "But do you remember when you and Eddie (her husband) were dating? He had that old Model T Ford and you all used to drive around on Sunday afternoons in the car and go to Laurel River?"

Wanda began laughing again. Oh, yes! She remembered that old car. There was the time our friend, Barbara, and I went for a long drive with Wanda and Eddie on the dirt roads along Laurel River. Barbara and I sat in the backseat of the Model T. I guess you could call it a backseat – it was a long board on top of a couple of small wooden barrels or something of that sort. There was not a backseat but Barbara and I managed to stay fixed atop the pine board as the car rambled along the road. There were ruts in the road that had us bouncing up and down with our heads touching the roof of the car. There wasn't a back to the boards for us to lean on. Around our feet were several gallon jugs of water. We barely had room for our feet on the floorboard, if you want to call it a floorboard. We could see the rocks and gravel below our feet as the car bounced along. Every two or three miles, Eddie would stop the car, get out and open up the hood. Next, he opened the back door of the car and pulled out one of the jugs of water, went up to the front, reached under the hood, and poured the jug of water into the radiator. He closed the hood and returned to the driver's seat and off we went. This was repeated every few minutes as he drove down the road until he was nearly out of water and then he drove to a service station and refilled the gallon jugs with water for the radiator. Now, that's an experience I doubt that many of you have had. Imagine that!

There was no doubt the old Model T had seen better days, but it served its purpose on Sunday afternoons. Young love didn't require much in those days. In recalling that day, I told Wanda I didn't think I could tell the story so that anyone could appreciate it. But we kept on laughing.

Wanda and Eddie married and her husband's next car was a Studebaker. I can't begin to say what model it was but it had to be one of the earliest Studebakers on the market and certainly had seen better days. As you read this, I hope you are able to remember the Studebaker. The couple's car was still running on a wing and a prayer. That was all that mattered to Eddie. He pulled into a service station one day for gas and overheard a young man say to another attendant, "That man's got a rope tied to his clutch." That young man was right. The spring under the clutch had broken and when Eddie pushed down on the clutch it would stick. He would grab the rope and pull the clutch back up and was ready for the next time he had to press down on the clutch pedal. Next stop, he pressed the clutch pedal down and then pulled it back up with the rope. Money wasn't easy to come by in those days and Eddie could always find a solution to his problems.

No matter the condition of Eddie's cars, he always managed to get where he was going, even if the car had to be pulled by an old mule. If this man bought a brand new car, he just wasn't comfortable with it. It ran too smoothly, no rattles, no screeching, and the brakes and windshield wipers worked. I've seen him lift the hood on a new car and see if he couldn't find something wrong with it. If he couldn't find anything out of order, he created something. It just wasn't normal to have a good running car.

After our little trip to the Cracker Barrel yesterday, my niece who was driving the car pulled into Wanda's driveway. We parked our car beside Wanda's station wagon. The first thing my niece said to me was, "Get your camera out of your purse. You've got to take a picture of this."

"Of what?" I asked. She pointed to the back of the station wagon. The windshield wiper blade was tied to the handle on the hatch of the vehicle with a Kroger plastic bag. Another of Eddie's solutions to car repairs. I grabbed my camera and got a couple of shots of the back of the station wagon. My niece and I broke out in laughter. After all these years, some people's habits just don't change.

YOUNG LOVE

I was a sophomore in high school; Wanda was a senior. This time she was courting hot and heavy. The relationship appeared to be serious. The whole family had high hopes for a singing career for her. She would be the first of us girls to go to college and music would be her major.

One day the phone rang. It was a girl from our past when we lived in Tennessee during the war. She and Wanda had created a friendship that continued through high school. Mary Lou was asking Wanda if she would come and sing at her wedding. This would be a wonderful experience for Wanda and she and Mary Lou could reminisce about their childhood days.

Wanda and her boyfriend drove to Tennessee. She sang at the wedding and as could be expected, with so much romance and drama going around, Wanda and her boyfriend decided they wanted to get married, too. She was still in high school! She couldn't get married! All the plans the whole family had for her singing career would go right down the drain. Something had to be done to stop this marriage.

My sister, Janette, was living in the same small town in Tennessee where the wedding had been performed. She worked at the telephone company as an operator. When she learned of the plans for a wedding, she got on the switchboard phone at work and called Mama. It was a three-way conversation between Mama, Janette as the arbitrator, and her husband at home trying to keep Janette calm. "Lock her in the closet! We can't let her get married. She's the only one of us who has the chance to make something of herself. She can have a music career. Mama, you've got to stop her! Lock her in the closet 'till she comes to her senses." Janette's husband was whispering, "Calm down now. Don't get so upset." And Mama was on the other end of the line trying to convince my sister she had done all she could do. Wanda was still going to get married. "Mama, you can lock her in a closet. Do I have to come up there and do it myself?"

Now, this was coming from a sister who was 20 years old and had been married four years. If anybody knew what to do, it was her! She hadn't even turned 16 when she married her soldier boyfriend and here she was, preaching to high heaven to my mother. No one was able to talk my sister out of the marriage and in December of that year, they got in her boyfriend's car which at that time may have been the Studebaker then drove down the street until they ran into one of her high school friends and Wanda yelled out the car window, "Get in the car. I need you as a witness. We've got to find another witness. We're getting married." A few blocks up the street, the car stopped, the friend ran up to the front door of a house and knocked. Harry answered, and she said, "Come on, Harry, Wanda needs another witness. She's getting married today." They hopped in the car and off to Jellico, Tennessee, they headed where they didn't have to wait three days after obtaining a marriage license.

COAL FOR SALE

It was the aftermath of a snow storm and still very cold. That Saturday morning Bud woke up to the sound of someone pounding on the front door. He stumbled out of bed and through the house and when he opened the front door, there stood his friend, Redd, shivering and shifting his feet back and forth. Redd was his nickname because his hair was carrot red and his face was covered with freckles. He stepped inside the house and said, "Get your clothes on! I've got a job for us where we can make a bunch of money today. A guy said we could borrow his coal truck and there's a place where they've been coal mining and he says we can shovel the leftover coal into the truck and take it and sell it."

It was the early 1950s when most of the young men were fighting the war in Korea and very few of them were left at home. Jobs were hard to find and if the young men right out of high school could find a job it was usually in a grocery store stocking shelves or at a service station pumping gas. The money made at these jobs was about enough to pay for their cigarettes, a few gallons of gas when they used their dads' cars on a date, and maybe enough money was left for a movie and a couple of Coca Colas at the local diner.

Bud shuffled back to the bedroom and hurriedly dressed, grabbing a windbreaker jacket because the sun was shining and it looked like the temperature would be rising that day. He and Redd found a couple of shovels in the old garage beside the house and off they went, to shovel coal. They filled the bed of the truck about half full and then had to decide where they would go to sell the coal. There was a small community across the river and about twenty miles up the road where they thought would be a good place to start. About an hour later, they were climbing the hill into the small town. It was one of those towns that didn't even have a traffic light on the main street. Not a sign of a soul was on the street. They planned to sell the coal by the bucketful going door to door. They would split up and go up each side of the street knocking on doors to sell their coal. They had left the truck sitting upon a hill out on the side of the main road.

What Bud and Redd had not given any thought to was that they were trying to sell their buckets of coal in what was known as coal country. Every house in the whole town had a big pile of coal lying out against a bank in their back yard.

Bud started up the left side of the street and Redd to the right. They began knocking on doors. It wasn't long before Bud had reached the end of the street. He had had no luck! He hadn't seen Redd for awhile and wondered what had happened to him. Then he looked across the way and spotted Redd coming out of one of the houses, fastening the gallous on his bib overalls with his windbreaker jacket hanging across his arm. Standing in the doorway was a lady in a long chenille housecoat. Redd was up to his shenanigans again! He hadn't sold a bucket of coal either.

It was getting late in the day and the sun was going down over the hills. The temperature was dropping and snow was starting to pepper down on the roads. They had better get back to the truck and head for home. Not one bucket of coal had either of them sold and they hadn't had a bite to eat all day long. They were starved and would have given anything for food and something hot to drink.

Reaching the top of the hill, Bud got in the truck and turned the key in the ignition. Nothing! He tried again. The engine wouldn't turn over. Oh, no! The truck wouldn't start and here they were stranded out in the cold in the land of nowhere wearing light weight jackets and without a bite to eat. Bud lifted the hood to the truck and gave all the parts a once over to see if he could find out why the truck wouldn't start. Once he had figured it out, he then needed new parts to make the repairs. That meant a twenty-mile trip back home to the service station to get parts. Bud and Redd had exactly eight dollars between them, most of it coming out of Bud's pocket. Fortunately, the parts would not cost much. Bud handed Redd the money and told him to hitchhike back to town and get the parts and he would wait by the truck for him to return. Redd started down the hill in a slow run. It was almost dark by then and still spitting snow.

Bud paced back and forth trying to keep warm. Not a sign of a car anywhere came by. Finally, he tossed a few lumps of coal on the ground, found some dry leaves and sticks, and using the book of matches he kept for cigarettes, he managed to get a fire going. He hunkered as close to the fire as he could, occasionally adding another lump of coal to the blaze. Hour after hour passed and Bud thought he was going to freeze before Redd got back with the truck parts. After awhile he was beginning to wonder if Redd was coming back at all. Then he saw the headlights of a car coming up the hill. A taxi cab pulled up and stopped behind the truck, and of all things, Redd stepped out of the Taxi. He had spent the remains of their eight dollars to hire a taxi cab to make the 20-mile return trip. Bud had the total sum of a dime in his pocket. And besides that, he had nearly burned all of the coal to keep warm while he waited for Redd to come back with parts for the truck.

Bud fixed the truck and his hands were stiff from the cold. He got behind the wheel and started back down the hill, heading for home. It was going on ten o'clock and in the distance he spotted a small diner on the side of the road. It was still open. They were so hungry their stomachs rumbled, but all they could buy with a dime was one cup of hot coffee.

Bud pulled up to the diner. They opened the door and strolled over to the counter, sat on the little round stools. The sign said, "Coffee—10 Cents a cup" so Bud ordered two cups of coffee. Redd jerked around and whispered, "What are you doing? We only have a dime, just enough for one cup." Bud looked straight ahead, never saying a word. The waitress brought two cups of coffee and Bud wrapped his cold hands around his cup trying to get them warm. Redd began twisting on the stool and shuffling his feet. Man, they were going to be in trouble when it came time to pay for the two cups of coffee and they only had a dime. Redd took a sip from his cup and looked down to the other end of the counter. There sat a state policeman drinking his cup of coffee. Again, Redd whispered to Bud, "We're gonna get arrested!" Bud kept rubbing his hands around his coffee cup then turning it up to his mouth. Redd was so nervous by this time he could hardly swallow the coffee. Bud appeared totally relaxed, never saying a word or acting like he had even seen the state cop.

They finished their coffee and it was time to leave. Redd's face almost matched his red hair. Bud stood up, reached in his pocket and then laid two dimes on the counter. Redd's eyes nearly popped out of his head. Where did Bud get an extra dime.

When the two first entered the diner, Bud spotted a dime on one of the tables, a tip left for the waitress. He slid his hand across the top of the table picking up the dime that a customer had left then casually dropped it in his pocket.

It was a little before midnight when Bud and Redd arrived home. They were dirty, hungry and extremely cold and tired from a long and unsuccessful day's work.

I WANT TO BE A MOVIE STAR

Growing up in a small town or the hills of Kentucky had its downsides as well as its advantages. If you didn't have relatives who lived in the cities that you could visit on occasion, you never had reason to ride the bus to places like Lexington, Louisville, Cincinnati, etc. Along with those big cities there was always the dream of New York City where all the movie stars lived. I certainly didn't have any relatives living in these places, so my chances of ever experiencing the great city life were nil. Now and then friends would tell about visiting relatives in the city and I couldn't help but be a bit envious as they talked about the fun they had.

I suppose the biggest thing in my life was the Saturday afternoon matinee movies at our local Hippodrome Theater downtown. The closest I would ever get to a movie star would be the 20th row back, sitting in an aisle seat on the left side of the theater. Mama gave me my quarter and off I went with my girlfriend, Julie, to see a double feature show with all the famous movie stars. I had my specials, mostly the stars that could sing and dance. I tap danced all the way home in my hard-soled loafers, dreaming of what it must be like to be a movie star, and when I grew up, I might get to go to Hollywood. I read all about the actors in my ten-cent movie magazine that I bought at Cottongim's Drug Store when I managed to save a dime. I even kept a large scrapbook of all their pictures cut from the magazines. I constantly thought, it must be wonderful to live in New York or Hollywood where you could see the stars on stage at Broadway shows, or by chance, see one walking down the sidewalk. Dream, dream, dream! Why did I have to live in a small town where movie stars were never ever seen? Oh, how lucky those city folks were!

It was the week of high school graduation when we heard that Burt Lancaster was going to be in the area filming a new movie called *The Kentuckian*. A real live movie star was coming to town! He was supposed to be at Cumberland Falls filming a scene above the falls. Only one girl in my class had access to her dad's car for driving around town, so a group of us girls piled in her dad's Hudson and off we headed, straight to Cumberland Falls. We were all excited over the mere idea that we might get a glimpse of a real movie star like Burt Lancaster. It had been rumored that one of our classmates was a stand-in for the boy who played the role of Lancaster's son. When we arrived, we discovered the filming had already taken place and the stars were gone. What a disappointment that was, but we hit the main two-lane road in hopes of catching up with the movie crew somewhere along the way. We could surely find them. Naturally, it never happened.

After high school, I married and moved to Louisville, Kentucky, where my husband and I worked and he attended college at the university. Exactly three years had passed and I had given birth to my first child. My husband's younger sister was visiting one weekend, and my husband said he would babysit so that I could take her downtown to shop and see sites. I had worked in the center of town so I had no problem with directions and anyway, we were going by city bus, which made a straight shot up Fourth Street a few miles and then we got off the bus right in front of Stewart's Department Store. Stewart's was the most popular place in downtown Louisville to shop. The building had about six floors.

We were browsing around the main floor of the store and I could hardly get through the aisles. I had never seen so many people before. Why had everybody picked that Saturday to go shopping? It was getting a bit too crowded for us so we decided to leave and find another store on up the street.

It was an effort plowing through the crowds of people to the main entrance, and when we finally made it to the sidewalk, we noticed that there were people six and eight deep, lined all up and down the sidewalk, facing the street. What was going on? Brenda and I nudged our way through to the front of the crowd and that was where we got the surprise of our lives. Cruising slowly at a snail's pace up Fourth Street towards the river was a line of the most beautiful Cadillac convertibles you ever saw, and in every color. All of the cars had their tops down and sitting high above the back seats were men and women. Oh, my gosh! They were movie stars. I thought I would either faint or swallow my tongue when I recognized the star in the very first car waving his hand in my direction. I couldn't get enough breath to speak. I was numb with excitement. I recognized most of the glamorous stars as the magnificent cars slowly passed in front of me. Some of the names I still remember. Lee Marvin, Eva Marie Saint, Rod Taylor, Ann Miller, some stars I couldn't name, and then there were Van Johnson and Jane Powell, their faces, both, were covered with freckles. I never realized they had so many freckles when I saw them in movies. What a time not to have a camera on your person!

Little did the two of us realize we had chosen the day for shopping when they were having the parade and premier showing of the movie, *Raintree County,* starring Elizabeth Taylor and Montgomery Clift. The movie had been filmed in nearby Danville, Kentucky. The two main stars did not arrive for the parade that day, but they appeared later for the first showing of the movie. I didn't even need to take the bus back home that day. I was already floating on Cloud Nine! If I had planned a day like that, it would never have happened. Those things only happen, and are the most exciting, when you least expect them.

Yes, I got to see movie stars that beautiful fall afternoon, lots of them! I had an experience I had long dreamed about, and for once in my life, it was no longer a dream. I was there in person!

I have a VCR copy of the film *The Kentuckian*. Burt Lancaster is shown with his son walking across the river on large rocks just above Cumberland Falls. The water was very low that day. Later in the movie, there is a scene where Burt and his son dive over the side of a steamboat. The kid actually taking the dive into the river was the boy's stand-in, and my classmate, Archie.

THE BLACK VELVETEEN DRESS

I had just graduated high school and was taking a business course to prepare for my future. The course only lasted three months. I didn't feel like I was getting my money's worth out of the course so I dropped out of the class. I didn't have a summer job and I felt guilty asking my mother for spending money to go to a movie at the Hippodrome Theater or stop at the drug store for a Coca Cola and a new ten-cent magazine. I needed a job until I decided whether I would go to college or get married. I was already engaged to a nice young man I had met a year earlier.

The stores were displaying their fall merchandise and I, like every young girl my age was admiring all the new clothes for winter. I was in Daniel's Department Store one afternoon browsing through their new dresses and spotted one I just had to try on. I knew I couldn't buy the dress, but it was so pretty, what would it hurt just to see how it looked on me. I still had the 23-inch waistline and a fairly decent figure so I took the beautiful black velveteen dress back to the dressing room. I didn't dare look at the price tag. The dress had an expensive look about it. There was no doubt it cost more than I had ever spent on a new dress. The slim fitting dress was sleeveless with no collar. The part that caught my eye when looking at the dress was the bright red poodle cloth bolero jacket with a black layback collar that complemented the dress. The dress and jacket fit beautifully. I put the outfit back on the hanger and placed it among the other new dresses. I was ready to leave the store but before I did, I just had to look at the price tag attached to the sleeve of the jacket. It was more than I had ever paid for a dress in my life, or I should say, my mother had ever paid!

I walked home with the picture of the black velveteen dress in my mind wondering what I could do to own that dress. I just had to have it. It felt like a dream as I admired my reflection in the department store mirror. I looked like a movie star with my dark auburn hair lying in folds of curls around my shoulders. I already had a pair of black suede pumps with rhinestone clips that would be perfect to wear with the dress.

I knew there was no point in mentioning the dress to Mama because she would immediately frown at the price and then tell me I didn't need the dress. As long as I could remember when one or two of us girls bought new clothes, and especially if they were Easter outfits, Mama would say, "Don't let your Daddy know you are wearing a new dress." We never understood why it had to be a secret from Daddy. Surely, he knew we bought new clothes and shoes now and then! So, we never mentioned our new apparel to him and he seemed never to notice. Daddy worked away from home so much that when he was home on weekends, he needed his rest. We knew not to bother him with trivial matters. Our day-to-day activities were Mama's responsibilities and we never even approached Daddy to discuss anything we did at school or church. We didn't think he would be interested.

That evening, Mama was in the kitchen cooking supper. Daddy was in the corner beside the window reading his newspaper as usual. No one else was in the house except us three. I pulled a chair up beside my dad and very sheepishly said, "Daddy, there's something I would like to talk to you about." He said, "What's your problem, Sis?" I answered, "It isn't really a problem but I just wanted to talk to you." I paused and he waited. "You know, as long as I can remember, I have never been able to buy a new dress without first looking at the price tag. If the price was more than I knew Mama would let me spend, I couldn't try on the dress. I was never able to buy the dress I really wanted. I bought the dress because of how much it cost, not because I liked it."

"Okay, is that what you want me to know? Why?" I continued, "Well, I was in Daniel's today and I saw the prettiest dress I've ever seen in my life and I tried it on. It fit me and looked so good and I really wanted the dress but I knew even before checking the price tag that it cost too much. I would like, just once in my life to be able to buy a dress because it is pretty, not because the price is right."

The whole time I talked and tried to be convincing with my story, I could see a glint in my Daddy's eyes. He didn't interrupt me at any time and appeared to concentrate on every word that came out of my mouth, and then he said, "How much is the dress, Sis?"

I took a deep breath and drew my shoulders together and very hesitantly said in an almost whisper, "It's $21.99." He drew back in his chair and lowered his head slightly as he looked at me and said, "Go tell your Mammy to write you a check in the morning and you go buy that dress."

There wasn't a prettier girl in town than I was when I walked down the street in my black velveteen dress with its red poodle cloth bolero jacket.

MEATLOAF FOR DINNER

It was love at first sight, and he was a sight to behold in his white uniform. My journalism teacher told me one day that I had snared the best looking young man in town. And she was right! He was extremely handsome. I met my husband to be when I was a senior in high school. He was home on leave from the Coast Guard.

My new husband finished his three-year tour of duty in the Coast Guard and was discharged two months before our wedding. We had been engaged exactly seven months. During that seven months I put all my efforts into learning how to cook, the way my mother did. Each night, Mama let me cook supper while she stood on the sidelines to assist me when I couldn't figure out what to do next, especially where the measurements were concerned. Mama always used a pinch of this, a smidgen of that, and just a dash of the other. Those instructions, to me, weren't easy to follow. I focused on a meal that had always been a family favorite—meatloaf, mashed potatoes, coleslaw, and cornbread. I had just about perfected the meatloaf recipe. Mama praised my efforts.

I knew when I got married I would be moving to faraway Louisville, Kentucky, a place I had visited only twice and that was when two of my sisters had lived there. Louisville was a big city compared to my hometown and I was frightened out of my wits at the thoughts of having to learn how to get around—on a city bus, something I had never done. What would I do if I got on the wrong bus, or missed getting off at my stop? My soon-to-be husband had the promise of a job with the Railroad and would be going to the University of Louisville night school. I was going to have a lot of time on my hands and would eventually have to ride the bus to find a job. Since I didn't know a single soul in the city who could befriend me, what would I do?

I was scared to death. I didn't know anything about marriage. I had only spent two out of the fourteen months of courtship with this young man. What did I know about him? Did he have a bad temper? Was he a spendthrift? Well that one was out of the question because we were setting up housekeeping in a furnished two-room basement apartment on his $300 mustering out pay. We would definitely be pinching pennies. I figured his knowledge as a sailor for three years had taught him enough about life to take care of both of us. He could teach me.

We were two weeks into the marriage. It was time for me to give my fabulous meatloaf dinner the test. In those days, meatloaf was made with a good grade of ground beef and half as much sausage. I was running a little short on the ground beef so I had to use extra sausage for the recipe. We had what I thought was a fairly decent meal. That night when we had settled into bed, we had just turned off the lights and were ready for a good night's sleep. It was quiet and suddenly, my husband said, "Did you throw out the rest of that meatloaf?"

"No, why?" He calmly said, "Well, you should have!" Oh, Oh, Oh! Wrong answer! I didn't even know I had a temper until that moment. Without saying another word, I threw the covers back on the bed, my feet hit the floor, and I was out of the bedroom and into the kitchen in about four long leaps. The poor little goldfish on a side table was even too frightened to jump out of his small round bowl like he was used to doing every night and I had to get up and place him back in the bowl. My husband was right behind me, trying to grab me from behind before I did something drastic. He discovered he had made a big big mistake! He was right at my heels as I reached for the refrigerator door. It was one of those refrigerators with legs and a motor on top. He kept saying, "It was alright. It was good." I pulled so hard on the refrigerator door it was a miracle I didn't jerk the handle off. He was still saying, "It was good." I grabbed the platter with the leftover meatloaf, made one swift turn, and both meatloaf and platter went into the garbage container sitting beside the sink. My husband was going into the garbage after it. I dared him to touch it.

While I was so worried about being the good wife, my husband had his first lesson on "watch what you say about your wife's cooking." Surely, his mother had the good sense to lecture him on the Dos and don'ts of proper criticism!

He walked on pins and needles for a while after that. It was a long time before he even worked up the nerve to say, "The potatoes need more salt."

AUNT RUBY

I was a very inexperienced young bride in the ways of the world and learning my way around the city was going to be a challenge. The only time I had ever traveled far from home was when two of my sisters lived in Louisville and I visited them during summer vacation.

My husband had been discharged from the US Coast Guard and had recently enrolled at the University of Louisville. I knew, with his three-year enlistment in the military, he had seen a good bit of how people in other cities lived. He knew his way around. I depended on him to show me downtown Louisville until I could go out on my own. I needed to learn the local bus transit system and I was scared of going out alone for fear I would take the wrong bus and end up in an unpleasant situation of getting lost. When I say I was innocent, I was like a twelve year old trying to find her way through a maze.

About six months passed and it was summertime. We learned that my husband's aunt lived in Louisville and one Sunday she invited us to visit her. I had never met Aunt Ruby but I knew she was the oldest of about six siblings. Aunt Ruby was older than my husband's mother who had eight children. I wasn't sure what to expect so I wore one of my Sunday dresses that day. My husband had a one-seater older

Plymouth he had bought while he was in the Coast Guard. The light blue Plymouth was in good condition and had been washed and shined just before we drove across town to see Aunt Ruby.

One thing I knew was that Aunt Ruby had grown children and was divorced from her first husband. She had recently married again. I was a bit nervous as we approached the house. I had no idea what to expect when I met this new aunt. Would she approve of me?

We knocked on the front door and when it opened, the lady standing before me wasn't exactly the small town aunt I expected to see, like Opie's Aunt Bea; in fact, I was more than shocked. Aunt Ruby had her carrot-orange hair up in curls and tied back with a kerchief. While I expected her to look like a middle-aged woman, a bit on the frumpy side, with very little makeup and wearing a modest shirtwaist dress like most older women wore, she was everything but that. Her makeup and lipstick matched her shiny orange hair, the same color as Lucille Ball's. It was the first time I had ever seen a lady wearing false eyelashes, and they were long ones! She wore a button-down-the-front shirtwaist blouse pulled up and tied like a midriff to reveal her stomach. She matched the blouse with a pair of short shorts, and I do mean "short"! Her long legs were well tanned. I couldn't help but wonder about her children, who were probably as old, or older, than my husband, and he was twenty-two. In my world, nobody's mother looked like that unless they were movie stars! She definitely wasn't the Ma Kettle type either!

Ruby wore a pair of very stylish sunglasses and woven wedge sling-back shoes. I had never seen anyone like her in my entire life. I could have caught flies with my open mouth. She didn't look anything like her sister, my new mother-in-law, who was a bit on the frumpy side and rarely wore cosmetics. I didn't have a clue about what to say to this unusually striking woman dressed like a teenager.

Ruby led us through another room of her house to meet her new husband. We walked into a sunroom and there sat a smiling, rather handsome young man. I just assumed he was probably her son and looked around, expecting to see her husband. Ruby walked over to the young man, gave him a hug and big slobbery kiss right in front of us then turned and said, "I want you to meet my husband." She gave his name which I have long forgotten, and again, my mouth dropped open from shock and my face turned the color of her hair. Her husband appeared to be about the same age as my own husband. Both of us nearly stammered in disbelief when we shook his hand. This was definitely a new experience for me.

We sat down and Ruby immediately plopped herself in the young man's lap placing her long tanned legs across the arm of the chair and her arms around his neck. I couldn't help but be embarrassed because I had never been around people like this before. I came from a small town family that never displayed their affections quite so openly, and besides, fifty-year-old women didn't wear short shorts where I came from! For me, this was my first life experience in the big city. I liked Aunt Ruby right off the bat. She was friendly, laughed a lot, and was definitely different from the rest of my husband's relatives, and I'm guessing was also the 'black sheep' of the family.

It was about two years later when I saw Aunt Ruby again. My husband's parents and six siblings were visiting for a weekend. We lived in a small apartment and with my husband attending classes at the university we had to count pennies at the end of each month to make ends meet. The day before payday I counted out enough pennies to buy a loaf of bread and a package of sliced bologna. My husband worked for the Railroad Company during the days and attended classes at night. The bologna sandwiches would tide him over until he received his paycheck.

I barely had enough pots and pans big enough to hold a can of peas or corn and I found myself suddenly having to prepare a dinner for thirteen people. After borrowing a huge iron kettle for the sauce and a large Dutch oven for the spaghetti from my neighbors, I set out to make spaghetti and salad. It was the only thing I could think of to fix that I could afford and would feed thirteen people. My friend had given me a family favorite spaghetti recipe which I had used and liked very much. It would do the trick and I could prepare a simple side salad to go with the spaghetti. I don't remember what I did for enough plates and utensils for that many people.

I was a nervous wreck while getting ready for the in-laws and younger children. Aunt Ruby had been invited to the dinner and she sat in my living room while I worked in the kitchen. My husband had gone to pick up the rest of the family at his sister's house.

I can't recall if Aunt Ruby was still married to the young man I had met two years earlier, but she came alone to our apartment that evening. I was working in the kitchen and all of a sudden, she heard me scream. She came running to the kitchen only to discover I had dumped all of the spaghetti in the sink while trying to drain the water off. It was one of those white enamel sinks that hung on the wall and had a drain board on one side. She looked at the situation and asked, "Is your sink clean?" I told her it was and then she said, "Just scoop the spaghetti back in the pot and they will never know the difference. And so, that's just what I did. No one would know except Aunt Ruby and me, although I knew my sister-in-law had such a weak stomach and was so particular, she would never have touched a bite of my spaghetti had she known it had been spilled in the kitchen sink.

The dinner went well and I was more than relieved when it was over. I never saw Aunt Ruby again until her father died, my husband's grandfather. That was about eight years later. We didn't keep up with her after that and I never knew if she was still married to the young man who I thought was her son. All I can say is that Aunt Ruby was not made from the same mold as the rest of her siblings. I really liked her, carrot-red hair and all!

SUNDAY IN DEFOE

The big snow we had about a week ago with so many travelers stranded on the interstate and people shoveling piles of snow put me in mind of a similar snowfall about sixty years ago, shortly after I married and was living in Louisville, Kentucky. By chance, my sister and her husband also lived in Louisville. They were living on campus at the Southern Baptist Theological Seminary where he was completing his ministerial studies. At the time he was pastor of a small country church in a farm community called Defoe, about thirty-five miles from where they lived. Every Sunday morning they were up early and traveling to Defoe with their eight-month-old son. My sister packed up his diapers, baby food, and necessities for the entire day because my brother-in-law would be preaching both morning and evening services at the church.

Each Sunday, different families in the small community hosted them for Sunday dinner and gave them a place to rest during the afternoon before preparing for the evening service at the little church. Most of the church members were full time farmers living in the old two-story farm houses they had probably inherited from their ancestors. My sister had made friends with a family who lived in a more modern day brick house that had electric heating and indoor bathrooms. It also had a telephone. Many of the other homes had not installed telephone service and still used the long-standing outhouses.

My sister had promised to take me with her to Defoe on a Sunday when dinner and bathroom facilities would be provided by the couple who owned the nice brick house. She was sure I would enjoy my visit with the family. It was wintertime when my sister called and told me to be ready to go early the next Sunday morning. We had to arrive before morning church services began.

Wouldn't you know—that was the weekend it happened to snow about twelve inches. But it didn't prevent us from driving from Louisville, because the roads had been cleared. My sister had to consider the weather conditions when going to Defoe on weekends with her baby.

When we arrived at the little country church, we learned that plans had changed. We would not be staying the day at her friends' house, the ones with the nice brick home and 'indoor plumbing facilities'. Dinner arrangements had been assigned to another family. We would go directly to their house after morning church services. This was a family my sister and brother-in-law did not know well; a very quiet family who lived in one of the quaint old two-story white frame houses on a large farm. The main parlor contained a pot-bellied stove for heating and bathroom accommodations were in an outhouse a good distance from the house. A snow path had not been cleared and my sister and I were not exactly prepared with the appropriate footwear. Neither did we wear the warm winter clothes that we should have worn. In fact, my sister was wearing a black sheath velveteen dress that had no sleeves. It had a pretty bolero jacket but she just happened to leave the jacket at home when she left Louisville. The dress was the one I bought at Daniel's Department Store back home just before I was married. I had loaned it to my sister.

While the two ladies prepared dinner for us in a section of the house which was an add-on called a Lean-to, we sat around the pot-bellied stove that was the only means of heat for the house except the wood stove in the kitchen. My sister warmed the baby's food on top of the pot-bellied stove. The outdoor temperatures were below twenty degrees, very very cold. We did not come prepared for such cold temperatures inside the house and we felt we could not sit around in our winter coats to keep warm. So we tolerated the cold by staying close to the pot-bellied stove.

Conversation was at a minimum. It was difficult to talk with the members of the family. They were very quiet and we could see that they were also very uncomfortable with us. It was obvious they were not in the habit of entertaining guests, especially when the guests that day were the church pastor and his family. With the tranquility, it appeared this was going to be a very long day.

While we sat in the parlor, the two ladies in the home were busy in the kitchen preparing Sunday dinner which had most likely been cooked on Saturday, the day before. I remembered visiting my Aunt Renie when she prepared all the food on Saturday that would be eaten on Sunday. There was no cooking done on the Lord's Day and most of the food was cold or room temperature.

My sister, her husband, and I had been left alone with the baby in the huge family parlor with high ceilings and only the pot-bellied stove for warmth. We were not aware that the family was eating their Sunday dinner in the dining room located in the lean-to at the side of the house while we waited. We were beginning to get hungry and wondered when we would get to eat. The baby had been fed, diaper changed, and he was placed in his little carrier near the stove for a nap. Eventually, the lady of the house called us into the dining room where the table had been set for the three of us. We would be eating alone. Up to this point, we had not been able to conjure up a conversation with this family.

We entered the room and the first thing we realized was that there was no heat in the dining room. It was so cold we might as well have been sitting outside on the front porch in twenty-degree temperatures– my sister in her sleeveless dress, and me in a dress almost comparable. I was not a coffee drinker but I knew my sister and her husband couldn't wait for that hot cup of coffee. The lady placed the room-temperature bowls of food on the table then they were followed up with three glasses of cold lemonade.

We looked at each other and not a word was said. The two ladies, most likely mother and daughter, removed themselves from the dining room, closing the door behind them and leaving us there to eat our meal. All we could do was stare at the glasses of lemonade and begin shivering. We were so cold in the unheated room that our teeth began to chatter. The only thing I remember about that meal is that the room was dark and there was a bowl of green beans and a plate of cornbread on the table. And, of course, three glasses of ice cold lemonade!

I look out the window on this cold winter day and see the remains of the big snow from last week and think about how cold it is outdoors. I can tell you now – you don't know Cold until you have had dinner in a twenty-degree room, wearing sleeveless dresses, and drinking ice cold lemonade!

These are my memories of a little place called Defoe, Kentucky. You can't imagine how many times this story has been told and how much we have laughed.

A DAY OF RESURRECTION

This may sound like my life's history, but it only hits a few of the highlights beginning after marriage and divorce. Ah, yes, Divorce!

I was clinging to the walls inside the courthouse to keep from falling through the doors of the elevator. My husband had just signed the papers giving him his freedom. "Divorce granted!" Yes, it was freedom for him; Hell warmed over for me. He had ended our marriage. And there was nothing I could do about it. Even the Orson Welles look-alike judge stepped out of my way as I flew through the doorway of his office.

If it hadn't been for two small children, I could have lost my will to live. Many people go through this stage after divorce, but I am here to say…you can get over it! I thought the hole couldn't get any deeper, but without realizing it, I had the strength to pull my way up and out of the hole. It took a number of years. Life wasn't peaches and cream by any means. There were many loopholes that followed. It was depression, sadness, struggle, lots of struggle, and two small children to keep me going. I had a lot to learn—a high school graduate going to work on a near minimum wage income was a challenge. I had no friends to offer support. I was learning how to survive without assistance. I searched for a sitter for my children and found one in the neighborhood. I bought a car then I had to learn to drive it. Today, I can laugh about that car – a Dodge Matador costing $500, the biggest and ugliest vehicle you've ever seen. It had tail fins! I mean, if it had had propellers I believe it could have flown!

My story isn't unique by any means. It's just my story! I went from job to job trying to hold my head high. Decision-making wasn't always easy; I stumbled and fell many times along the way. There were more bad times than there were good. I was out of work as many as four months at a time. It isn't easy when you have no income to fall back on. You lose a lot of sleep at night, and when the car breaks down and you can't afford to get it fixed, you cry a lot. Such a silly thing to cry about – a car! But we all know, life isn't easy when you have no transportation to work, or to the grocery, or to take your kids to activities. The answer to feeling sorry for myself showed itself after buckets of tears. I always wondered why you had to plummet to rock bottom before the problem could be solved.

Fortunately, my sewing skills kept me busy around the house. My daughter became one of the best dressed girls in her peer group because I could take remnants and build her a fashionable wardrobe. I was able to design new outfits for her to wear to school. I also fashioned my own work ensemble.

A few years passed then someone told me about an organization called Parents Without Partners (PWP). A couple of my friends and I decided to join. They, too, were divorced with children. I finally had a social life. It was a good organization with activities for both the parent and the children. Meetings and monthly socials were planned, plus, new friends came into my life. Eventually, I was elected president of the organization. That was a busy year for me, supervising programs, socials, and other activities, including those for the children. After my year as president ended, my interest in PWP ended. I never attended another activity or monthly meeting.

It took about fourteen years to get over the stigma of divorce and the lack of self-worth, and my participation in PWP was a great help. About three years passed and by then, my children were out of high school, going to college and working. I thought my troubles were over. Not by any means! I resigned my job of seven-and-a-half years, put my house on the market and found a residence in my home town that had an extra building where I could open a craft shop and go into business for myself. Things were coming together for me. My daughter had to move out of the house and find new living quarters for herself. My son was busy getting ready for his first year at the university. I advertised my house for sale on a Friday and it was sold the following Sunday. Things were moving faster than I expected. I asked the new owner to allow me two months to get ready to move.

Next, the house caught fire three days after it was sold. No one was home at the time and our little miniature poodle died of smoke inhalation. I spent two months alone sorting through rubble and deciding what could and couldn't be salvaged. I lived nearby in the Springs Motel while I labored daily clearing the house. My son's new wardrobe for college was ruined and had to be replaced. Insurance provided the funds for him. While he entered the University of Kentucky, I moved back to my hometown, into a nice little house that was built in 1907. I dearly loved the house and its arched doorways and old architectural features. It had a screened front and back porch. I opened my own craft shop and became an entrepreneur, a word I'd never heard of until I became one!

Almost a year later, I was getting ready for Christmas production and sales when a knock came at my back door. It was drizzling rain. I'll never forget that night. I was busy with my craft projects in the kitchen and watching *Mork and Mindy* when I answered the door. Standing there was an old high school friend. "Pat, smoke is pouring out of the window of your shop (located right behind my house)." Ah, yes, just another little nose dive. My shop was on fire. I lost everything except the gutted building—one month before Christmas. Two fires in one year. Three days later I called my children to give them the news. That wasn't a happy day!

A second time in one year, I was feeling the stench of smoke in my nostrils as I inventoried the situation day after day. Another cleanup job and I was working alone! The insurance adjustor left it all to me. He didn't have any idea how to describe craft items on an itemized list of losses. No job, no income—déjà vu. I finally found another secretarial job with no benefits offered. I could barely cover my monthly expenses. Time passed, and I sold my house and moved to Tennessee, living the first year with my sister. I would reside the next 19 years in the same small town where my family had lived during World War II. I learned a lot during all those years, most of which was about failure. My daughter had married and had two children. My son completed his education at the University of Kentucky then married a girl from Wisconsin. They all lived in Kentucky. I lived in Tennessee. It was during those last 19 years that I learned to accept the setbacks and obstacles that came my way. I didn't expect great things. They weren't going to happen. I became content with my way of life. I had my sister living nearby and several good neighbors and friends to rely on for companionship and fun.

When I left my home and my children behind those many years before, the doors to a new life opened up. It took a few years to discover I could laugh again. I never searched for a new man in my life. If it was meant to happen, so be it. Living alone teaches you that life is what you make of it. If I didn't learn anything else from all of my drawbacks and troubles, I learned how to enjoy life while living alone. I taught myself many things and enjoyed what I was learning along the way. I was talented and I could create. I was good at crafts and interior decorating, and I knew how to sew. My investment in the Singer 2000 sewing machine had paid off. I enjoyed the process. I found that humor was one of my most positive and beneficial characteristics. I loved a good laugh and along the way, I learned to laugh at my failures. I made others laugh with me. I became interested in genealogy and my own family history, the best use of spare time anyone can have. I started telling short stories to my friends and co-workers. They seemed to enjoy my tall tales, and I enjoyed passing them along. More and more, I found that humor and busy hands kept me steadfast and contented.

As I began looking back at my life, I discovered I hadn't done so bad after all. There were no big accomplishments but I was satisfied with the little ones and my way of life suited me although I wasn't financially able to buy another home.

My kids were busy building their own families, and I was fortunate to have them for weekend visits. They always supported me in anything I did. I also looked back on my life and realized the best thing my husband did was sign those divorce papers and instead of giving himself his freedom…he had given me my freedom, the freedom to be myself and do what was best for me. I was no longer held back and ruled by another being. Naturally, the divorce had many adverse effects on my children, things I couldn't change or correct.

I was nearing retirement and then one day, due to my explorative habits and my continual interest and love for decorating, I won a decorating contest through a national magazine. It was the day life changed for me…again. I gained more confidence than I had ever had before. I acquired new friends and a new life. I sailed on a ship for the first time, the largest ship in the world. I traveled to other countries for the first time. I saw Broadway shows in New York City and London, England, for the first time. I became a regular customer with Delta Airlines, etc. and wasn't afraid to fly the skies alone. My children supported me and made my life more fun because they were enjoying my adventures as well. I remember their surprise when they answered the phone early one morning and heard my voice, calling from the Queen Elizabeth 2 in the middle of the Atlantic Ocean. That was an extremely expensive phone call, but worth every penny! They are not only the best kids a mother could have, but they have become my companions. They laugh at me and with me and never put me down; well, almost never! They constantly encourage me to do the things that make me happy. They help build my confidence.

I wrote a book, a task we all dream of accomplishing. It isn't a best seller, but it is "my story" and mine alone. Nobody can ever take that away from me. So, today, as I look back, all I can say is that I am grateful to the big fat judge in divorce court and the man who walked out of my life many years ago. I never got the chance to tell him, "I was reborn." It was a day of Resurrection. I can knock on his little box at the Lexington Cemetery mausoleum and smile as I say, "Life is great! Sorry you aren't here to enjoy it too." (Always end a story with a smile.)

MY NEIGHBORLY NEIGHBOR

Every day when I arrived home from work, I was never sure if I was going to face a challenge after I opened the front door, or if I was going to have a peaceful supper with at least one of my two children. That day, I saw immediately it was going to be a challenge. Both Jan and Greg were sitting on the couch. It was a rare thing when the two of them were both there when I arrived home after work. One of them had to be rounded up in the neighborhood or from the small park down the street.

I sat my purse on a chair and removed my jacket and that was when Jan said, "Mom, there's something I think I aughta tell you." Every time she ever said those words to me, I knew it meant trouble!

"Okay, what is it?" I could tell this was a story I didn't want to hear, so I took a deep breath and said, "Go ahead, out with it!"

"Well, ya' know those people that moved in the house back behind us?"

"Yeah, I know who you are talking about. What happened?"

"Well, ya' know that every morning I take a shortcut through the back yard and walk along the fence in his yard to meet Robin at her house and go to school with her?"

"Yes, I know that!"

"Well, this morning I took the short cut and was walking in that man's yard and he ran out of his back door and yelled at me, 'If you don't quit goin' through my yard and killin' the grass, I'm gonna call the po-leece!"

I suppose that was enough to make the average kid leap to her feet and run, but it didn't work exactly like that with my daughter. She didn't say anything to our new neighbor and continued on her way to meet her friend, Robin.

Next, she said, "I kinda think he might be comin' up here to talk to you and I thought I'd better warn you before he gets here." Just what I needed!

There's something about the bravery of a man when he knows a woman lives in a house alone with her children. My husband and I had been divorced several years. Women aren't supposed to be smart enough to know how to challenge the masculinity and forcefulness of an angry man. He knows when he is in the winning corner if his opponent is a woman.

It wasn't fifteen minutes until I heard the hard knock at my front door. Well, girl, it's time to face the music! Okay, breathe deeply! I opened the door and there stood a redneck, I could see immediately he was a redneck, with arms folded across his broad chest, a Marlboro cigarette pack rolled up in the sleeve of his tight fitting T-shirt, and feet widespread as though he was ready for the fight. He looked to be about five feet, eight inches tall, and was wearing that bully expression. I believe I was supposed to fall back in fear at the sight of him. But, I didn't; I stood my ground. This man reminded me of the days when comic books had ads on the back cover of a little skinny guy that was always being bullied and then he took a Mr. Atlas course and developed big muscles and was able to defeat the bully.

I was staring at what appeared to be Mr. Atlas, but he wasn't the friendly one. I looked him straight in the eye and said, "Could I help you?"

"Are you the woman who has the little blonde headed girl that's been a'goin' through my yard and killin' my grass?"

"I don't know, sir! Who are you and where do you live?" That answer ought to get the best of this redneck bully standing before me, ready for the first swing of the fist! Actually, I think it only frustrated him and made him even angrier. "Well, if she don't stop goin' through my yard and killin' my grass, I'm callin' the po-leece and puttin' a stop to it."

Now, he knew he had me right where he wanted me—scared and shakin' in my boots! I think I disappointed him when I politely replied, "Don't worry, sir, I'll take care of the situation. The little blonde headed girl won't be goin' through your yard anymore and killin' your grass." And then I closed the front door.

That was when the lecture began. "Don't even think of going through that man's yard again—ever! I can't be at home after school to see everything you do and protect you from idiots like him. It would be your word against his and who do you think the judge will believe? I have to trust you to follow my rules, and this time the rule is—don't get near that man's yard."

Jan O'Neal

All of the neighbors around me had built chain-link fences around their back yards, but there was about a twenty-foot break in the fence between my back yard and Mr. Atlas's yard. That's where Jan found the opening for her shortcut to Robin's house. I had already planted Forsythia bushes in that expanse to hide the opening. I didn't see the need for additional fencing. While the man was so concerned about my child killing his grass, he had two junk cars sitting in the middle of his yard where he had been working on them for weeks and months. Talk about an eye-sore and a grass killer—and he was worried about one little girl killing his grass!

I wasn't certain the matter would end there, and of course it didn't! The next afternoon I came home from work and Jan was there with her girlfriend. This twelve-year-old child just had to get back at the neighbor for being so mean and hateful, so what did she do? She and her friend decided to walk around the back yard while her brother, Greg, played basketball with his friends. The basketball goal was located at the side of the driveway. The boys played ball almost daily.

The neighbor's two young boys just happened to be playing in their own yards. Jan and her friend casually walked to the back about three or four feet from the fence line and in front of the Forsythia bushes. Pure aggravation is all it was. Jan had to get back at this country redneck, so she would tantalize him a bit. Her plan worked!

The neighbor's two boys took off running towards the back door of their house, yelling to the top of their voices, "Mama, Mama, that girl's gonna come in our yard," and out the door the mother came, with hair to her waist and bangs flapping so long they covered most of her face. You couldn't even tell what the lady looked like. She began squalling out, "You better not come in our back yard. I'll call the po-leece." Naturally, Jan didn't look their direction and she and her friend moseyed up the back steps and into our house, giggling under their breath.

I arrived home from work that day to be greeted by the second chapter in this drama. Now this time, I was angry. I began my lecture about following the rules. My lectures had never worked before; why did I think they were going to take effect this time? I thought maybe if

I threatened her within an inch of her life, she might get the message —"don't tantalize Bubba! I can't afford a lawyer to keep you out of a detention center!" The kids' dad, also my ex-husband, drove up about that time and I explained the matter to him, saying, "Tell Jan she has to stop pulling her little pranks. She is going to get herself, and me, in big trouble." I thought maybe he could put a little more emphasis on the seriousness of the situation.

Dad lectured his daughter but I knew she wasn't really listening and taking the matter seriously. Also, that evening, Dad decided to find out who this neighbor was and give him a call and clear up the whole ordeal. He also wanted to impress upon this little pea-brained Bubba that he didn't threaten the mother of his children. Come on, Dad!

That turned out well! Dad called the man and said, "I understand you are having a problem with my daughter going through your yard. I can assure you there will be no further problems."

He thought he had done the manly and neighborly thing, but he wasn't quite ready for the response he received—"Your little blonde headed girl has been goin' through my yard and killin' the grass and I'm gonna call the po-leece and have her arrested if she does it again." The neighbor should have thought before he spoke. The little blonde headed girl's dad wasn't taking the threat too lightly when he raised his voice and said, "And you can go to Hell!" He then slammed the phone down.

Now, was that the way to solve a neighborly problem? After that, the neighbor put up a farm fence, unlike the other chain link fences, as a barrier between the two houses. There was still enough space at the end of the fence for a kid to slide through. Greg and his friends continued playing ball and each time the basketball rolled towards the fence, the two little boys went running and yelling, "Mama, Mama, that boy's gonna get in our yard," and out would come Mama with her long dog-hair mane flying in the wind and squealing to the top of her voice, "You better not come in my yard."

One day I was standing at my kitchen window and noticed one of the young boys walking towards the break in the fence with his bicycle. He pushed the bike through the opening and started across my back yard, heading around the side of my house to the street. I hurried to the back door, stepped out onto the deck just as the boy went across the yard. When he looked up and saw me, the color drained completely from his face. I thought the kid was going to faint. I smiled to myself and never said a word. I really didn't have to speak!

The problem eventually solved itself a few months later when the neighbors moved. And yes, the two rusty junk cars had killed the man's grass!

A BIRTHDAY PRESENT FOR MY MOM

I have reached an age where a birthday is something I'd rather forget. My birthday falls on May Day, a day that when I was young I always figured was MY DAY. When I made my own birthday plans last year, my daughter said, "We were planning to give you a surprise party." I told her, "You can't surprise me! Nobody has ever been able to surprise me."

As you can guess—they surprised me! Yes, my children gave me an early surprise birthday party because I fouled up their plans by scheduling a short trip to Nashville on my birthday.

When I was growing up, there was never a birthday party; not even a few girls coming to my house to spend the night, listening to our favorite music, popping corn, telling jokes, and seeing who could stay awake the longest. Mama would bake a white cake for me and cover it with seven-minute icing, but there was no hoopla or celebrating. I don't even remember blowing out candles.

I remember the year I was turning thirty-one. My son, Greg, was seven years old. He was small for his age, had light brown hair with a big cowlick, a few freckles across his nose, and his eyes had the shiniest big black pupils you ever saw. You might say he was a little

Opie Taylor, the kind of kid with that innocent look that made you want to hug him.

We lived near Turfland Mall, walking distance in fact. Sometimes Greg would ride his bike to the mall with his friends to get an ice cream cone, taking a shortcut through a field of weeds and then they would stroll through the mall. On this day, he was there alone, hands in his pockets, walking back and forth past Zales Jewelry Store, and then he walked into the store and began viewing the jewelry in the cases. He knew every mom liked jewelry but he didn't know there was a price tag attached to the kind of jewelry sold at Zales. There was only one lady clerk in the store and she approached him. She appeared to be the age of a grandmother, so naturally, this little boy caught her attention. What was a child his age doing wandering around in a jewelry store by himself? Why not a novelty shop like Spencer's Gifts, or Grant's next door that sold lots of toys? She asked, "Can I help you?" He answered, "I'm lookin' for a birthday present for my mom." She responded, "Okay, how much money do you have to spend?" He kind of lowered his head and in a soft shy voice said, "A dollar."

The clerk was so taken by this little freckle-faced boy, knowing he was serious as his eyes gazed over the glittery jewelry in the cases, she said, "You stay right here. I think I can find a present for your mom." While he waited, she walked through a curtained doorway to the back of the store. Now, just exactly what did the clerk expect to find in the supply room of the jewelry store that would cost less than a dollar?

She returned carrying a small square box. When she opened the box, it held a set of salt and pepper shakers made of crackled glass with chrome plated screw-on lids. She showed Greg the set and asked, "What do you think of these?" He shook his head in approval and said, "They will be good, I'll take 'em. How much do they cost?"

The lady said, "I believe you have enough money; they're seventy-nine cents. I'll wrap the box for you."

"How much does that cost?"

"Oh, the wrapping is free. You don't have to pay for that."

"That's good 'cause I don't have but a dollar."

She proceeded to take the time to carefully wrap the small box in floral giftwrap paper and then added a big red bow to the top. She said, "I believe your mom will like your birthday present." and then Greg reached in his pocket and pulled out his crumpled up dollar bill. The lady placed the box in a small Zales gift bag and gave it to him. She watched as Greg walked out of the store with one hand in his pocket and the other swinging the gift bag. I suppose the lady was more proud of finding a suitable present for this little boy than he was.

A short time later, Greg walked into the kitchen where I was washing dishes and he plopped the box on the table and said, "Mom, I've been to the mall and bought your birthday present. It cost seventy-nine cents and I had enough money left for an ice cream cone and two pieces of bubble gum. You can't open the present yet, though!"

Greg O'Neal

I, of course, asked Greg where he bought my birthday present and you can imagine my thoughts when he said, "At that jewelry store in the mall." I have often thought about the lady who waited on my child that day and wondered how many times she has told this story herself. I wish I could thank her for her attention and kindness to a little freckle-faced boy who only had a dollar to spend for his mother's birthday present. Yes, I still have my crackled glass salt/pepper shakers and they sit right at the front of the kitchen cabinet shelf.

ANOTHER BIRTHDAY

After being surprised with a birthday party last year, and I do mean "surprised," I was headed for Nashville with three of my best friends, my daughter, Jan, her friend, Nina, and of course, my traveling companion. I was reminded of another birthday many years ago. It, too, was a surprise party.

I was turning 33. Jan was almost 12; Greg was 9. Nothing had been planned for my birthday until a co-worker made the mistake and let it slip that my kids had planned something special. My friends were frustrated with her because the co-worker had spilled the beans and told me, but in the long run, it worked out best. I was prepared! And it's a good thing I was!

I got home from work at 5:30. Before I could close the front door both kids said, "Mom, we need to go somewhere." Any other day I would have complained and said, "I don't feel like going somewhere. I'm tired."

"Well, where do you have to go?"

"We'll tell you. You just drive and we'll tell you which way to go. Don't ask us where we're going." I noticed as we went out the door that Greg reached back and pushed the door open slightly. That was so the next door neighbor could get in and be there when my friends arrived. My neighbor had the birthday cake and would set things up while we were gone.

As I drove, I said, "You're gonna have to tell me where to turn."

"Oh, we will! Go that way at the corner. And, don't ask where we're going."

"Okay! Okay!" I already knew we were headed for the Springs Motel on Harrodsburg Road. "Keep goin' straight – now turn here (onto Larkspur)."

The kids' dad had helped them with their plans by giving them money and he showed Jan how to call and make reservations for dinner. We walked into the large dining room at the Springs and not a soul was there except us. Who needs to make reservations for dinner at 5:30 in the evening?? The waitress could tell this was a special occasion so she was exceptionally nice. We had the whole dining room to ourselves.

Going out to dinner for me and my kids meant stopping at Frisch's Big Boy for a fish sandwich, so it was obvious that Jan and Greg were extremely nervous. This was new to them—a fancy dining room, making reservations, folded napkins in the lap, stemmed glasses of water on the table, the whole works! The waitress seated us and handed us the menus. I could see their eyes widen as they looked at the prices on the menu. Jan was trying to whisper to Greg, "What'll we do? What if we don't have enough money?" She turned to me and said, "Mom, don't order anything too expensive 'cause we don't have much money.

I said, "How much money do you have?"

"Ten dollars."

I agreed to keep my choice on the menu at a low price. I said, "If you don't have enough money, I'll pay the extra if it goes over ten dollars." She breathed a sigh of relief.

Out of the corner of my eyes I could see the kids trying to whisper to each other and make hand and eye motions. I pretended I didn't notice. They kept looking at their watches and finally Greg said, "I have to be home by seven o'clock. I have some homework I have to do." I nearly laughed out loud because I had yet to see the child bring school work home with him.

Time after time, Jan looked at her watch and gave eye motions to Greg. I was keeping track of the time because I knew my friends were probably sitting in my living room, waiting for us to return for my surprise party at seven o'clock. Rosemary from next door was obviously there handling the situation.

When the waitress handed the kids our check, I could see them swallow. It was just under ten dollars. I said, "I'll tell you what. I'll leave a tip for the waitress." Their eyes nearly popped when they saw me lay a dollar and some change on the table. The places we were used to going to for dinner didn't require tipping.

We still had time to spare. Knowing it was too early for us to go home, I suggested we go through Turfland Mall for a few minutes. "Okay, okay! That's a good idea!"

While we were there Jan said, "I need to go to the drugstore for something." I knew she was probably going for a carton of cokes or ice cream to serve later. The cake was already in the fridge. I told her that Greg and I would be in Grants Store when she finished. She returned carrying a bag down to her side hoping I wouldn't ask what she bought. A couple of minutes later, I saw Greg whisper, "It's fifteen 'till seven. We gotta go!" I still couldn't believe he had used homework as an excuse to be home by seven. I turned and said, "Are you all ready to go? I'm getting tired." Their nervousness was so obvious it was almost funny. I did my best to pretend I didn't have a clue what was going on. I certainly didn't want them to discover I was aware of their birthday plans. I wasn't sure if they were going to make it through the ordeal. You never saw two kids so nervous. We arrived home at seven on the dot and of course, several of my best friends were waiting to surprise me. They were all so tickled that my children were able to pull off a surprise party on their own, making all the phone calls, ordering a cake, and with the help of their dad, making dinner reservations. That was the year Greg gave me a cigar box covered in macaroni then sprayed with gold paint. Jan gave me a bobble-head doll for the coffee table. It was 'Betty Boop'. You don't forget things like that.

IRRESISTIBLE SLEEP

A Story that is not a tall tale, but one worth reading:
My, My! This was one of those days when we should sleep in. I got up late only to find it was still dark enough to turn on the lights in the house, and it was pouring the rain outside. It's not the kind of day that tells me, "Oh, Gee, this is a good time to clean house." For me, there is never a good time to clean house. That's what I do when company's coming! So, since it was going to be one of those dreary, depressing days, I thought I would write a story.

This isn't the expected folklore tale you are used to reading, or one that will make you laugh, but more or less, an educational, informative personal story.

The situation began back when I was in high school. Mama just thought I was lazy because I had little energy and took lots of naps. Every morning in second period English class with Mrs. Pope, I would find myself fighting to stay awake. As soon as the class ended, I was wide awake again. At the time I didn't know it was a physical condition or anything I should worry about. It wasn't until years later when I had been married several years then divorced, and had to seek employment to make ends meet for me and my two children that the

WAIT 'TIL YOU HEAR THIS ONE!

condition excelled. I took a job at the University Medical Center in the medical records department. I had to read lots of medical charts for insurance purposes. One day I was reading a summary on a businessman where he was explaining his problems to the doctor. He had a severe sleep problem. The summary held my attention to the very end. The man had just described me to a T. And then the word "narcolepsy" popped up like a neon sign. I suddenly realized there really was a name for what was wrong with me. I had narcolepsy.

Several years passed and the sleep problem became an issue for me. When I explained to my doctor what was happening, his answer was "When you get sleepy, just take a nap". Now, if that wasn't the thing to say! I thought to myself, "If this was your receptionist and she left her desk to suddenly take a nap, what would you do? You'd fire her, that's what!" Well, that was the end of that doctor for me!

My job entailed lots of typing and reading. One thing about narcolepsy is, a sitting job is not recommended. A person should seek employment that keeps them moving and active, therefore, keeping the energy built up and preventing the issue of falling asleep on the job. Even at that, you may find yourself leaning against a post or table to keep yourself steady and on your feet.

I should stop here and explain a little more about Narcolepsy from the patient's point of view. Many people think Narcolepsy is connected to Epilepsy and sometimes the reactions are similar. The difference is that the true condition is simply called "irresistible sleep." This means that a person does not feel sleepy and does not know he is going to fall asleep at any inopportune time. There are stages of Narcolepsy and those who have severe cases are considered handicapped. They can't hold down a full-time job. They usually work out of their own homes where they can take breaks from their work and take naps during the day. You might see a person walking down the street and you think they are having an epileptic seizure, but no, they have been struck suddenly and unexpectedly by an episode of irresistible sleep. It also affects the muscles. Unexpectedly, your knees will double, almost taking you to the ground. It can't be controlled. In my case, the condition was moderate but still enough to drive me crazy. AND, no one understood!

You have seen people with Narcolepsy and probably laughed at them, which was the ordinary thing to do. I have been laughed at many times by family and friends because I would fall asleep in church, in front of the television, and just sitting in a group talking. I can remember being with a friend in an elegant upscale restaurant and got so sleepy in the middle of the meal that I had to ask him to take me home. A very embarrassing situation! I can rarely sit through a movie without falling asleep. I don't know it's going to happen, it just happens.

I remember when Tom Snyder had his late late show and one night his program was about sleep problems, basically Insomnia. He said to his guest, "I can't think of anything worse than Insomnia and not being able to go to sleep." I whispered to myself, "Oh yes, there is a much greater problem than Insomnia. It's not being able to stay awake when it is necessary!" His guest had brought a small dog on the show. He then showed a video of the dog running and playing in the yard. This little dog had Narcolepsy. A person threw a stick and the small dog started running across the grass to retrieve it. About twenty feet away, he began weaving and fell to his side, sound asleep. A few seconds later the dog jumped up, continued running, and then he stumbled again and fell to the ground asleep. He did this five or six times in his chase to get the stick. That's when the guest explained to Mr. Snyder that the dog had Narcolepsy.

It was the first time I had ever seen anything on television concerning Narcolepsy. When I said the word to people, ninety percent of them had no idea what I was talking about.

A few years later, my job entailed a great deal of typing because I was preparing material for publication. I needed to be alert and conscious of any errors in the documentations. I took short naps during my lunch hour in a small lounge and each afternoon, I took a ten-minute nap during my break. My co-workers were amazed that I could lie down on the sofa, be asleep within two minutes, and wake up ten minutes later. I had conditioned myself to do this and when I woke up, it was the same as if I had taken a two-hour nap. This was the only way I could make it through a work day.

The situation was beginning to be very frustrating and by the time I left work each day, I was strained. I couldn't take it any longer. One morning at seven o'clock I grabbed the phone book, found the number I was seeking then picked up the phone and called a friend from high school. I hadn't seen him in years. He was a practicing physician in town and I explained to him that I wasn't sick, but I had a problem and I needed to talk to a doctor who would listen and take me seriously. He said, "Come to my office on your lunch hour." I was there at noon and I will always remember his treatment as I explained my situation.

I didn't want to use the word Narcolepsy, so I asked, "Are you familiar with Irresistible Sleep?" He was so kind! He said to me, "Yes, and Pat, the average person has no conception of what you feel when you get sleepy." I had finally found someone who took me seriously when I spoke of my condition. That was Vernon Hart. We called him by the nickname 'Mutt' in high school. Even after the passing of so many years, it was difficult for me to look him in the face and call him "Doctor," but for me, he had earned the title many times over. He prescribed medication that became a life-saver to me. It not only helped keep me awake during my daily working hours, but also gave me a boost of energy to help me make it through the day. There were no side effects indicated.

When I moved to Tennessee, my new doctor would not prescribe medication for me until I entered the hospital for testing. I told him my symptoms, etc., etc., and I think I knew more about Narcolepsy than he did, but still I was required to be tested. Two thousand dollars later, he said, "Yes, you have Narcolepsy," and gave me a prescription for the same medication I had been taking for twelve years.

After I retired, I decided I no longer needed the medication because I spent most of my time at home and could take naps any time I felt an attack of Irresistible Sleep. I am sure there are many people suffering from Narcolepsy who have never sought treatment from a doctor. I believe the medical establishment has become more aware of the disease, which has no cure and they don't know what causes it, but at least, they can treat it.

So, when you see a person nodding and falling asleep in church, a meeting, theater, or elsewhere, please don't laugh and make fun of them. In most cases, they may suffer from Narcolepsy. There is no pain with this disease, but it has a great effect upon their lifestyle.

BITTERSWEET

The fall season is the perfect time of year for taking scenic drives and enjoying the change of colors in the trees. It pays to have a driver who is familiar with the territory and can lead you along the winding country roads where the scenery is at its utmost in beauty. I am not the person you want to count on as your guide unless you are interested in every dead end road in the county that has a sign saying "no outlet." I can definitely find those for you!

It is a time of year when Bittersweet, a vine that grows 15 to 20 feet high, can be found in wooded areas and thickets alongside rural roads. The reddish-orange berries are sought for their beauty and versatile use in fall decorating. I remember many years ago driving the two-lane road along US-25 near the old Wigwam Village at Rockcastle River in Livingston, Kentucky, and seeing the Bittersweet tied in small bunches and hanging from a rack on the roadside at the Indian Village. I loved to stop and buy a couple of bunches to take home and hang in my kitchen.

It was a Sunday afternoon and my kids were gone for the day, so I decided to go for a scenic drive. I was still wearing my Sunday clothes and I saw no reason to go home and change since I had no plans for getting out of the car. It was a beautiful fall afternoon, just the time of year for finding Bittersweet. I knew nothing about the country roads but what would it hurt to find one, and maybe I could run across some Bittersweet in a thicket nearby. I drove down a two-lane road and turned at the next place that looked like a country road. I hadn't driven more than fifty feet when I realized, I had made a mistake. A big mistake! I was driving into a wooded area on a very narrow road that was nothing but deep ruts high enough on my car that I couldn't even open the doors. I doubt that the road had ever been used by an automobile. It was probably cut out for tractors. There was no place to turn around so I just kept driving. I figured the road would eventually run into a paved street and I could continue on. I drove less than a quarter of a mile over huge rocks expecting to puncture a tire at any moment. The next thing I knew, I had come to a dead end. Surrounding me on three sides was farm fencing. "What do I do now?" I thought. I got out of the car in my black wool sheath dress and suede high heel shoes and decided to look for some Bittersweet berries while I figured out a way to turn my car around and go back the direction I came.

I found a few straggly sprigs of Bittersweet, returned to my car, turned the key in the ignition and nothing happened. I gave the key another turn, nothing! My car wouldn't start. The sun was going down and I knew it would soon be dark. I was stuck out in the land of nowhere with no way of calling my children to let them know where I was. Even if I had had access to a phone, which, by the way, was long before "cell phones" became common language, how was I going to tell them where I was if I didn't even know myself? It would take a helicopter to find me. Yes, I had pulled a good one this time. I was in big trouble. On the other side of a barbed wire fence was a large field and beyond the field, I could see headlights of cars in the far distance. But how was I going to climb the fence and trek across a mile or more in my best high heel shoes?

I walked around the car and looked across the field to my right and spotted a farmer a good distance away, out walking with his dog. If only I could get him to look my direction, maybe he would realize I was in trouble. Actually, it was pretty obvious since I was parked at the end of a dead end road that led to nowhere. That's when you pray! "Please Lord, tell that farmer there's a crazy lady over here whose car won't start and she's stranded and needs help." I kept watching and finally I noticed the farmer looking my direction. Then he started walking across the field, headed my way—proof that the Lord does answer prayers, even those of a crazy lady.

The man came up to the fence and opened a wide gate. How do you explain to a farmer that you happened to drive onto a narrow dead end, rocky road that really isn't even a road, and in your Sunday clothes, to pick Bittersweet? When I explained that my car wouldn't start he told me to try it again. It still wouldn't start. The farmer said I had flooded the engine. I should wait a few minutes and then try again. He said that I could then drive across the field and around the side of his house to another gate that led to the main road. "But, be sure and lock the gate back so that my cows don't get out," he said.

Cows? I couldn't see any cows and I really wasn't anxious to see them, either! The farmer returned to the house with his dog following along at his heels. I waited about fifteen minutes while watching the sun drifting lower and lower behind the hills, and then tried starting the car again. This time the engine turned over and I breathed a sigh of relief. I slowly drove through the gate, got out of the car to lock the gate back, and then went bouncing across the field towards the farm house. I made the turn at the side of the house and suddenly, standing before me in a huddle like an opposing football team facing a quarterback, were about twenty cows chewing their cud and staring at me with their big sad eyes. I didn't know cows were that big! Now, I wasn't born and raised on a farm so I didn't know anything about cows or how to talk them! They just stood there. I kept waving my hands hoping they would understand, that meant 'move.' How was I going to get past them so that I could drive through the front gate? They didn't offer to budge. I kept patting my fingers against the steering wheel and then I decided to try inching the car closer and closer to the cows. Little by little they parted enough to let me get through, still chewing their cud and still staring at me. I knew what they were thinking. "That lady doesn't know anything about how to get cows to move." I suppose it took ten minutes to get through the huddle. It wasn't going to be my day to make a touchdown! I suddenly realized I had reached the big fence gate, got out of the car hoping the cows would keep their distance, and then I opened and closed the gate. About fifty yards away I could see a paved two-lane road. At the moment, it was the most beautiful thing I had ever seen!

The farmer had instructed me to turn right on the road and also gave me directions that would get me back to the main highway.

It was dark when I got out of the car carrying my muddy black shoes and a few straggly sprigs of Bittersweet. I was relieved to be home. That experience taught me that from then on, when I wanted Bittersweet, I would drive to a floral shop and purchase it.

GOLDEN WEDDING ANNIVERSARY

Nothing is more exciting and uplifting than eight children celebrating their parents' 50th wedding anniversary. We all gathered at home to make preparations for the event. Invitations had been sent to relatives and friends and we had no idea how many people would show up that Sunday afternoon, December 19, 1965. We could only hope the weather would be such that it wouldn't interfere with those who had to travel several miles to attend. The cake had been ordered, refreshments prepared, Inez's wonderful banana punch was chilling in the refrigerator, and her house was spic 'n span spotless. That was no surprise to any of us because Inez's house was always spotless. I put my floral arranging expertise to work and created a beautiful gold and white centerpiece with white candles.

All eight of us kids arrived and were on hand to take care of all the plans. Our thoughts for many months had been that our parents' health would be good so they could enjoy their big day. They weren't in the habit of celebrating birthdays and anniversaries from year to year, so the whole idea of a party was giving Mama the jitters. Daddy, in his natural manner, stayed out of the way. He didn't want any part of the celebration, so he tried to make us think, but we had an idea he was looking forward to the occasion as much as we kids were. By the time the in-laws and all the grandchildren gathered in both Mama's house and Inez's, it would be quite a congregation. Inez lived directly across the street from my parents which helped with all of us running in and out of one house or the other.

50th Wedding Anniversary, 1965

I had even gone to the trouble of making my own dress for the occasion. My teal green velveteen dress and white lace jacket made an attractive combination. I even had teal green shoes dyed to match my dress. My six sisters, each, looked just as pretty. Mama and Daddy had raised a beautiful bunch of girls, and my brother, Don, was quite handsome as well. Thirteen of the soon to be fifteen grandchildren would be present and my niece, Brenda, was there with the first great-grandchild.

That morning the entire family joined my parents at Park Hill Baptist Church for services. It was the church Daddy had built. Mama couldn't wait to show off her family. We had all been, more or less, raised in the church because we were there for Sunday school, Baptist Young People's Union, (BYPU), Training Union on Sunday nights, Prayer Meeting on Wednesdays, and we girls belonged to the (GA's) Girls' Auxiliary. Then there were Sunday evening church services, and whatever other groups that could be created. Off and on, one or two of us sang in the church choir. Yes, I suppose you could say we were raised in the church! I, for one, had broken the habit and was not attending a specific church where I lived. In fact, it had been a good while since I had entered the church doors.

Everyone was hustling through Mama's house, and those who weren't there were getting ready at Inez's house. I was sitting in the living room, dressed and waiting for the others when Daddy sidled up to me, pecked me on the shoulder with the back of his hand and said, "Sis, there's something I think you aughta know!" I looked up at him as he crooked his finger and pointed at me. I grinned and said, "What is it, Daddy?" He tilted his head down and said, "They don't take up tickets at the door!" It was obvious he didn't have to say anything else. His message was well received.

Mama was strutting her stuff when we arrived at the small mission church. She was so proud of her family. This was the first time any of us had attended services with our parents at Park Hill.

We hurried home to prepare for the visitors who would be arriving in about two hours. There was hardly time for lunch because we had to get all the refreshments ready and placed on Inez's pretty dining table.

The Lord was looking down on us that December Sunday. It was one of the most beautiful days of the year and the temperature was 70 degrees. Everyone was wearing sweaters and jackets. The guests arrived two and three at a time. The house was overflowing with my mother's sisters and brothers, and their children who had driven from Middlesboro, Kentucky. My cousin, Walter, Mama's favorite nephew, and his family were there. Lifetime neighbors followed each other through the front door, delighted to share in the celebration.

I could tell that all the people at my parents' golden wedding anniversary were enjoying the activity and warm fellowship. Pictures were taken and when the crowd slimmed down, I could see Daddy beginning to fidget. He wasn't in the habit of getting all dressed up in his Sunday suit and having to stay that way all day. He wanted to get home, take off his suit and tie, and fall into his comfort chair. It was time to read the Sunday newspaper and take a nap.

Estep 50th Wedding Anniversary

Mama was so pleased to have three of her four sisters present. The oldest of the Rowlett girls, aunt Rittie, who lived in Oklahoma had already passed away. Mama received several anniversary gifts. All went as planned and my parents' 50th wedding anniversary was a success.

THE OLD-TIME FAMILY

hen I read this poem written 85 to a 100 years ago, I feel as though he knew my family and wrote this beautiful rhyme just for us.

"The Old-Time Family"

It makes me smile to hear 'em tell each other nowadays
The burdens they are bearing, with a child or two to raise.
Of course the cost of living has gone soaring to the sky
And our kids are wearing garments that my parents couldn't buy.
Now my father wasn't wealthy, but I never heard him squeal
Because eight of us were sitting at the table every meal.
People fancy they are martyrs if their children number three
And four or five they reckon makes a large sized family.
A dozen hungry youngsters at a table I have seen
And their daddy didn't grumble when they licked the platter clean.
Oh, I wonder how these mothers and these fathers up-to-date
Would like the job of buying little shoes for seven or eight.
We were eight around the table in those happy days back then

Eight that cleaned our plates of pot-pie and then passed them up again;

Eight that needed shoes and stockings, eight to wash and put to bed

And with mighty little money in the purse, as I have said.

But with all the care we brought them, and through all the days of stress

I never heard my father or my mother wish for less.

— Edgar A. Guest

TORNADO OF 1974

Working nine miles out in the country one hardly ever knew what was going on around town, especially when it came to changes in the weather. For whatever reasons, nobody seemed to keep a working radio on hand at the office. It was 1974, the year of the thirteen tornadoes that swept through Ohio and Kentucky one afternoon. Nobody in our office building was even aware that bad weather was approaching. At five o'clock, nearly everyone in the building was gone. Even I hurried home before realizing the tornado was coming down from Louisville through Versailles and on into Lexington and Richmond.

Everybody had left the office building except my friend Pansy. She was working late that evening and left the building about seven o'clock totally unaware of the dangerous weather conditions. At that point, the tornado had traveled all around the area, bypassing Lexington altogether except for the downpour of rain and high winds. It was pouring buckets of rain when Pansy got in her car and turned on the radio only to discover that tornadoes had already passed through from Xenia, Ohio, traveling south through Louisville, and it wasn't until later that she discovered a tornado had already leveled Stamping Ground, Kentucky, just a few miles away.

Pansy's eighteen-month old baby was with his babysitter as usual. Pansy's drive home was about thirty miles ahead of her. As she drove the two-lane road towards home, she could barely see the road and the wind was thrashing the tree limbs from side to side. There were no cell phones in those days so she had no way of getting in touch with her husband, or her babysitter who lived in a mobile home, the most dangerous place to be during storm and tornado warnings. Her first thought was that hopefully, her husband had advance warning of the tornado and had sense enough to go to the sitter's mobile home and get the baby. Pansy lived in a brick house in town which was much safer.

The drive along the road was slow and dangerous, but she kept plugging along. At one point she saw a pickup truck ahead of her lifted off the road. It nearly scared the life out of her. She kept on driving. The road remained clear and her only thought was to get to her baby. There was no other traffic on the road to slow her down then suddenly, she spotted a car off the side of the road in a ditch. Climbing the bank was a lady and her young son. Pansy stopped and said, "Where are you headed?" The lady said, "I live in Cynthiana." Pansy replied, "Get in, that's where I'm going."

She hadn't gone much farther when the most dreaded thing happened. A tree was lying across the road and she couldn't drive around it. So, in the downpour of rain, she and the lady got out of her car and they began pulling on the tree. With the wind and rain slashing back and forth, finally, they moved the tree far enough off one lane of the road so that she could drive her car past it. Pansy was wearing a pink polyester pant suit that day and when she climbed back into the driver's seat, she was soaking wet with mud clear up to her elbows. But still, her thoughts remained on the safety of her baby. Surely, her husband would have enough foresight to pick up the child from the mobile home and get him to safety. She prayed and she prayed, "Please Lord, let my baby be safe."

The remainder of the drive seemed like forever. Was she ever going to get home? Of course, the first thing she had to do was take the lady and child to their home which happened to be on the opposite end of town. That delayed her another thirty minutes of not knowing where her child was and if he was safe. She was nearly in tears as she drove. That, she didn't need since she had to focus on the falling tree limbs across the road ahead of her.

The rain was still pouring like drops of hail and she felt like someone had stuck a knife in her back, but Pansy continued on up the road. At last, she could see her house up ahead and the lights were on. She pulled into the driveway of her home, got out of the car, shaking mud from her feet and feeling the cold of the dripping wet pink pant suit sticking to her skin. Her hair was shedding droplets of water down her face. She looked and felt like a drowned rat. In her mind, she knew her husband must be worried sick about her, wondering where she was and if she was safe from the tornado that had already hit Louisville, Frankfort, Versailles and leveled Stamping Ground. Would she be able to get home without having an accident or being blown off the highway into the land of Oz? Hopefully, she would come straight home instead of going out of her way to the babysitter's.

The normal thoughts any mother would have in a situation like this were the concerned feelings of a loving husband! He must be worried out of his mind! Pansy drug herself from the car with rain still spattering down on her then hurried to the front door of the house. She opened the door. There wasn't time to remove her mud covered shoes, and the first thing she saw was her husband and baby on the sofa in the living room. As she breathed a sigh of relief, her husband looked up and said, "Thank God you're home. This kid has shit all over himself!"

Yes, her baby was safe from the tornado, but I think they are still searching for Pansy's husband!

DOGWOOD SHORES

It was time for a change in my life. I had had it with my job. I think it's what they call "job burnout." My daughter was working and my son would soon be entering college. Daddy had died a year earlier so I began thinking of moving back home and opening a craft shop. I was good at arts and crafts and was an experienced seamstress. Since my family and friends were encouraging me and thought it was a great idea for me to become an entrepreneur, I, too, thought it would be a great idea but even better, if they would offer to help finance the project. I had no other means of support and would have to depend on my success to pay the bills. Now, if this wasn't something, I was plunging into an endeavor I knew nothing about. But what the heck, you only live once!

I had access to a piece of property where I could build my shop and have room for living quarters. I needed an architect to draw up suitable plans for me. My brother-in-law had a friend who had just built log houses in a new area outside of Knoxville, Tennessee, and he was willing to provide blueprints that would work for my plans. He suggested I drive down to Knoxville and see one of the houses he had built in a new resort area called Dogwood Shores.

It was February and we had just been through three weeks of

below zero weather with snow that wouldn't melt. On the weekend I was to drive to Tennessee and meet the builder. The temperature rose to 40 degrees when I left home. The snow on the ground was beginning to melt. I stopped and picked up my mother to make the trip with me to Tennessee.

On Saturday morning the four of us piled into the big Mercury – Mama, my sister, Bena Mae, her husband Raymond, and me. A close friend, Blessing, was going along with us. Dogwood Shores was a new subdivision, rather barren and appeared to have only about a dozen completed houses. None of the houses were occupied because they were meant to be used as summer vacation homes. Roads had yet to be paved and we were following gravel and dirt roads. Since the heavy freeze was letting up, the ground began to thaw causing the roadways to be very muddy. We hadn't a clue where we were headed, but Raymond was sure he could find the house we were seeking. We hit a low lying spot that was quite muddy. As he drove along, my sister kept saying, "I wouldn't go that way. You'll get stuck in the mud." He was sure he would have no problems. Famous last words! You've known those men who never want to take the advice of their wives, well Raymond was one of them. He wasn't one to listen to my sister when it came to driving instructions. He started up the rise; his wheels began spinning. The big car was soon stuck in mud, deep mud.

It was about five o'clock in the afternoon and the sun would be going down soon. We were all dressed in windbreaker jackets and if the temperature started dropping we would be in trouble. Our biggest worry was Mama. Would she be able to bear the cold, and if so, for how long? If we kept the car running and the heater on, we would eventually run out of gasoline. Mama stayed in the car while the four of us worked at trying to drive out of the mud, one at the wheel; the other three pushing the car.

I was wearing my new crepe soled shoes and they were getting covered with mud each time I got out of the car to help push from behind. The car didn't move an inch. Finally, Raymond said he would walk back to the entrance of the subdivision and maybe someone would come along in a pickup truck with a tow, or they might have a

CB radio and could call Triple A and have them send a tow truck. CBs were quite popular at the time; all the truckers were using them. The problem with that idea was that we could give no directions to where we were and there were no road signs.

While Raymond was gone, Mama, Blessing, my sister and I sat in the cold car making jokes and telling stories. We were afraid Mama might get upset and with the cold setting in, we had nothing on hand to keep her warm. We waited and waited for Raymond to return. It seemed like it had been hours. At one point, I started the engine and Bena Mae and Blessing got behind the car and began pushing. What we discovered was that the car was just going deeper into the mud. It was above the rims over the wheels.

We were not prepared with food or drinks and suppertime had long passed. Blessing had a small box of raisins and we laughed as she counted them out to each of us. We continued laughing and told funny stories to keep Mama in good spirits. Blessing was a very funny person and she could always make Mama laugh. The only problem with laughing was that it would make us want to use the bathroom. Blessing even suggested she try one of the houses to see if she could open the door so that we could use the bathroom. Our feet were covered with mud. Wouldn't that be great, us tracking through someone's house, dropping mud every step we took? My sister said to Blessing, "If you really have to go, just find a little mound of grass and go. Who is going to see you? We are the only ones out here in the land of nowhere!"

We began worrying about Raymond because he had been gone so long. Finally, about 9:30, we saw headlights coming towards our car. We didn't know whether to be scared or grateful. We locked the car doors and waited to see if it was friend or foe approaching. Blessing's sense of humor cut in and she said, "If that is somebody who is going to rape us, let me go first." Just what we needed at a time like this—Blessing and her jokes. A young man in a Volkswagen stopped and said Raymond was in someone's house where there was a CB radio, he was trying to contact Triple A and was waiting for them to respond and come to the rescue.

Triple A never responded to Raymond's call. The young man assisting him called friends on the CB and they were coming to help. About ten o'clock they drove up in a large truck with a tow attached. It had already started to rain, causing more clay mud. While we sat in the car, the young men attached cables to our car and pulled us up the rise onto high ground. The car was covered in loose clay and so were we.

As we drove out of Dogwood Shores, we passed the log house we had originally gone to see. It was about a hundred yards over the rise from where we had been sitting for hours. All of us were starved when we walked through the doors of a Krystal Burgers restaurant at 10:30 p.m. The clerks glared at us as we walked across the freshly mopped floors with mud packed on us from our hips to our toes.

When I returned home, my new crepe soled shoes were thrown in the trash. That was my one and only trip to Dogwood Shores.

DRIP, DRIP, DRIP

The street where I lived was only two blocks long. It was not a through street so we saw little traffic which gave the kids a chance to play touch football in the middle of the block.

I was a pretty handy person when it came to painting, wallpapering, laying tile, and just general household sewing and decorating. But when it came to plumbing and electrical repairs, I knew nothing. That's where the professionals took over, that is, when I could afford the cost, which was very seldom. That not only upset me but made me angry at times as well. There's nothing can get a woman's dander up like that of trying to fix something in the house and she can't make it work. When those television programs show a lady crawling under a kitchen sink with a wrench and screwdriver then removing a connection and replacing it with the flip of the wrist, don't believe it for a minute. I was never able to loosen those faucets and screws. I didn't have the strength.

It was a Saturday morning when the neighborhood boys were playing touch football in the street in front of my house. My neighbor, Kenny, who lived a couple of doors down the street, was right in the middle of the boys, more or less in charge of the game. I had been in the bathroom observing my plumbing problems. I could feel my temperature rising. I couldn't afford to call a plumber but repairs were necessary. The faucet in the sink was dripping, the tank in the toilet was whistling and using up the water, and the bathtub faucet was running. I'd had enough. The plumbing problems in my bathroom had to be fixed—or else!

I stomped through the hallway to the kitchen and reached under the sink and pulled out a wrench and a clawfoot hammer. I was going to fix the leaks in the bathroom. I headed back to the bathroom and as I passed a bedroom door, I could see the kids through the window playing in the street, and right in the middle was Kenny. Wait a minute! He was a healthy young man and I decided he could fix the leaks for me, so I turned around and hurried to the front door. I yelled at Kenny and told him I needed his help. I told him I was about to destroy my bathroom. He took the wrench and hammer from me, for fear I was going to start swinging them.

About twenty minutes later, the sink quit dripping, the toilet stopped running, and the bathtub no longer leaked. And as they say, "That's what good neighbors are for!"

SUNSHINE YELLOW

What can you do to a 6' x 6' bathroom to give it an uplift—white tub with shower attachment, white toilet, and a decorative light fixture above a white sink that hangs on the wall with a mirrored medicine cabinet. There wasn't even room for a dirty clothes hamper or shelves for towels and washrags. This decorating project was going to require a very creative mind, so it was time for me to put my decorating skills to work. That little room needed to be bright, cheery, and inviting. Inviting? Well, I'll use that word for want of a better one!

Off to the paint store I went for a gallon of Sunshine Yellow paint. Yes, that was the color I chose and if that didn't brighten my bathroom, nothing else would! Of course, waterbase paint was what I requested, it being the preferred medium, whether or not it was the right medium. I always hated having to clean brushes with turpentine and paint thinners, such a smelly mess!

I figured if I did a neat job, I wouldn't even have to go through my rubble of old clothes to find the right ones to wear for the paint job. And, why should I put a shower cap on my head of dark auburn hair? I had no plans for spattering my hair with sunshine yellow paint.

First I had to clear the bathroom of all unnecessary items,

including the removal of the light fixture above the sink. I gave the gallon of paint a good stir and placed it on the lid of the toilet, the only flat surface available for a bucket of paint

I figured I might as well paint the ceiling yellow, too, since it was such a small room, and besides, that would keep me from having to be careful about ceiling trim. I don't know why it took me so long to realize I had bought oil-based paint, but I had already given the walls a first coat of paint. I wasn't satisfied with the oil-based paint, so I cleaned the roller, a hateful job, and decided the paint was going back to the store for replacement. Since it was the clerk's mistake in giving me oil-based paint, he made the exchange at no extra cost.

I had all weekend for my decorating project so there was no rush to get it completed. That evening I got out my equipment and paint rollers that I had washed out the night before and the pan for the paint. I was using a step ladder which wasn't easy to maneuver in that small space. Two legs sat in the bathtub and two in front of the toilet. I had to scoot in and around the ladder. I had already removed my shoes but didn't see the need to take off my navy polyester pants and pantyhose. I was a neat worker! Then I began the removal of the decorative screws around the light fixture. I was down to the last screw and suddenly, it dropped from my hand. Plink, plink, but no plunk! Where did the screw go? It should have hit the floor but it wasn't there. I didn't even have to search; I knew where it was and the little swirl in the top of the paint was evidence the screw was in the bottom of the can. How was I going to get it out?

There was only one way, so I pushed up my shirt sleeve, removed the rings from my fingers, and reached to the bottom of the can to retrieve the screw. It worked, but I still had a hand to be scrubbed and fingernails to clean.

I was ready to paint the ceiling so I turned my paint roller round and round until I was sure it was covered with an adequate amount of paint. I stood on a rung of the ladder and made my first swipe across the ceiling and over the bathtub. Not realizing I had failed to squeeze the water completely out of the roller, paint plopped into the bathtub, down the tile wall, onto the tile floor and then speckled my hair.

If that wasn't a good start! I stepped off the ladder right into a big blob of yellow paint. How was I going to get the paint off my foot? I would have to remove my navy pants before I could take off the pantyhose. As you can guess, the only way I could remove my pants was to pull them down over the soaked foot. There went my good polyester pants and pantyhose!

I hadn't even started the paint job and I had a mess to clean up. I had to get the paint off my foot then off the tile walls and floor before it dried. Now, I had bought the kind of paint that only takes one coat for good coverage. I completed the walls and ceiling and something wasn't quite right. The finished walls looked streaked and terrible.

Any good painter already knows that you can't use water-based paint over an oil base finish. The clerk failed to mention this to me as he mixed another gallon of water-based Sunshine Yellow paint. I was about to learn that one coat would not do the job. I let the paint dry and proceeded with another coat, this being the third coat of paint. The room was beginning to look better, but still would require one more coat of paint; it being the fourth covering. That wasn't good! My eyeballs were beginning to turn yellow!

It's bad enough when you have to 'do it yourself' household decorating and repairs, but when four coats of paint are required—that will put you into a coma, but I wasn't ready to give up yet. Things were beginning to look up when I purchased a window and shower curtain in yellow stripes. Since the shower curtain was much too long I had to trim about six inches from the bottom and re-hem the curtain. I hung the window curtain which happened to be over the bathtub. Then I placed the shower curtain on the rod with its new hooks. They looked beautiful until I read the tag on the side of the shower curtain. "Dry Clean Only." Whoever heard of a shower curtain that had to be dry-cleaned? How ridiculous! Shower curtains were supposed to be waterproof, plus, how was I going to keep the window curtain from getting wet when taking a shower? I spent more than usual for the set of curtains and there was no way I could return them —I had cut and re-hemmed the shower curtain! Maybe I could remedy the situation with a liner and a threat to my kids that they were not to get the shower curtain or window curtain wet when they took a bath.

My decorating job was finally coming together in spite of the few stumbles along the way. Last, but not least, was the blank wall facing the toilet. It needed something pleasant and appealing to accent the room. What better than a collage of family photos for everyone to study while they did their business! I thought the family pictures were quite lovely. I won't repeat what my kids thought!

Finally, my Sunshine Yellow bathroom was completed. I was happy with the finished results. When I returned to work on Monday morning, my co-workers kept asking me why I had yellow specks all over my head.

My daughter went through the back yard each morning to meet her girlfriend on the street behind us so they could walk to school together. I got home from work on Monday, and the first thing Jan said was, "Mom, you don't even have to turn the light on in our bathroom in the morning. I can see the yellow walls all the way from Robin's house."

MIRROR, MIRROR ON THE WALL

I was in a decorating mood. I had already wallpapered five rooms and that left the living room. I was living in an old house that had been built in 1907. It had its good features such as once having French doors leading into the living room, arched doorways from room to room, and even a slanted ceiling in one bedroom to match the slanted floor. My laundry room had the convenience of deep double sinks which came in handy for craft projects and bathing the dog.

The old wallpaper in the living room really needed replacing. I don't know what I had in mind at the time but for some reason I needed to see if the wallpaper covered the space behind a large 4' x 4' mirror above the mantle. I didn't like the mirror and was considering a replacement. It was a very plain, unframed mirror with sharp edges, and I can tell you now, also very heavy. The only way I could see behind the mirror was to take the two-inch screws out of each corner of the mirror and pull it away from the wall a couple of inches. Being the Do-It-Yourselfer that I am, I did just that. There was no wallpaper behind the mirror so that meant I had to put the mirror right back in its place. I pushed the mirror back, holding my hand against it to keep it from falling forward then picked up the four screws and started placing them back through the holes in the mirror. Uh-oh! Something was wrong, very wrong! The screws slid in and out of the plastered wall. They were not going to hold the mirror in place. When I pulled my hands away, the mirror fell forward.

What was I going to do? I stood there holding the heavy mirror against the wall with both hands spread from side to side. The only thing left to do was slide the mirror over the edge of the mantle and down to the floor. How was I going to do that? I knew if I placed my hands over the edges of each end, the heavy mirror would slide down and possibly slice my hands in two. That's when it would have been nice if a pair of heavy-duty work gloves happened to be lying handy on the mantle, which, of course, they weren't!

It looked like I was stuck! And I do mean Stuck! I couldn't reach the telephone to call someone for help and even if I could use the phone, my doors were locked and no one could get in the house to rescue me. There was a small wooden kitchen chair sitting nearby. If only I could reach the chair with one foot and pull it towards me, maybe I could slide the mirror over the edge of the mantle and down onto the chair. There again, I was taking a chance on the sharp edges of the mirror sliding through the fold of my hands. It was obvious the small chair was too lightweight to hold the mirror. It would fall backwards onto the floor, possibly shattering the mirror.

I stood there spread eagle against the mantle with blood draining from my arms and they were beginning to ache. Of course, I had to tackle this job at night when there was no chance of anyone knocking at my door, and even if they did, the only way to get my back door open would be to call the fire department or Glock the Lock Man! How many hours would I have to wait for that to happen?

Yes, only I could create a predicament like that. I stretched my leg as far as I could, trying to reach the small chair. Why couldn't the Lord have given me longer legs and a brain that didn't appear to be developed from wet noodles? The chair was the only thing close enough to be of any help. It isn't easy maneuvering with one leg while spread eagle against a mirror. My reflection was beginning to get on my nerves. I really didn't like what was looking back at me at that time.

After about thirty minutes, it appeared no miracles were going to materialize. I scooted the kitchen chair in front of me with one foot. The mirror was awkward and must have weighed thirty-five pounds. I started inching it towards the front edge of the mantle. Scratching the paint off the mantle shelf was the least of my concerns. It was time for the test. I had to prove how strong I was. In one swift movement, I held each side of the mirror and pulled it over the edge and down towards the chair. I held tight as I pulled it on down to the floor. I did it! No injuries to my hands, but I was shaking like a leaf.

I often ask myself why I have to be so smart and find the need to tackle the Do-It-Yourself projects. The mirror never went back on the wall. I replaced it with an antique oak mantle that had its own mirror. That Do-It-Yourself project required chopping off the brick on each side of the fireplace. "Another story!"

I THOUGHT I SAW A MOUSE

When panty hose was a part of my daily apparel, I had a regular habit when I removed my clothes after I got home from work. I took off my slacks and panty hose both in one action rather than one at a time. When I finished I didn't separate the two articles of clothing, I just laid the slacks across a bedroom chair with the panty hose still stuck down inside the slacks. One morning, I decided to go shopping. I was in the bedroom dressing. I had already applied a clean pair of panty hose and then reached for the same slacks I had worn the day before. I pulled up the pants. They seemed a bit snug and bunchy but I paid no attention to that. I finished getting ready and headed out the back door to the car.

When I arrived at the shopping center, my first stop was Rose's Department Store. While browsing through the aisles of the store, a couple of times I got a glimpse of something going past my right foot. The second time it happened I looked down. Was that a mouse running past my foot? I kept walking and then I saw the shadow again. I looked down and what I saw threw me for a loop! Hanging out of the right leg of my slacks was about 12 inches of one leg of my panty hose—the ones I had worn the day before. I forgot about leaving the panty hose inside my slacks and didn't notice them still stretched out inside the pant legs as I was getting dressed.

I was so startled that the first thing I did was quickly look up and down the aisle to see if anyone was watching me. I could already feel my face flushing. Was it possible that a customer had seen something hanging out of the leg of my slacks, flopping back and forth, as I walked around the store? I bent forward and grabbed the toe of the panty hose and started pulling, thinking they would slip out quickly into my hands before anyone saw them.

That isn't what happened! Once I gave a hard tug on the panty hose, they began to stretch. They hadn't just gotten caught in one leg of my slacks but crossed over the crotch in back to the other leg. I pulled and I pulled and the panty hose seemed to stretch and stretch. There was nothing I could do except keep pulling. I just knew that any moment a customer or a clerk was going to step up in front of me and wonder what in the world I was doing all bent over like that. I expected a camera to be pointed directly at me and monitoring my every move. I worked as fast as I could trying to pull the extra panty hose out of the right leg of my slacks but they just seemed to grow. Finally, the end of them popped out at me. I curled them up as fast as I could and shoved them into my purse. At that point, I could imagine the store manager walking up to me and asking what I had placed in my purse. Was I trying to shoplift?

I was sweating bullets as I exited Rose's Store. I can't even go into the local store today without remembering my chaotic experience. From that day on, I removed my pants and then took off my pantyhose separately and placed them far from the pants.

KENTUCKY HORSE BISCUITS

Bill Gates made his fortune in computer technology. A lady made her millions when she created a little item that was a savior to all secretaries—Wite-Out—and then there are all the famous designers I envied.

Well, this is my story, a creation that was going to be a showstopper. I had left my job to go into business for myself, the craft supply business. My shop had been open a few months when one day a couple from my previous job came to visit me. They had a proposal for me. She had promoted the Bluegrass Music Festival in Lexington that was held once a year and had become quite successful. The Horse Park was rather new and located right down Iron Works Pike about a quarter of a mile from where I was previously employed. The lady had come up with an idea for a new product that she felt would be a big seller at the Horse Park, and the Kentucky Training Center, the place where they auction the million dollar thoroughbreds every year. And, of course, knowing that I was a good crafts person, the couple decided I was the perfect person to provide this product: "Kentucky Horse Biscuit."

I would come up with a way of marketing the Horse Biscuit, otherwise known as 'horse manure'. I gave it some thought and soon presented my ideas to them. They went for it! Marketing the horse biscuit as a Kentucky souvenir to tourists who visit the state for horse racing would be a winner for sure. That was going to be my claim to fame . Move over, Bill Gates, Bob Mackie, and Heidi Klum, and the lady who created Wite-Out! I would soon have my own show on television!

First, I had to have a source for the horse manure, something I had never dealt with in my life. One of my customers in the craft shop had the answer and she also had a pickup truck for hauling the 'materials'. Blue-ribbon winners were boarded about fifteen miles up the road. I wanted nothing but the best product for my endeavor. She and I jumped into her pickup and off we went with shovels and boxes. If you've never been around horses before, you are probably unaware —"that stuff stinks!" I watched while my friend shoveled (a good time for claiming back problems!). We hauled the manure home and I stored it at the back of my garage to dry out. I lay in wait for complaints from the neighbors concerning the horrible odor coming from behind my garage, but none came. Believe it or not, once manure is dry, it doesn't have an odor. I was learning as I went – a city girl who'd never been on a horse in her life—or cleaned up after one!

I designed two styles of plaques: one had a walnut wood base with a desk pen and a horse biscuit applied to it. A small brass plate identified it as "Kentucky Horse Biscuit." Now, that should be a big seller at the parks, right? The second plaque was oval and had a stenciled horse on it along with the horse biscuit and brass plate. The stenciled horses were hand cut from wood grained paper and looked quite nice. I won't go to the trouble to give you my formula for the biscuits, but I will tell you that my two deep sinks in the laundry room of my house were where production began – along with the use of my blender. Don't hold your nose…it wasn't that bad and the blender ceased being used for cooking! It had a more productive use.

My creation met with approval from my 'partners'. The first sales went to the Horse Park, the Kentucky Training Center, and to Cumberland Falls State Park's gift shop – two gross each. I didn't try marketing the souvenirs anywhere else. I didn't have time to spend on them and run my craft shop too. I soon received a second order for the craft item then the local Lions Club held its annual syndicated TV auction, so I offered a couple of the plaques to the auction. My brother was an auctioneer for the show. When the desk plaque came up for bid, they had to cut off the time for it because so many bids were coming in and they needed to give time to the other items being sold. I had no idea the area had so many horse lovers and my horse biscuit would be so popular.

A short time later, my craft shop burned and I went out of business. I called my friends and told them I would not be making any more of the souvenirs. And then one day, my nephew approached me and asked if I could provide him with a small number of the horse biscuits for the Rotary Club. It seemed that a European Equestrian group would be visiting the Club and my nephew wanted to offer a token gift to each of them. I went back into production and provided the number requested. I couldn't believe my horse biscuits would be going to all parts of Europe.

THE HOOSIER WALL CABINET

Everything was in place in my new apartment. This was my second move since I sold my home in Lexington and I was beginning to tire of packing and unpacking. I had cleaned up after two fires during these moves and it was time for a little relief to come my way. The inventory of all of my household furnishings plus the inventory of all of the items in my craft shop after it burned had taken its toll on me, and now I was moving into a new apartment. Hired help came cheap because my sister worked in the local sheriff's office and she acquired the assistance of three inmates at the jail to help unload my furniture. They were allowed to leave the jail for special assignments. Upon completion, what I needed at that point was a long vacation but what I got was the unpleasant task of searching for a job. I could smell smoke every time I drove down the street. It was the after effects of experiencing the tragedy of two fires in one year, to the point of constantly feeling the stench of smoke in my nostrils.

Since I was now living in an apartment in a new complex, everything was clean and quite nice. All of my furniture was in place except one wall cabinet. It was the top half of an old Hoosier kitchen cabinet that had been stripped of paint and refinished. It looked like a new piece of furniture. There was only one place the cabinet would fit in the apartment and that was on a wall over my washer and dryer next to the kitchen.

By chance, my sister and her son came to visit that weekend and I asked my nephew if he could help me hang the cabinet. It was much too heavy for one person to handle. Long toggle bolts would be required to keep the cabinet attached to the wall. Between the two of us, we were able to hang the cabinet on the wall and it looked very nice. I was pleased with the finished product.

My sister and her son left the following day. My laundry was beginning to pile up so I decided to do a wash load. I gathered my clothing and carried it to the washer and when I reached for the handle on top of the washing machine, it would only open about four inches. My nephew and I had not measured the space between the cabinet and the washer, as to how close the bottom of the cabinet was to the lid. I couldn't get my laundry in the machine. Just another of my Do-It-Yourself projects.

THE ANTIQUE BABY BED

My first grandchild was about to be born. I was driving up the street one day and spotted a beautiful white wrought iron baby crib in someone's front yard. It was for sale. I could see it was an antique and appeared to be in excellent condition. I backed up my car and the next thing I knew, I had bought the baby bed, complete with mattress.

A few months later, I put my house up for sale and moved to Tennessee. I rented an apartment in a new complex. The living room was large so I placed the baby bed against a wall behind my sofa. It worked well there but then one day I decided I wanted the crib in my bedroom.

The living room was carpeted making it difficult to maneuver the small bed across the room. It was quite heavy so I positioned myself on one end and began pulling the bed. Little by little I reached the doorway to the bedroom. That's when I discovered the bed would not go through the door. Great thinking! I didn't even bother to measure the width of the bed before beginning this little endeavor. It was one inch wider than the open doorway. There was no way of twisting and turning the bed to get it through the opening.

The only thing left for me to do was move the bed back to the wall behind my sofa. I stood in the bedroom and started pushing the bed. It wouldn't budge! The nap of the carpet worked for pulling the bed across the room but trying to push it back definitely wasn't going to happen. What was I going to do? This beautiful little antique bed was blocking my bedroom door. I was stuck in the bedroom and there was no way to get out.

I had just attempted another one of my Do It Yourself (DIY) projects that wasn't working. When would I learn? I needed help. I had already gotten myself in a similar predicament not too long ago when I tried taking a large mirror off the wall above my mantle. It seems I should have learned a lesson from that incident. Again, I couldn't get to my telephone, which was in the living room, to call for help, and even if I'd had a phone in the bedroom, I couldn't get out of the bedroom to open the locked front door and nobody could get in the apartment. There had to be a solution to this problem.

Maybe I could crawl under the small bed and wiggle my way into the living room where I could pull the bed away from the bedroom door. There wasn't much space between the bottom of the bed and the floor and I didn't have the body of Twiggy! What if I got stuck under the bed and couldn't crawl out? I didn't want to be found days later by the fire department lying on the floor under a baby crib. My epitaph would probably read, "She died trying…"

I began shifting the bed back and forth on one end. Little by little it began to move. After about thirty minutes, there was barely enough room for my pleasantly plump body to squeeze between the corner of the bed and the door facing. I tried drawing in my breath, hoping that would help. I finally pushed my body past the door facing, not removing paint or strips of wood.

It's a long way from one wall to another when you are getting there inch by inch. I later decided the baby bed looked great right where it sat, back against the wall behind my sofa. I also decided to call the telephone company and ask them to send a technician to install phones in every room of my apartment!

RHODA

All of us can recall a teacher we had in school that was special to us, our favorite teacher. But the teacher I will tell about was not only special for her ability to teach and capture the minds of her students, she was also unique for the person she was away from school. She had interests above and beyond anything her students could have imagined. Her name was Rhoda. She taught high school algebra and geometry.

While watching an episode of the Antiques Road Show, I was reminded of a time a number of years ago when I went with a friend to visit Rhoda. She had long since retired from teaching school. She had been married to a farmer and the couple led a very simple life. Rhoda wore shirtwaist dresses to school every day, kept her hair short with a kinky perm and wore very little makeup. The lady was without a doubt, one of the best math teachers a kid could ever have. To keep order in the class she would look very stern and try to scare the students, but it didn't work. There were three comedians in my class and all were straight A students. That alone allowed them the privilege of getting by with anything they wanted to do. They would start their little comedy stunts in the middle of class and it got Rhoda every time. She would turn towards the blackboard so that we couldn't see her face. We knew she was laughing because her body shook and she kept her arms folded in front of her. When she was able to compose herself, she turned towards the classroom and gave that stern look then she would ask someone to close the classroom door. Once the boys had captured her attention, the class went from a lesson in math to a comedy routine. Rhoda was afraid the commotion we caused would draw the attention of the school principal down the hall.

I loved that lady! One day, many years after I graduated from high school, a friend of mine who was as interested in antiques as I, said, "I want to take you to see someone. Do you remember your geometry teacher?" Of course, I did! "You won't believe her collection of antiques." I was totally surprised because she was the last person I would think of collecting antiques. My friend captured my attention immediately and I was very anxious to make the trip. She called the lady first to let her know we were coming because she lived way out in the country and didn't trust people driving up to her home unannounced. She was widowed and lived alone. As the years had passed, her memory had begun to decline.

It was hotter'n blue blazes that day as we pulled up beside the little shake shingle house. Stacks of wood were beside the house. Even though we had called ahead, we weren't sure she would remember and might possibly greet us at the door with her shotgun. It hadn't been very long since the lady had been robbed. It seems she drove down the road a couple of miles to the small country store and while she was gone, someone broke into her house and stole all of her Ray Harm original paintings. Anyone familiar with art knows Ray Harm was famous for his many bird paintings. I was lucky enough to have met the artist once at a show at Jenny Wiley State Park. He gave a great performance with his art demonstration and had a delightful personality.

Rhoda was a lady who, even when I was in high school, spent her weekends traveling through Kentucky and Ohio attending estate sales. At the time, she wasn't considered a collector of antiques. She just bought things because they were old and she appreciated their quality. Salesmen who came to the little store where she traded would tell her about the estate sales and auctions. She would hop in her husband's pickup truck and off she would go, no matter the distance.

Rhoda greeted us at her kitchen door and was very glad to see us. I knew she didn't remember me from high school although she pretended she did. We entered the house at her back door and walked directly into her kitchen. There was no sign of a fan or air-conditioning and it was hot enough to boil water in the sun. My mouth fell open when I looked around the large country kitchen. Her massive boarding house table had a chair of every kind lined around it. Sitting on the floor beside the back door was a beautiful bust of Dolly Madison carved from soap stone. A long shelf was attached to all four walls and covered with vintage cake stands, honey stands, and cut glass bowls. I couldn't say a word for looking. A huge glass front cabinet was filled with Fostoria dishes. I think she had every piece ever made in the American pattern. Against one wall was a large open fireplace. Above the fireplace was the most beautiful round, beveled mirror framed in mahogany I had ever seen. I couldn't believe my eyes. She had hauled the huge mirror from Ohio on bales of straw in the back of her pickup truck. This little country lady, living as simple as anyone could, had a fortune in antiques. When my friend and I inquired about certain items, she had no idea of their value and didn't even know they had any worth at all. She bought them because they were old and she thought they were beautiful.

Rhoda wanted to take us through her house. We stepped up one step and through a curtain covering the doorway into what must have once been the living room or an entrance hall. Things were piled everywhere. There was a chandelier sitting on a table, more beautiful glassware and Duncan Phyfe furniture. On into a bedroom, there were two gorgeous cherry and mahogany beds. One had the spool twist posters and carved acorns on each post. She informed us that two different presidents had once slept in those beds. As I recall, I believe Thomas Jefferson was one of the men. My eyes wandered from side to side in the room. There was so much clutter everywhere that we had to follow a path through the house.

I was sweating from the heat. The windows of the house were boarded up for protection. On one bed was an old featherbed. Rhoda invited us to spend the night with her; we could sleep on her featherbed. I could just imagine suffocating in the featherbed from lack of air.

I was so taken by this lady's lifetime collection of antiques that I felt I was living in a dream. After we left her shake shingle house and were driving down the country dirt road, my friend asked me what I thought the value of the lady's collection might be, the lady who didn't know there was any value at all to her things. These were things she loved and bought them for that reason only. I thought about the question and answered, "I would venture to say she has hundreds of thousands of dollars worth of antiques in her house." That was when my friend said, "There were two rooms off the kitchen that you didn't even see!" My mouth dropped!

I don't know why I tell this story. The little old lady who was my geometry teacher died a few years after my visit with her. I have often wondered what happened to the abundance of antiques that she loved so dearly, without ever giving any thought to their worth. Would the new owners have any appreciation for Rhoda's collection? Would they love them for their beauty or for their value? And to think—I could have spent the night in a bed where Thomas Jefferson once slept!

POST OFFICE MURALS

Mural on Corbin Post Office Wall

I was quite surprised when I answered the phone to the voice of a friend, also my cousin, living in Phoenix, Arizona. It had been a long while since we had communicated and I was very pleased he had called.

My cousin said, "There's something I've been thinking about and I figured you were the very person who could answer my questions." Such faith this young man had in my down-to-earth common knowledge. But this time, I didn't have the answers. He said he remembered as a young boy entering the local post office week by week and while he was there, his attention focused on a wall mural. He was wondering if the mural was still there. I told him I would do a few inquiries and call him back. I did a bit of research and soon had the answer for him.

The murals were often mistaken for Works Project Association (WPA) art. Many of the post offices were built by the WPA. The main function of this program for post office murals was to select art of high quality to decorate public buildings where funding was available. This made the art accessible to all people. I discovered the oil on canvas mural was placed in my hometown post office in 1940. The title was derived from the Indian word *Kentucke,* meaning "Dark and Bloody Ground." The mural painting still hangs in the old building which is now used by the local Board of Education. The oil painting in the old Lexington post office was done in 1938 and entitled "Daniel Boone's Arrival in Kentucky." It seemed highly appropriate since Boonesborough State Park is just a few miles away.

The list is long of towns in Kentucky where the murals were painted. The great Depression had a tremendous bearing on families. Jobs were unavailable everywhere and unemployed artists who painted the murals were paid for their work. Building of post offices was just one of the major projects provided by the Civil Conservation Corps and the Works Project Association to keep people employed.

KLONDIKE GOLD

"The tallest of the three Indians was known as Skookum Jim, the brother of the Tagish Chief… He was known as the best hunter and trapper on the river. Tagish Charley was also a fine specimen of the northern Indian, lean and lithe as a panther, keen in his perception, and as alert as a weasel…"

This is a story about George Washington Carmack, the man credited for his discovery of gold in the Klondike. You can find all sorts of stories about him in books that have been written in recent years, and I am sure there were many newspaper reports about GW Carmack as well.

I write about George Washington Carmack because somewhere back in my ancestry, his name appears. My grandmother was a Carmack. Her father, Enoch, was the youngest of Levi Carmack's thirteen children. George Washington Carmack was born ca. 1860, the same year my gr'uncle Abraham Carmack was born. The following segments were written by GW Carmack himself:

"…On a very early morning in the latter part of May 1896, I was sitting on the bank of the river of Fort Selkirk. The sky was above the eastern rim of the Palisades and was glowing with a soft light, presaging the birth of a new day. As I watched the flaming banner thrust forth their streamers of scintillating fire above the mountains (this was probably the northern lights as we know them), I felt my blood begin to tingle with new life and strength. I had a premonition that something unusual was going to take place in my life…"

The story continues, "One day in the latter part of July, as I was in the act of taking a large salmon out of the trap, I saw three Indians coming toward my camp. As they came closer the Indian in the lead raised his hand and shouted, 'Kla-how-ya George'. I answered the salutation and at the same time I recognized two of them. They were Indian friends whom I had not seen in several years…

"Both of the Indians were looking over my shoulder. Charley, with an inquiring expression on his face said, "Wa fo you talked dat cults wa wa? I no seeum' gold." "That's all right, Charley. I makum' Boston man's medicine." With that I began to pan again until there was only a couple of tablespoonsful of black sand left in the bottom of the pan. I raised the gold-pan up to the Indians and said, 'Spit in it boys, for good luck.' They complied and I put the pan in the water and began gently to whirl and tilt one way until a streak of bright yellow gold showed up…

"Why the Canadian Government awarded a pension to Bob Henderson for making the first gold discovery in the Klondike district is a mystery to me…unless it was because he was a Canadian, and my name was GEORGE WASHINGTON CARMACK… Now I have never claimed to be the original discoverer of gold in the Klondike, but on August 17, 1896, one of the most startling and far reaching events in the history of gold discoveries took place when I uncovered the frozen bosom of the Klondike and set forth from Bonanza Creek the astounding cry, "One hundred dollars to the pan."

NOTE: A few years ago I had a young neighbor who was the author of history books for young people. He had a talent for writing stories about famous generals in the Revolutionary War in a manner that was interesting to the youth of today. One day I was talking to him about his books. He later gave me one he had authored, *The Story of John Paul Jones*. Even I, who never liked history in school, loved his book. In conversation one day, he mentioned that he had written a book entitled *Klondike Gold*. I drew a deep breath. He was quite surprised when I informed him that the discoverer of gold in the Klondike was one of my ancestors.

THE PEOPLE WE MEET

The letter read: *"I have just completed reading 'Room at the Foot of the Bed' and it is absolutely beautiful! Pat is a most interesting and wonderful writer. I can't imagine anyone remembering so many details from childhood. This work (which I know must have taken a tremendous time) is a beautiful legacy not only for your family, but all families of this age. So many things in this book were really common experiences to all of us... In relating the story of one family, Pat has recorded the experiences of many families. I would so love to meet her."*

Her name was Margaret Anderson. She had read my book, ROOM AT THE FOOT OF THE BED, accounts of my family history. At the time, I had yet to meet Margaret, but she would eventually become a dear friend. I learned that Margaret was very much involved in genealogy and had read the first edition of my book.

The lady was born in Kentucky but spent most of her adult life in a small town in Tennessee. Much could be said about her. She was a high school teacher, one dedicated to the education of our children. While I was just a new bride and mother of my first child in the mid-1950s, busy each day with changing diapers, preparing formula, rocking my baby and preparing dinner for my husband at the end of every day, little did I know there were events of turmoil taking place not so far away from me that would have a bearing on the future of all children being educated in the public school systems.

Across the country, courts were ruling on the desegregation of all schools. The governor of Tennessee had dispatched troops to see that all Negro children could attend high school in Clinton, Tennessee. There were twelve black students who registered for school in the year 1956-57.

Margaret Anderson was a teacher in that high school. I remember a Baptist minister, Paul Turner, a close friend of my family, who happened to get involved in the stormy uprising. Resistance from within and outside the community resulted in the bombing of the high school in 1958. Margaret and Reverend Turner accompanied the twelve high school African-American students each morning on their walk to school. Local law enforcement officers walked with them. The local citizens eventually came to support the school principal, affirming that desegregation was the law of the land.

Ten years later, in 1966, Margaret wrote a sensitive account of the desegregation of the Clinton School and the long process of integration. Her book was entitled "The Children of the South." Ralph McGill, editor of the *Atlanta Constitution*, wrote the foreword to the book, saying "This excellently written book will be remembered and kept when many other books coming out of the fever and ferment of the South will be forgotten."

Margaret Anderson appeared on several television shows such as *The Today Show, Good Morning America*, and others. By the time I met this gentle lady at her small town home by the river, she was about eighty-four years of age, devoting her time to her continued interests in genealogy. She encouraged me to continue my writing and to consider sending copies of my book to the Kentucky Historical Society in Frankfort, Kentucky, and the Filson Club in Louisville.

My friend, Margaret Anderson, died at the age of 90. She lived her life in Tennessee and was returned to her birthplace of Glasgow, Kentucky for burial. She was a shining example of a great lady. I am blessed to have known her.

FROM A SCHOOL NEWSPAPER TO A NATIONAL MAGAZINE

It's amazing how times have changed, and the advantages young people have today in the school systems. It seems that someone is continually complaining about the way the schools are run. If the parents of today's children could go back 65 years, they would come to appreciate the education and privileges offered the students. The high school I visited recently had beautiful tile floors throughout, unlike the old smelly, oil treated wood floors where I went to high school. The new school had an up-to-date modern cafeteria for the students, also unlike my high school which had no cafeteria or lunch room. Students who lived too far away to go home for lunch either carried a sack lunch to school or went across the street to Tom Smith's small store to buy snacks. They usually ate Moon Pies and RC Colas to go with the sandwich they brought from home. Can you imagine what today's nutritional system would have to say about that? Then they had the choice of sitting alone in the school library or on the steps outside the building. I'm not complaining. That's just the way it was!

But we had our good memories. I remember walking down the hall one day in the old high school and hearing a noise that sounded like a plane had crashed into the school. I looked around and discovered a huge chunk of the plastered ceiling had fallen to the floor within inches of me, just missing my head. The ceiling was 15-20 feet high. You may not think of that as a good memory, but at least I remember it!

I was a senior that year and chose two of the elective classes. One was a Speech class taught by the junior high principal and the other class was Journalism. In both classes we were required to write articles and stories. I didn't lead the most exciting life in a small town so just how many stories could I conjure up since my attempt at fiction writing was an absolute no-no? I recall the time my journalism teacher asked the class to write a one-paragraph article creating our own subject. It was hard enough writing a story when she gave us the subject matter, but when I had to come up with an idea of my own, that was a bit troublesome.

I noticed the girl across the aisle began writing immediately while I sat there trying to generate my thought processes. What in the world could that girl be writing about considering she had two rungs missing on her ladder, so to speak? I couldn't come up with a single idea. I watched as the girl turned to the second page of her notebook. After all, the teacher only asked for one paragraph. She was writing a novel. She was beginning the third page and I hadn't even come up with a subject to write about. I had to create something so I started rambling with about ten minutes left in the class. It was like that every day. What was there to write about? We didn't even have television to give us ideas.

Several of my journalism classmates published the school's monthly newspaper which had several pages of news articles. The fact that the walls of the girls' restrooms were being painted wasn't exactly my idea of a news article. The most popular one was the "gossip column" exposing the newest dating couple in the class. One day, I decided to write a "fashion" column indicating the new color for spring was Blue. It wasn't a bad article considering I got most of the information from my newest edition of *Seventeen Magazine*. It was my favorite magazine and I saved up my spending money to buy it every month. My prettiest blouse had been ordered from the magazine. Ms.

Chestnut, my teacher, thought it was a good article so it was featured in the next issue of our school newspaper.

The school received copies of a regional newspaper that was published quarterly and included the best articles from all the schools in the region. Well, whatta' ya' know, my true blue fashion story appeared in the newspaper. Ms. Chestnut was so proud of me. That was the beginning of my journalism career, and I might add, the ending!

I regret to say it was thirty-nine years later before my career picked up again when I entered a magazine contest. All I had to do that time was submit photographs and the magazine wrote the story, only if I won the contest! The subject matter that time was "Interior Decorating." As you have probably already guessed…I did win the contest! A photograph of my breakfast room was on the front cover of the magazine and I received five pages of coverage with more photographs. My sister's house was also featured in the magazine. The article was entitled "The Sisters Act." Oh! You want to know what the winner of the contest received as a prize besides having her pictures in a national magazine? What do you think of a first class, all-expense-paid, ten-day round-trip voyage for two on the luxury liner ship, the Queen Elizabeth 2, between New York and Southampton, England?

Two years later, another magazine, *Country Decorator*, featured another three-page story showing pictures of my house. Of course, I bought all the magazines I could find and gave them to family and friends, only to discover I forgot to keep one for myself. So, I don't have the article from that magazine. However, as a gift for me, my son had the first magazine framed.

Page from Country Accents Magazine

IN BRITAIN

This short story will introduce you to a wonderful magazine published monthly in London, England by Premier Magazines Ltd in association with the British Tourist Authority. The magazine is entitled *In Britain*.

Appearing in the magazine one month was a special letter to the editor. I wrote the letter never dreaming it would be chosen and published as the "Letter of the Month." It reads:

LETTER OF THE MONTH

Through a magazine competition three years ago, I won a voyage from New York to Southampton on the QE2. I had always wanted to visit Britain, the homeland of my ancestors. It was a dream come true. On the voyage I made the acquaintance of a lovely couple from Ohio – an instant bond was created which would develop into a lasting friendship. Leaving my friends after a tour of London, I travelled by coach through England, Wales and Scotland. Nine days later we met again for the return voyage to the US. We said our goodbyes at the airport in New York City and returned home. Upcoming months would bring us together again for frequent weekend visits and holiday excursions. Being an avid craftsperson, I made a keepsake St Nicholas doll for my friends as an early Christmas gift in 1996 when they were making arrangements for a return visit to England for the holiday season. On 5 December, two days after receiving my gift, the husband died suddenly from a cerebral aneurysm.

In January 1997 I received my first issue of IN BRITAIN. It was a welcome surprise. Again, in February, another copy arrived in the mail, then another and I had no idea who had provided the gift subscription or why. It wasn't until May that I finally discovered my benefactor – when he received the St Nicholas doll, my dear friend was so delighted that he immediately subscribed to IN BRITAIN in my name. He knew I would enjoy the magazine. And he was right! Now, when it arrives every month, it has special meaning. Through each issue, I can continue to enjoy a little bit of Britain and also be reminded of the delightful times shared with a wonderful friend.

Patricia O'Neal, USA

THE OLD TAYLOR HOUSE

T he house with a sign out front bearing the name "Old Taylor House" and a date, ca. 1876, still stands on three acres of land located on a road called Lone Mountain. It has quite a history behind it. The house once stood on the lower side of the road midst a wooded area of trees and lots of bushes and undergrowth. You probably wouldn't even have noticed the house at one time because it was so well hidden and slowly deteriorating. It drew no attention from people driving past.

But the house caught the attention of one lady. She was mesmerized by the big old two-story white house. Well, at one time it was white; it was very weathered gray when she spotted it. My friend, Ann, and her husband had bought the three-acre plot of land across the road that backed up to a grove of trees – a perfect spot for an old two-story frame house dating back to the mid to late 1800s. And, that house stood right over on the other side of the road on Lone Mountain.

Ann began investigating and discovered the original owner of the house had been the parents of a Tennessee governor in the early part of the 1900s. Being a lover of old things and an expert at choosing quality antiques, Ann researched the history of the house and its early occupants. Two Taylor brothers who both ran for governor of the state of Tennessee had once lived there. One was a Democrat, the other served on the Republican ticket. They would even travel together campaigning across the state and each carried his fiddle for entertainment – a very entertaining pair. One of the brothers went on to serve three terms in the House of Representatives. Before I delve too far into the lives of these men, this story isn't about the history of the Taylor brothers, it's about the house they once occupied as young boys.

Ann had made up her mind that she was going to buy that old run-down house, but it would have to be moved to the three acres of land she and her husband had recently bought. Richard was a builder and was the best at remodeling old houses. That little factor was in Ann's favor but every time she mentioned moving the big old house, she was met with controversy and dissention. "It can't be done," they said! That response wasn't good enough for Ann. She said, "They put a man on the moon. I can move a house across the road!"

And that she did! Ann found farmers who owned tractors and trucks that pulled the long open flatbeds behind them. The next thing you know, the old Taylor house, once owned by the family of two governors, was transported to the upper side of Lone Mountain and deposited on the flat, open ground facing the road.

Ann and Richard went to work renovating and putting back

together the pieces to the house, including all of the Victorian gingerbread trim along the roofline. Richard removed all of the old crackled paint by using a small blow torch and water. When he finished, there wasn't a speck of the old paint left on the house.

When I first met Ann and Richard, they had already moved into their renovated home. Ann had excellent decorating taste and had collected the antiques perfect for their new dwelling. The interior of the house had high ceilings with beautiful old gaslight chandeliers. The wide plank floors were finished to perfection and covered with oriental styled rugs. I had never been in a house before this where the kitchen and L-shaped adjoining family room had brick floors. An open fireplace divided the two areas. You could sit on the sofa and see the covered back porch where Ann hung her towels and sheets to dry. She loved the scent of the open air as the linens blew in the breeze. It was a very homey atmosphere.

The window above the front door revealed an exposure from a small sitting room decorated in blue and white floral striped wallpaper. The room was enclosed with old white wicker furniture. The first time I saw the room, I envisioned Scarlet O'Hara on the beautiful chaise lounge with a book in one hand and a tall glass of lemonade or a mint julep in the other. The large dining room with added fireplace made my eyes sparkle. The open living room also had a fireplace with tall walnut wood doors encased on either side. The doors covered a tall area of library shelves. With Ann's decorating skills and Richard's eye for recreating the beautiful interior carpentry and moldings of a Victorian house, they had brought to life the old Taylor home of the 1800s.

Years passed. The old Taylor house was sold and Ann and Richard moved to Alabama. My sister and I had just won the "Country Accents" decorating contest and while the photographer and stylist were in town photographing our homes for the magazine, I told them about the old Taylor House. I took them for a drive to Lone Mountain and when they saw the exterior beauty of the house and the gorgeous gazebo a few yards away, they were very interested in seeing inside the house. I called the new owners and explained the situation and the lady was more than delighted to have the couple come and visit. We hurried back to Lone Mountain and were given a tour of the revised home featuring the new owner's personal decorating style.

It was a few months later when I received a phone call from the current owner of the Taylor house telling me that the freelance decorator and photographer had submitted photos and biographical information to *Country Sampler* and they published an article on the house. During this time, Ann had never been told about the house being considered for a special feature in a magazine. One day, Ann was browsing through the magazine stands at the book store and picked up a *Country Sampler*. What were the chances of her opening the magazine to the page displaying a picture of the old Taylor house and the sign out front, the house she had saved from ruin and moved from one side of Lone Mountain Road to the other? The magazine fell open to that very page.

Each time I visited Ann at her home on Lone Mountain, I headed straight for her den facing the open log fireplace. With my feet folded under me in the comfort of her sofa, a decorator magazine in my hands, I waited while Ann prepared my tall glass of lemonade (in summer) or hot chocolate (in winter). I sure miss those visits.

HEAR THE TRAIN A-COMIN'

If you are over the age of 60, you will probably agree that the fascination with trains was a wholesome part of your childhood; whether it was the train set you received at Christmas with a little black engine that blew smoke and had several cars that hooked together and formed a circle around the tracks that filled the center of the living room floor, or the real train that passed through town near your home several times a day and night. The sound of the train whistle was warming and to many, it meant Daddy would soon be home for supper.

My Uncle Will worked for the L&N Railroad Company when I was a kid and oftentimes, when the train had a layover at the Roundhouse for a few hours, he would walk from the depot to our house to visit with my mother. They would sit on the front porch and talk until it was time for him to leave. Sometimes he was there long enough to have supper with us. Uncle Will was a sweet old man. His limp when he walked was the result of having been hit by a train in his early years requiring one foot to be amputated. He had served in WWI and lost his wife in childbirth shortly thereafter. My mother was the one who came to his aid in taking care of his three young boys. She was a new bride at the time and my dad also worked for the railroad company and was gone days at a time. My uncle remarried and his job with the railroad became his life.

I was married the first time I rode a train. I boarded the train in Louisville, Kentucky, and it took me from there via Cincinnati, Ohio, to Corbin, Kentucky. It was a very long ride with a little two-year-old in tow. My second train ride, years later was not a pleasant one. I had joined my former sister-in-law on a journey from Louisville to New Orleans, Louisiana. My niece, Diane, had just died of a diabetic cerebral hemorrhage. I was accompanying her mother, Margie, on the long train ride to New Orleans to collect my niece's personal belongings and bring them back home. My niece was 27, and just a baby herself when her father died in a B-17F plane crash; such a beautiful girl, petite, with long dark hair, working as a medical technologist and in the prime of her life when she hemorrhaged one Sunday afternoon and was transported to the hospital. She died within the hour.

That extremely long train ride was anything but enjoyable. It was the one that has always brought bad memories to my mind. The journey back home was even longer and more bleak and desolate as I listened to every chug chug chug of the train wheels, mile by mile, during the return trip. I never rode a train again!

It just so happened, frequent visits back home on weekends before the interstate was built took us down US 25. It was usually dusky dark when we drove between Berea and Mount Vernon, a long straight stretch of highway that ran parallel to the railroad tracks. My children knew nothing about trains but when we were driving down the highway, the big black engine pulling dozens of cars behind it was also going south and we kept time with the train. The lights were on in the passenger cars and my kids would wave and wave and the engineer would see them and blow his whistle, again and again. That was the most exciting thing that could happen to them. That was more than fifty years ago and every time we drive along old US 25 going south, my kids bring up their remembrances of racing with the train. Good memories.

But the focus of my story goes back more than seventy years ago.

If you sat at our kitchen window and looked out over the field of weeds behind our house, you could see Elsie's Store down on the corner of Poplar and Tenth Streets. Standing in the middle of the road beside the little grocery store, you could see through from Poplar Street all the way over to the railroad tracks beyond Main Street. The train tracks ran parallel to Main Street. There was a time when kids would hear the train whistle blow at the far end of town and they would run down to Elsie's store to watch the train whiz past. The days of the big black engine with smoke trailing behind it were dying out. Someone had created a more modern, very sleek engine that traveled much faster than the old black engine. It looked like a big long silver bullet pulling the many cars behind it. And it traveled very fast. It was the new diesel engine that ran on its own power and, you might say, went "faster than a speeding bullet."

A new diesel engine

People around town were very excited about the new diesel engine. It usually came through town once a day and we knew when it was coming. We could hear the long, loud wail of the whistle as it passed through the south end of town.

My friend, Bobbie, lived about four doors up the street from Elsie's Store and she thought the diesel engine was the most fascinating thing that had ever been invented. When that long, loud whistle began blowing, my sister and I ran to the kitchen window.

Always, without fail, when we heard that whistle, we could spot Bobbie running down Poplar Street to Elsie's Store to see the train. Bobbie was a tall, skinny girl. She usually wore her hair in pigtails, and she had the longest legs I had ever seen on a girl. She was like an antelope running with outstretched legs to get to Elsie's in time to see the beautiful speeding bullet. The diesel was there and gone again in the blink of an eye, but nevertheless, Bobbie never missed a day seeing the beautiful piece of machinery fly by.

My children never really knew the thrill of trains, hearing the hum of an airplane's motor high above them, and standing, staring for minutes at a time, hoping to spot the glint of the sun on the silver metal of the plane in the sky. They never felt the excitement of flying kites at the top of the hill just to see how far away they would fly, kites that had been made with sticks, newspapers, and put together with flour and water glue. No! Children in today's world will not know what real fun can be, fun created by their own hands.

I became a grandmother and lived in a small Tennessee town. I moved into an old frame house built about 1920 that faced the railroad tracks. It took awhile to get used to that long whistle that awakened me every night about 2 a.m. just outside my window, making me think it was coming right through my bedroom, but after a few weeks, I could sleep right through the noise.

A person waited to see the little red caboose that followed behind every train telling them it was the last car on the train. And then, it was no longer! They did away with the one thing that had attracted all of us and our children, the little red caboose. My grandchildren would visit me on occasion and when we heard the sound of that whistle at 2 a.m., I could look towards my living room door and see the shadowy outline of a little girl holding the curtain back to see the train go by. It gave me a very warm feeling. She stood there watching until the very last car went by. And then, during the day when my grandchildren heard the train coming, they stood on my front porch and the six-year-old counted every car that passed my house. I can always remember her saying, "Whew, that sure was a long one!" Those were the days!

Freight Train passing through Clinton, TN

I can't conclude my story without telling about the time, only a few years ago, when the Norfolk Southern Railway provided an annual event offering a train ride from Lexington to Oneida, Tennessee, on one of their old steam engine trains complete with about six passenger cars. My daughter, Jan, decided it was time she took that train ride. A friend joined her and they prepared a picnic lunch to eat on the train. She kept me informed by cell phone exactly the location of the train before it passed over the railroad viaduct on Southland Drive. I drove over to see the big black engine with smoke pouring out above as it raced past. I stood at the side of the road holding my video camera steady and waited. I could hear the train coming and just as it appeared at one end of the viaduct, I began filming. Jan was standing at the window of one of the silver passenger cars looking out.

We had a second reason for filming the train as it chugged across the viaduct—my dad had built the railroad viaduct back in the 1930s. I remember him telling me that the area now filled with shops and businesses was then a huge farm with fields of corn all around. The old farmer was working his cornfields and told my dad he had just sold three acres of land to the Kroger Company to build a grocery store. Trains continue to cross the viaduct and each time I drive through, I look up and say to myself, "My Daddy built that!"

HOUSE BY THE RAILROAD TRACKS

I was living in a small rental cottage in Tennessee. My landlord who was also my friend lived right next door to me. The cottage was located at the edge of an old cemetery. Many of the headstones had broken and were thrown into the woods behind the cottage. Stones in the graveyard dated back to the early 1800s. I found myself strolling through the cemetery at various times, always carrying my box of tissues with me. I loved reading the epitaphs on the headstones. Sometimes there were rows of small stones and you could see by the names and death dates that the children were from one family and had died of diphtheria, cholera, typhoid, or another dreaded disease. While living in the cottage, someone told me that it had been built over a cave.

After a few years, I began outgrowing the cottage. I had an obsession for collecting things, mostly little things that took up space. I was ready for expansion. One Saturday morning my sister called me and said there was going to be an estate auction nearby and we should go. The old frame house facing the railroad tracks had been empty since the homeowner entered a local nursing home about two years earlier. All of her furniture was still in the house. I hurried to the bank to withdraw $100 in case I found any small irresistible treasures at the auction.

People had already arrived when I met my sister in front of the house. It was very hot that day so she and I sat in the shade of a huge tree in the front yard of the old house. Not only were the contents being sold but the house itself was going up for auction. I could see the house was definitely in need of renovation. We had been told that the couple living next door planned to bid on the house. They wanted to purchase and use it as rental property. If they bought the house and renovated, there was the chance that I could rent the house. It was one with lots of character; just what I was looking for.

A small crowd had gathered for the auction, including my current landlord. First up for bid was the house. Bidding was slow and the initial bids were quite low. Heaven forbid we could watch someone else steal the house at such a low price! My sister nudged me in the ribs and whispered, "Pat, bid on the house!"

My hand flew up and I was in the bidding. With a purchase like that, a ten percent payment is demanded at the auction site. Suddenly, it hit me, "What am I doing?" I hadn't even been inside the house to see its condition and how much work it would need. I didn't have any idea how many rooms it had. I broke out in a heavy sweat and turned to my sister and said, "All I've got is a hundred dollars." She responded, "That's alright! I brought my checkbook."

Finally, I got control of my senses and withdrew from the bidding. I never could understand how that woman had such control over me. She would say, "Do it" and the next thing I realized, I was wading knee deep in muck! And, of all things, I was bidding against the couple who had planned to purchase the house and rent it to me. Had I lost my mind? No, I just had a very influential sister who could talk me into anything!

The couple was high bidder for the house. I walked away from the estate auction that day having purchased a few pieces of linen and a round, drop leaf kitchen table. I loved the table with its scratches on the surface where it showed signs of many years of chopping cabbage for making kraut. Let's see now! A hardrock maple drop leaf table; a large oak round dining table with a huge pedestal; an enamel kitchen worktable; an old oak table with five legs and three leaves; and now another drop leaf kitchen table? Don't ever ask a woman what she is going to do with it! "You can never have too many tables."

I did end up renting the old 1920s frame house that faced the railroad tracks. It had a small front porch surrounded by banister railings and gingerbread trim, and it sat thirteen steps above ground level. The original front door had long arched windows. There was a large covered porch at the side of the house with a row of Rose of Sharon trees along the banister railings. Hummingbirds loved the blossoms.

House by the railroad tracks, Clinton, TN, built ca. 1920

The house was arranged so that you had to go through two bedrooms in order to get to the kitchen. When you walked from room to room you couldn't help but notice the ceilings were different heights. They varied from eight feet in the laundry room and bathroom to ten feet in the living room, and the most interesting of all was the fifteen foot ceiling in the small hallway beside the bathroom. There was a square door on the upper wall, so high that I couldn't even reach it with my stepladder. I tried and tried to figure how I could get through that door and into the attic of the house. When the executors of the estate went through the house, they discovered thousands of dollars in CDs and twenty-dollar bills hidden in books and other places. I knew my treasure was hidden somewhere in that attic. Month after month I would look up at that little door and think, "There's gotta' be a way to climb up there."

On occasion, my brother-in-law would stop by for a short visit and he never failed to tell me, "You know, the old man who used to live here died right where you are sitting!" And then he would leave my house with a big smile on his face.

I lived in that little old house facing the railroad tracks, watching many freight cars roll by and listening to the screech of the wheels and loud whistle of the train in the middle of the night as it approached the railroad intersection. There were times it felt and sounded as if the train was coming right through my bedroom. But that is something you get used to and learn to love. Seeing the joy on the faces of my grandchildren as they watched the train go by is worth living by the railroad tracks. Watching them stand on my front porch counting the cars one by one until all 100 of them had passed is worth it.

I lived 15 years in that quaint old gray painted house with its warm morning heaters, its warped floors, a claw foot bathtub, and a small sink that stood under a square window instead of a mirror. It had one tiny closet built in the days when Ma and Pa hung their Sunday clothes and winter coats on nails at the back of the closet. The kitchen window faced a blossoming crab apple tree with a clothesline where the next door neighbor aired her handmade quilts. It was a house filled with history and lots of character. Eventually, I moved away from that house without ever getting to see what was in the attic!

BLESSING

How do you describe a person with a name like Blessing? Somehow, you picture a child with the beauty of an angel and a personality that goes with it. But my Blessing was anything but that! She was plain and tall and her weight was a fraction above normal. When she opened her mouth, no matter how big the crowd or how loud the thunder, you could hear Blessing's voice sounding like cymbals above it. She purposely wore long sleeved blouses two sizes too large so that no one could see the extra fat on her arms and around her middle. She figured it was better to wear an oversized blouse so people could wonder how big she was rather than wear a tight fitting shirt, and remove all doubt. She never met a stranger and could tell you the life history of every resident of Marlow, where she was raised. Marlow was a small country community of farmers. Everybody who lived there farmed, raising corn and tobacco. There was no such thing as a proper dress code for the residents of Marlow. They all dressed alike, bib overalls with blue shirts and red railroad handkerchiefs around the neck. The men wore lace-up Brogan shoes. The women wore shirtwaist calico dresses, always below the knee to cover the wrinkled cotton stockings held up with garters. They didn't mind wearing their bib aprons even when they went to town. The men would be spitting tobacco and the women dipping snuff. When they drove down the road in their red pickup trucks that hadn't seen a waterhose more than twice a year, you had better be standing a good distance away if you didn't want a spray of tobacco juice aimed your direction from the window of the pickup.

Blessing was a friend of the family and she was always fun and had a story to tell about someone in her home community. I don't think anybody in the state of Tennessee could top her flat country drawl.

I remember the story she used to tell about when she was a little girl. She had learned that a man and a woman in the neighborhood were getting married. This was a second marriage for both of them after losing their spouses. The woman and man each owned their own homes, so they decided to move into her house, combining their furniture, and then sell his house.

Blessing came running into the house all out of breath and anxious to tell her mother the latest good news. Her mother was already aware of the marriage plans. She was busy at the kitchen sink when Blessing blurted out, "Mama, did you know Ms. Smith and Mr. Jones is gonna get married and put their thangs together?" Blessing's mother whirled around and swung the dish rag across her face saying, "You hush that filthy talk and I don't wanna' ever hear you say nothin' like that agin'." Blessing could never figure out what she had said wrong.

On occasion, my sister, Bena Mae, Blessing, another friend named Mabel Farmer whose name fit her perfectly, and I would take short weekend trips together. Mabel had the driest sense of humor of anyone I have ever known. Everything she said was funny. She could make the recipe for three-day old bread and lumpy mashed potatoes seem funny. No matter where the four of us went, it became a rolling in the floor kind of laughter.

It was the early 80s, an era when every female in America wore a gold chain around her neck. Status depended on how long the chain was and how thick the gold. Even I had a gold chain, only because my son gave me one for Christmas that year.

Every time I went shopping with Blessing, we had to look in the jewelry cases at gold chains. Blessing always wanted my opinion on which chain she should buy, which one looked best on her, a short one or a long one, but she never bought one. This time, Mabel was with us and we were in a department store in Knoxville. Again, Blessing was lifting one chain after another from the jewelry case and saying, "Which one do you think looks the best?" Before I could answer, Mabel walked up and said, "Blessing, what differnce' does it make which one you buy? It'll just git lost in the wrinkles of yur neck!" I didn't think I was going to make it to the nearest restroom. Blessing didn't buy a necklace that day either!

One weekend I was driving to Lexington from my home in Tennessee so I asked my sister and Blessing to go with me. My daughter and son both lived in Lexington. My son was going out of town and he offered his house to us for lodging. We arrived on Friday night and got up early Saturday morning to plan our day. Blessing had never been to Shaker Village at Pleasant Hill, so that was where we headed first. We toured the entire village and had lunch there as well. The straight-from-the-garden vegetables were wonderful. We enjoyed a delightful meal. Blessing got to sample the Shaker Lemon Pie for the first time. The waitresses were in standard Shaker dresses to the ankle covered with aprons, and mesh caps on their heads. I had to explain to Blessing that the waitresses were not real Shakers; that the community practiced celibacy and died out about a hundred years ago. Blessing loved the history of the Shakers and the efforts being made to keep the legacy alive.

Returning to Lexington that evening, we stopped off at Fayette Mall. All three of us were so tired it was an effort to even walk, so we sat on a bench in the middle of the mall watching shoppers parading back and forth. Not a word was spoken between the three of us. We were too exhausted to say anything so we just sat and watched the people stroll by.

Extreme exhaustion can make any situation funny. We must have been sitting on the bench about thirty minutes with no interest in anything except resting. About that time, a couple came walking across in front of us. The man was tall, somewhat overweight with the typical pot belly and dressed in bib overalls, one shoulder strap hanging loose down his back which was typical of anyone wearing bib overalls. The lady, obviously his wife, also wore the typical faded calico dress and lace-up tennis shoes. There was no doubt they were a farm couple. They walked slowly. My sister, Blessing, and I were observing them very closely when Blessing suddenly spoke up and said in her standard country drawl, "I believe thur' frum' Marlow." Our muscles relaxed and we could not control our laughter.

Blessing lived next door to an elderly couple who, every Saturday evening at six o'clock, turned on the television to the Lawrence Welk Show. Blessing was right there with them every week. They would have been very disappointed if she didn't show up. As she used to say, "Just how much of Larnse' Welk can ye' take?" Well, she took him every Saturday evening until the old couple had passed. I see the re-runs of the show today and think of Blessing.

No matter the occasion, when Blessing was with us we could count on an outburst of laughter. Each year at Christmas, I receive a greeting card from this fantastic lady bringing me up-to-date on her life and family. She has challenged and defeated the 'cancer monster' many times. At the age of 93, she has had spirit and strength to conquer all her battles.

TEA IN AN ENGLISH COTTAGE

My friend, Carole, and I planned another trip to England together and this time we would join friends we had met on our first cruise who lived at Chatteris, near Cambridge, England. It was March and a cold month with scattered showers in parts of England, but after we arrived in London, we didn't let that stop our trekking from one place to another.

It was Sunday morning when we left our flat to hurry to Euston Station to take the train to King's Cross. I had never climbed so many stairs and taken so many escalators in my life. The flights of stairs were many and London had the longest escalators I had ever seen. We hurried to the platform to board our train to Cambridge where we would meet our friends, Terry and Heather Simpson, a newly married couple we had met on the Queen Elizabeth 2 four years earlier. It was quite cold and windy that morning and there were only occasional glimpses of the sunshine. Our friends were waiting at the train station when we arrived in Cambridge. They drove us into the village to King's College where we went for a brief walk. Even for March, the grounds were glowing with yellow daffodils and purple floral ground coverage. We stopped at a small café for coffee and hot chocolate.

WAIT 'TIL YOU HEAR THIS ONE!

Terry described every building in the village in detail. He was well versed on the history of Cambridge as well as British history. We passed the greens where *Chariots of Fire* was filmed. I had my camera ready for any and all of the interesting sites.

From Cambridge, we drove through the countryside to a place called The Five Miles from Anywhere Pub. The Pub served buffet dinner on Sundays. It was my first time to eat lamb and Yorkshire pudding. The pub was adjacent to a canal and overlooked many acres of flatland. It was also my first time to stand beside an English canal.

We drove on to Ely after filling ourselves with the wonderful English dinner. There, we toured the Ely Cathedral, a sight to behold. The architecture was like nothing I had ever seen. Stained glass windows glowed from the sun's rays.

We had covered a bit of ground during the day, so about 4:30 that afternoon, Terry drove us to Heather's sister's home at Cottenham. Her sister's name was Patsy. When we arrived, Carole and I were surprised to see a quaint, five-bedroom, two-story brick house dating to 1835. It had a walled courtyard in the back where a rose garden was beginning to blossom. Two grown sons lived in the home with Patsy and her husband. Since we entered at the back of the house, we were taken straight to the large dining room where a fire was blazing in the open fireplace. It was warm and cozy. The room was large and very simple in its décor. The furniture was old and quite worn. A large oriental area rug covered the hardwood floors beneath the long dining table. Patsy had prepared English tea with a display of coffee, tea, scones, cookies, tuna/cucumber sandwiches, jams and clotted cream – everything you would expect at an English tea, and desserts I had never eaten before.

I was busy exploring every item on the table. Patsy had served us on antique gold-rimmed chintz patterned china plates. Cups and saucers were made of ironstone. The cream and sugar containers were her prized possessions of a pattern resembling blue Delftware and called Norfolk ware. And best of all, she came from the kitchen carrying a teapot covered with a cozy. The jam and clotted cream were served in crystal comports. Nothing on the table matched but Patsy made it so charming and appealing, Carole and I couldn't help but notice how comfortable and relaxing an atmosphere the lady had created. She had us feeling like a couple of friends who had dropped by unexpectedly for a cup of tea. The crackling fire at the end of the room only added to the warmth of the occasion.

As the afternoon progressed, Patsy's sons told us humorous tales of their experiences in a musical group. One of the young men worked with musical electronics, the other played in the band. The two were quite handsome and had vibrant personalities. I fell in love with their jolly British accents. I was so relaxed with this family, I wanted to stay longer, but it was already past six o'clock and we had to get back to the train station to catch the last train into London.

We left the house the same way we entered, by way of the courtyard. One of the sons had built a new square-stone patio. A selection of flowers was growing along the border of the patio and centered by Patsy's beautiful roses. A large outbuilding stood behind the patio and appeared to be in much need of repair. Only structural repairs were permitted. The historic building could not be changed in any manner to affect its original appearance.

Arriving at the train station just in time to step aboard the train, Carole and I took separate seats where we could lay back and soak up our thoughts regarding the day's events. When we arrived back at the flat, we prepared a snack of toast, Brie cheese and ham. We talked and reviewed our day in Cambridge and Cottenham. It was a day I shall always take pleasure in remembering, and when I set my table with scones, jams and, instead of clotted cream, cream cheese appetizers, and using my vintage teapot with its cozy, I will relish the thoughts of the day I had tea in an English cottage. Wonderful memories and wonderful people.

A CHURCH BAZAAR

It was the hottest week on record, 103 degrees, and there I was, walking the streets of London, England. I could feel the heat through the soles of my ballerina shoes. And to beat it all, people were sunning themselves in Hyde Park. I thought they were crazy, and soon discovered they weren't used to such high temperatures like we sometimes have, and they loved it. Yep! They were still crazy!

My friend, Carole, and I decided to take the train to Cambridge, a beautiful place to visit. There was King's College and the campus of Queen's College, the mathematical bridge, quaint churches and homes, and flowers everywhere. After we arrived at the train station in Cambridge, we began walking. We had no map and didn't have the slightest inkling as to where we were headed, but we eventually wound up in the center of the business district of the village. Along the way we passed a church where a wedding party was leaving so we stood on the sidewalk to enjoy a bit of their festivities and photography in front of the church.

We stopped at an open market hoping to find something cold to drink. As we had already learned, the English never use ice in their cold drinks. In fact they don't refrigerate their drinks. We soon came to another old church that was having a bazaar that day. All women like bazaars so why not check it out! There were tables outside the door with trinkets for sale. Then we entered the church where there were more tables inside the vestibule. The sun was beaming through the beautiful old stained glass windows. I looked down at the flooring to see if there were inscriptions telling who had been buried under the slabs of stone. Up at the end of the aisle (you know the kind, like the one where Princess Diana had her wedding) were more tables with refreshments. That's where I was headed because I was thirsty enough to drink the water from the canals if I didn't find something cold and wet soon. Beside the refreshment tables were a couple of folding tables covered with floral cloths and facing the auditorium where we could sit and eat. I had already downed a glass of room temperature lemonade and was on my second glass. At least it was wet!

Carole was having a conversation with a little old gentleman who was working the refreshment tables. No other customers were there. We gathered our refreshments and sat down at the front table, ready to sink our forks into our desserts. Just as I lifted my fork to my mouth, I heard the blare of the church organ. It was enough to raise me off the seat of my chair. I looked up and there was an organ sitting up high against a wall directly in front of us. Huge pipes ran the distance of the wall to the steep ceiling. A young man dressed in a black robe was seated at the organ and I could see his arms moving back and forth. I looked to the left of the organ and discovered the church auditorium was filled with people. Where in the Sam Hill did they come from? There I sat with my fork at my mouth in front of all those people, and I could feel my face turning a glowing red! Oh, my land! What had we gotten ourselves into? Was it a wedding, a funeral? Carole was holding her coffee cup to her mouth. It suddenly dropped to the table. She and I glared at each other. Her eyes looked like they were going to pop out of her head. We didn't know what to do—drop our forks, or continue eating and drinking while we sat there staring down at the entire congregation. Did you ever have that feeling of getting caught with your hand in the cookie jar? Well, then you know how we felt!

I looked to Carole's right and noticed a small office a few feet from us. With my hands covering my mouth, I whispered to her, "Is there a door on the outside of that little room?" She shook her head no. Then I whispered, "How are we going to get out of here?" She said, "We're not, unless you want to walk down that long aisle." In my mind I could imagine the wedding march playing!

So, there we sat as if we were on exhibit. And actually, we were! There was nothing we could do. If only we could just fade into the background and disappear. That wasn't going to happen. No miracles were going to be performed that day! The Lord wasn't willing! The people began singing and the little old man sitting at the foot of the organ stepped up and handed Carole a book opened to the page of the song. He smiled; she smiled. We mouthed the words. Afterward, the organist climbed down the steps beside the huge pipe organ, walked across in front of us a few feet and to our left where there were two young men, also dressed in black robes. One of them spoke a few words, and then the other, while Carole and I sat there mortified. Again, the young minister (we assumed he was the minister) went back to the organ for another song. The congregation stood and this time, the little man came up the steps and handed me a song book. Carole and I stood with the others. Neither of us knew the song but again, we mouthed the words. The minister returned to his podium. I could hardly hear what he said since I was sitting to his back side. The congregation all held papers in their hands. The minister began reading then the people would read. Back and forth, back and forth, and turning to the next page to continue reading. I couldn't understand a word they said due to my hearing impairment and their British accent. I whispered to Carole, "How many pages are there to this thing?" She answered very quietly, "I don't know but we aren't going anywhere until they are finished."

You can't imagine what it was like being on display before an entire church congregation with a dry throat, and so thirsty, with a piece of cake, a cup of lemonade sitting in front of you that you can't drink, and staring down a long church aisle that you can't use for escape. Every time the congregation stood, we stood, waiting to see if it was a wedding or funeral we had attended. I'm sure the people were wondering what part we played in their Saturday afternoon program.

Three songs and thirty minutes later, the program ended. No bride and groom appeared, and no coffin! As people began leaving the sanctuary, the little man approached us and thanked us for being present at their 100th anniversary celebration. It was a Methodist church. Carole and I gulped down our lemonade, quickly left the church and hurried up the street in search of the Mathematical Bridge.

THE MATHEMATICAL BRIDGE

A trip to England is one of the best gifts you can give yourself. There are so many historical sites to enjoy and places to go. Their flowers are perfection and grow extremely large. The British put lots of love into their gardens. If you like theater, London is the place to be. I remember being in London with my friend, Carole, and the first theatrical performance we saw that week was *My Fair Lady*. I believe the play is a favorite with everyone, as well as the movie itself. If you can believe, we were seated in the center, front row. We could actually prop our feet up on the edge of the orchestra pit.

The play began with all the performers dancing and Eliza Doolittle singing and then Professor Henry Higgins came on the scene. As he came closer to the front of the stage, I sucked in a long breath and leaned over and whispered to Carole, "That's Anthony Andrews!" She shrugged her shoulders and said "Who's he?" I should have known she didn't recognize him because she had never been a movie buff like I was. I knew all the old movies and the stars that played in them. I said, "He played with Jane Seymour in *The Scarlet Pimpernel*, one of my favorite romantic movies." I couldn't believe I was actually looking at him from only a few feet away.

We would attend other shows before leaving London that week, but our trip to Cambridge was at the top of our list of places to see.

After browsing the bazaar in the historic church of Cambridge, we had yet to find the Mathematical Bridge, so we went in search of it. The record-setting heat that day was about to get the best of us. We had to do a great deal of walking if we wanted to see the historical sites and the beautiful scenery. The heat from the streets felt like beds of fire to my feet, but that didn't stop me from walking.

I thought I could find the Mathematical Bridge because I remembered it being near a pub called The Anchor, and the Anchor was beside a canal.

We wandered up and down narrow streets with unique names like "Up the Street" and "Down the Street." We saw the bridge from a distance and searched for an entrance to the canal where it was located. Up and down more streets and we came to an entrance to Queen's College. There were signs for entry. We bought our tickets and were directed to the small tunnel taking us to the Mathematical Bridge crossing the canal. We walked through the tunnel and then we came to an opening. There it was—the famous Mathematical Bridge, the one we had seen in magazine photographs and articles many times. Look at us! We were finally standing in the center of the bridge.

Mathematical Bridge, Cambridge, England

Finding a bench along a walkway where we could watch the small boats drifting up and down the canal and under the Mathematical Bridge, we relaxed and enjoyed watching visitors in the small kayaks laughing and drinking their wine. We didn't notice how long we were there. I started getting a bit sleepy so we decided it was time for us to leave. We had already explored several parts of the village that day. We crossed the bridge again and walked through the little tunnel which was actually a breezeway through one of the buildings. We found our way back to the entrance of Queen's College and when I reached for the handle to the door, I discovered it was locked. I tried again and again. It wouldn't budge. The heavy wooden door had a lock with a huge chain like something you would see in a Robin Hood movie. There was absolutely no way we were going to get out. Carole checked a sign on a wall and it showed the closing time to be six o'clock. It was six-fifteen.

Queens College is surrounded by a brick wall at least ten feet high. We looked around and walked up and down and could find no exits. We were locked in! It would soon be dark and it looked like we would be spending the night at Queens College. I could see us lying on the grass during the night using our handbags for pillows. There wasn't a sign of life anywhere around us. We could hear music nearby, so we followed the sounds and saw an open door. We went through the door and stepped into a back room of a small church. Looking through a doorway, and up the aisle, there stood a bride and groom embracing for their kiss at the end of the marriage ceremony. We couldn't be caught peering in at the couple's wedding so we backed out the door we had just entered.

We had better come up with an escape route because it would be getting dark soon, and then what would we do! Okay, let's go back across the mathematical bridge. The canal was bordered by a very tall wrought iron fence and I remembered seeing a Volkswagen just beyond the fence earlier, so there must be an exit through the fence somewhere. Luck was with us. We found the opening in the fence. Beyond the fence and facing the street, the same street where we saw The Anchor, was a long brick building. There was no way to tell if it was a business office building or someone's home. How were we going to get to the other side of the building to the street? I noticed a door at the very end. It had a window at the upper half. I slowly crept up to the door and peeked inside. It looked like a small foyer but it could very well have been someone's living room. I tried the knob and lo and behold, the door was open. I could see another door across the room facing the street. I turned to Carole and said, "I'm going to go inside and run across the room and see if that door is unlocked." I had my fingers crossed that I didn't get caught because I hadn't planned that far ahead. Carole wasn't in favor of my idea, but I plunged forward anyway, holding my breath as I slipped through the room. I grabbed the second door knob and it opened. I motioned to Carole and she followed me through both doors and out onto the street. We were safe! Thank goodness, we wouldn't be arrested for breaking and entering.

It was hurry, hurry, hurry! We had to get back to the train station by eight o'clock to catch the last train back to London that day. Just one little problem—we didn't take note of the directions coming into Cambridge. What streets did we follow? As we walked Carole would say, "I don't remember coming this way. Do you recognize anything?"

"Oh, yes! Don't you remember? We passed that little church coming in from the train station. A wedding party was leaving and having photographs taken."

"Oh, okay!" Again, "I don't remember that building, do you?"

"Oh, yeah! I remember that big flowering bush."

"Are you sure we are going the right way?"

"We have to be. There's no other way to go!"

We continued walking and pointing out buildings we remembered and by this time it was almost dark. Finally, Carole spotted a sign behind a big tree limb with a great big arrow pointing in the direction of the Cambridge Train Station. We picked up speed and arrived at the station then hopped aboard our train back to London.

Returning to the states at the end of the week, we had reservations on the Queen Elizabeth 2. Our dining companions on the ship were a couple from England. We made our initial greetings and as we talked, the lady asked if we saw any stage shows while in London. Carole named the three we had seen and when she mentioned *My Fair Lady*, I saw the lady raise her eyebrow. I casually mentioned the change in her expression and asked if the play had any significance to her. She answered, "As a matter of fact it does. Our daughter played Eliza Doolittle in the play." I thought Carole and I were going to swallow our tongues. It was an earlier production of the play and as we talked, Carole said, "I believe I saw that production. She was wonderful and had a beautiful voice." Her name was Joanna Ridings. We continued our discussion about the play and the lady's husband said, "Paul Newman was at one of her performances and asked to go backstage and meet Joanna. He said she had the most beautiful voice he had ever heard. Joanna Ridings received a British award, one equal to our Academy Award, for her performance in *My Fair Lady*.

IT'S ONLY A SPRAINED WRIST!

This time I was in London with my friend and traveling companion, Carole, and wouldn't you know, I had Plantar Fasciitis in both heels. If you have had it, I don't have to explain the pain and discomfort. We had walked all over London and at times, I would begin limping, but I wasn't going to let the pain in my feet stop me from seeing all of the sites we had planned.

It was the month of March and our last day in London. We had just come from Harrods of London. I was wearing my all-weather coat and my arms were filled with goodies for all the kids back home. Of course, my video camera was with me wherever I went. Carole and I had left the tube and were walking back to our flat near Euston Station. We had rented a cute little efficiency apartment in a very old hotel, still decorated in the vintage style. The kitchen was so tiny, only one person at a time could get in it. We didn't even have an oven in the little stove, so we toasted our bread in a skillet. You learn how to live very simply when you are trying to conserve and keep expenses low. The bathroom had a long claw foot tub and pedestal sink. I loved the heated towel bars. There were no closets in the bedroom, only what we would call 'shiffrobes' with mirrored doors. Our breakfast each morning would get our day started. It consisted of scones, toast and jelly. I drank orange juice and Carole had her cup of coffee.

I had packed a set of adapters to use with my hair dryer, curling iron, and video camera. The second morning in London I was sitting on my bed curling my hair. Carole had plugged in an adapter for my curling iron. I pulled my hair up on top of my head, rolled it down to the scalp with the curling iron and when I finished, I noticed the section of hair seemed very brittle. The curling iron was too hot, but I went ahead and tried the second curl. This time I was looking in the mirror and saw smoke rising from the top of my head. Before I could unroll the curl, my hair broke off all the way to the scalp. Oh Heavens, my hair was burned. Carole had given me the wrong adapter. There was nothing I could do! My hair was ruined.

It was one of those days when it was rain awhile then sunshine, back and forth. That evening as we returned to the flat on the train, I whispered to Carole, "I think I smell my hair." She leaned forward and placed her face against my head, sniffed, and said, "You do!" The smell was disgusting and there was nothing I could do to remedy my hair problem. There's nothing like burnt hair so short that it can't be cut anymore! I had the rest of the week to go and the only good thing in my favor was that no one in London knew me!

It was our last evening in London. We were walking along a sidewalk a good distance from the busy thoroughfare of Harrods of London, my favorite store. All of a sudden, my toe hit a break in the sidewalk and I fell face down, 'splat', spread eagle on the concrete. My packages went flying. My knee and my hand got the brunt of the fall. Pain? Of course, but I wasn't about to let it show. I pulled myself to the curb where I could sit and try to ease the pain in my knee and wrist. Naturally, as you could expect, I had sprained my wrist—and I was to fly back to the states the next morning.

I looked up and there stood two young men. A lady had also appeared from her small shop. They began assisting me while Carole gathered all of my parcels and my video camera. They wanted to take me to the hospital and I kept saying I would be okay if I could just sit for a couple of minutes. The lady insisted I go into her shop and try to relax until I was able to walk. Now, this is to say, don't ever let it be said that people of other countries are not kind and helpful. These residents were doing everything they could to assist me.

I managed to pull myself together and Carole and I continued on to our flat. We had to pack our luggage — two large, heavy pieces each. We were both flying out of London on separate airlines and at different times. I would be leaving first. I decided to pack my purse in the suitcase and wear a fanny pack, or whatever you call those pockets that wrap around the waist! My airline tickets and passport were in the pocket worn under my coat. I was in no condition to be able to carry a purse and manage two pieces of heavy luggage.

The next morning, with a swollen hand, a bruised knee, and two large suitcases to carry, off I went, walking to Euston Station to catch the train to Victoria Station. Carole helped me until it was time to board the train. She hated having to leave me fending for myself the rest of the way to the airport. She, herself, would be leaving for the airport about three hours later.

This is where the fun began. We have talked about the underground stairs and escalators to the Tube and how busy they can be. You certainly don't interfere with other people who are in a hurry because they can run you down if you get in their way. So there I was, one-handed, limping from Plantar Fasciitis pain in my heels and a bruised knee, lugging a large suitcase and a heavy duffle bag. I managed fairly well until I reached Victoria Station, the main hub of London. I started up the longest escalator I had ever seen, trying to keep to one side of the narrow stairway so other passengers could hurry past me.

Whewww, I made it to the top. Oh, Lordy, I looked ahead of me and there were two long stairways with a platform between them. I lugged the suitcases off the escalator with people clamoring around me, and headed for the stairs. I would have to use both hands even if one hand was out of commission. At this point, I had to pick up the luggage by the handles on each end in order to get them up the stairs. I could see that I wasn't going to make it. By chance, a lady observing me walked over and said, "I believe you need some help." She grabbed one handle and I, the other, and together we reached the top of the stairs with the duffle bag balanced on top of the big piece of luggage. Another escalator and, oh no, another set of stairs. Could I make it? I struggled, with the duffle bag flip-flopping from side to side, and finally reached the top step. I purchased train tickets, and after a long walk across the station, dragging my luggage behind me, I reached my train.

Try boarding a train with two high steps, a turn through a narrow doorway and on into the car, and then positioning your luggage out of the aisle—with one hand and not a soul around to help you! I struggled and pulled and pushed and finally, I plopped down in a seat, huffing and puffing. All that was bad enough, but I also didn't know diddly-squat about what I was doing, or if I was even on the right train to the airport. Thirty minutes later the train entered the terminal. Again, it was pull, tug, push, and drag two heavy pieces of luggage down the steps and off the train with one hand, and a heavy duffle bag still flipping and flopping.

Next, was the tram! Where to get on, where to get off, and hopefully, the tram wouldn't start moving before I got through the door and into the main terminal. Now, I was in the middle of people shuffling through in every direction. I sought the first uniformed person I could find wearing a name tag and asked for directions to my airlines, which happened to be Delta. I was flying nonstop to Cincinnati. At this point my throat was dry and I was thirsty so I began looking for a refreshment stand. Oh, no! All of my American money was in my purse inside the suitcase. I had no money on me! I found my way to the Delta reception desk and the line of passengers was so long, I vowed I would not get up to the check-in desk in time to board the plane. I was getting nervous. A family right in front of me must have had ten pieces of luggage and a couple of kids. It would take forever to get them checked in. I could see myself still standing in line while my plane flew over the airport.

Suddenly, I felt a nudge at my shoulder. A young airport representative said, "Are you traveling alone?" He could see I only had two pieces of luggage. I answered "Yes." He said, "Follow me. I can get you through the check-in faster." He led me to the Business fare desk where there was no one checking in. The representative processed my ticket, took my luggage, and I was directed to a waiting room. I breathed a huge sigh of relief.

Thank the Lord, I had finally reached my destination area and had time to relax. Forty-five minutes later, I saw the family that had been in line ahead of me walk into the room. A few minutes after that we boarded the plane and I was safe and on my way back to the states. When I arrived at the Cincinnati airport, my daughter was waiting on a balcony and saw me limping along, dragging my luggage one-handed through the long corridor. I motioned her to come. She came running. I said, "Take my luggage! My right hand is sprained and I don't think I could drag this luggage another ten steps." "What happened?" "Oh, I had a little fall on the streets of London and bruised my knee and sprained my wrist."

SAVANNAH

We were vacationing at Seabrook Island, South Carolina, a beautiful place for relaxing and enjoying the beach and watching dolphin strand feeding. Strand feeding is a sight that can only be seen in a few places at certain times of the year. Things were slowing down for us, so Carole and I decided to drive to Savannah, Georgia, for one day. We started out early that morning and arrived in Savannah before noon. We walked the historic district and it was soon time for us to seek a good restaurant for lunch. Naturally, we would try Paula Deen's but we had no idea how to get there. After walking a few blocks, I spotted a lady walking down the street and called to her to give us directions. She was very kind and told us how to get to Paula Deen's and then she said she was on her way to Mrs. Wilkes Boarding House to meet friends for lunch. That sounded interesting. She described the restaurant to us and it sounded much more inviting than fried chicken, and reservations were not required, so we followed her. When we arrived the waiting line was halfway down the block. The crowd seemed to be moving along, so we took our place in line and were soon inside and being seated at a table for nine in the Boarding House. It was delightful. I watched as the waitresses filled the table with bowls and platters of food. I counted twenty-one different vegetables, meats, and breads. I can truly say it was the best $15.00 I had spent in ages.

Later, in the afternoon we browsed more of the historic district of Savannah and our last stop was an antique shop down by the river. Realizing it was beginning to get dark, we decided to head for home. Before leaving the shop, the owner suggested we turn our diamond rings to the back of our fingers; there had been a run of theft and vandalism in the vicinity and it wouldn't be a good idea for our jewelry to be easily seen. We followed his advice and hurried to our car. The drive was about 113 miles and we had not traveled very far when we passed one of those huge service stations where they have places to purchase snacks, souvenirs, and about ten or twelve gas tanks. The place was well lit so you couldn't miss it if you were planning to stop for gasoline.

Carole must have driven a couple of miles on past when she said, "I should have stopped for gas at that big service station."

I said, "What is the gas gauge setting on?"

She answered, "Empty!" I squealed, "Empty? Are you crazy?"

She said, "I think I have enough gas to get us back to Seabrook." I, of course, replied, "The devil you have! You are stopping at the very next gas station we see."

That two-lane highway was the straightest, darkest highway I had ever seen. The sky was black, no moon, and not a single twinkle from a star. The sides of the highway were lined with tall pine trees. I was beginning to think every pine tree in South Carolina was along that road blocking our view of everything. There wasn't a light from a house or building anywhere and we seemed to be the only vehicle on the highway. I was getting nervous.

"What will we do if we run out of gas and are stranded on the side of the highway?" I asked.

"I guess we'll call Jan and ask her what to do!" Jan is my daughter and she always has an answer for every dilemma, but I could just hear her voice when we called her and said, "We've run out of gas and we are stranded on the side of the highway. What do we do?"

"Are you nuts? You expect me to come and get you from 400 miles away?" Well, that idea was out of the question, so we kept driving and looking right and left for a service station. Still no sign of life anywhere. Finally, we spotted a light up ahead on the opposite side of the two-lane highway. It was a small two pump gas station with a gravel drive. A little white building stood to the back of the lot. It didn't look very appealing and we could see no sign of life except for three or four men inside the building. None of them looked like they had shaved in a few days and they were wearing bib overalls. One guy was quite a bit larger than the others. Carole said, "I don't think I want to pull into that station. It doesn't look safe." I answered, "You are going into that station. We need gas. What's the worst that can happen?" What a question to ask at a time like that! I insisted Carole cross the road and drive into the station. We pulled up to the gas tank and she took her credit card out of her purse and said, "I'll just get $5 worth of gas. That'll get us back to Seabrook. I don't want to stay here any longer than we have to." Imagine how much gas $5 would buy when gasoline prices were over $3 a gallon! Carole got out of the car and a sign on the tank said "Go into the station to pay for gas." Well, if that wasn't just what we needed! I looked at Carole and said, "Leave the car keys with me. If you aren't back here in three minutes, I'm leaving without you." She said, "A fine friend you are. You don't get the keys." We were doing our best to humor each other.

I sat in the car and never took my eyes off the little white building. It's times like that when a minute feels like a lot more than sixty seconds. The door opened and one of the guys started across the gravel drive to our car. He was the big guy. I checked the locks on the doors and started sliding down in my seat. Where was Carole? What was taking her so long? And what was I going to do when the big guy reached the car? Fear can create all kinds of thoughts and sensations and I began to perspire. The big guy walked past the car and didn't even look my direction. About that time, I saw Carole coming. She reached for the gas nozzle and put about five gallons of gas in the car, and then she hustled back to the car door. We were out of there like a flash of lightening, spitting gravel behind us.

It takes all kinds of experiences to make some situations

memorable. When someone mentions Savannah, Georgia, this is what I remember, not the unique little shops, the pretty historic homes and buildings and the nice little antique shops. But, somehow, amidst all the turmoil and fear experienced during that leisure trip, I also remember Mrs. Wilkes Boarding House. You would love it!

THE QUEEN ANNE STYLE HOUSE

My mother would gather up all the kids like a mother hen does her chicks. Off we would go again to wherever Daddy's job took us. This time, only the five youngest kids were in tow. It was the summer of 1942. Daddy worked for the Works Project Association building schools, court houses, bridges and whatever needed building. He had recently completed the construction of Dry Land Bridge and Dupont Lodge at Cumberland Falls State Park, only 20 miles from home. From there, he was sent to Clay County, Kentucky, to build a court house. This time he was building an elementary school in Campton, Kentucky. A lovely house had already been rented for the summer. It was a Queen Anne style house, the kind a child remembers, like remembering a vine-covered cottage in a fairy tale. Everything was pretty. The long shaded walkway leading to the front steps, the beautiful field of golden grass, the garden on the hill behind the house, tiny white rabbits nesting under a large flat rock next to the outhouse, a water pump outside the kitchen door, and the lovely wraparound porch with gingerbread trim and banister railings. All this and more are the memories I have of the yellow Queen Anne house in the little town of Campton when I was six years old. My sister, Wanda, who was eight, recalls the beautiful cherry secretary and oriental rugs that were left in the house by the owners. We never had fine furniture like that at our house, or pretty French doors separating the living room from the dining room.

None of the streets were paved at the time and our house faced a dirt road with an abandoned school building across the way. Little did I know as a child that the summer in Campton would become a childhood dream.

Driving up the two-lane road, my older sister, Janette, and I had slim hopes of finding the house from our early childhood. We were certain it had been torn down. Too many years had gone by since we last saw the place. We didn't even know what street it was on so we made a quick stop at the City Hall to see if anyone remembered the old yellow Queen Anne style house. The only identification we could give that would be a clue to landmarks was a description of the schoolhouse that stood across the road. I recalled playing with friends in the building.

A couple of phone calls later we were directed to the street where the house once stood. We came to the location where the old schoolhouse had been and standing in its place was a modern brick home. Across the street was a gray frame house, not the pretty yellow Queen Anne house I had hoped to see. We were disappointed. Our dream house was no longer there. It had been replaced and sitting in the shade of the small front porch was an elderly lady. We decided to stop and visit with her. She might know something about the house that once was there. We parked our car in the driveway down below the side of the house. I walked up that same narrow walkway leading to the front porch, but somehow, the sidewalk didn't seem to be nearly as long as I remembered. The porch was small and had black wrought iron railing along the front; nothing like the low standing wrap-around Victorian banister railings enclosing a side porch where Wanda and I had played. I identified myself to the lady and explained the purpose of our visit.

I noticed the paint on the house was chipped and appeared to have been repainted many times. Could I have been mistaken? Could this be the place where we lived in 1942? "Ma'am," I said, "could you tell me when this house was built?" She replied, "It was built in 1928, but we added a section onto the side." Oh, my goodness! Was I actually standing on the porch of my dream house? I didn't recognize it because so many changes had been made through the years. I asked her about the wraparound porch and she said, "Oh, that! The side porch was removed so we could add extra rooms to the house."

At first, the lady was slow to conversation but as we continued making inquiries, she loosened up. When I told her my Dad had rented the house back in 1942 from a man who may have been a doctor, she said, "My husband was a dentist and went in service back in the early Forties. While he was away, I went to Lexington to work. We put the house up for rent." I was dumbfounded when I realized I was talking to the original owner of the Queen Anne house. Was there a slim chance that the lady would allow us to see inside her house? At that point, my sister and I were practically on our knees ready to beg. Was it possible that we might recognize something from our past? The lady welcomed us inside and the first thing I saw was a wide open doorway between the living room and dining room.

"Did this doorway once have French doors?" I asked. She said, "Yes! We took them out."

Then I spotted an antique cherry secretary standing in one corner. "Do you mind if I ask how long you have had that secretary?" "Oh, it has always been around." The lady took no offense to our questions so I continued, "Do you remember if the secretary was left in the house when you rented it in 1942?" She said, "Probably! The house was partially furnished when we rented it that summer." I couldn't believe my eyes. This was the same secretary my sister, Wanda, had used to lay her tablets and pencils on and practice her writing and drawing. Janette asked if she could look out the back door and the lady kindly obliged. Janette wandered to the closed-in back porch and looked out the window. When she returned, she said she felt like she had gone back sixty years in time. Everything looked the same. The lady's modern refrigerator sat in the same spot on the enclosed porch as the old Frigidaire with the gas motor on top. I pointed to the bathroom between two bedrooms and commented that it was just an empty room in the early days.

"The house didn't have electricity back then, or a bathroom," she said. "That's why we used an oil stove and oil lamps for lighting. There was an outhouse not far from the kitchen door." Janette and I remembered the outhouse with a two-holer and the long-handled water pump under the kitchen window. She told the lady about the time the oil stove caught fire and she ran down the hill to where some men were doing construction work on the road and yelled for them to come and put out the fire.

How could I possibly forget the day the storm came up so quickly Wanda and I didn't even have time to gather our dolls and playthings from the front yard before the strong winds were upon us. Mama was inside the house and didn't see the storm approaching. Wanda ran to the front steps and hurried up to the porch. The wind was so strong I couldn't make any headway. I could feel myself being propelled backwards then swept off my feet and back, back, towards the road. I could hardly breathe when suddenly I was thrust into the air. I wasn't aware of Daddy walking up the sidewalk and grabbing me around the waist just after my feet left the ground. He hustled me inside the house to safety.

And then, there was the day my brother, we called him Bug, came to visit us. We were sitting on the front steps when suddenly a beautiful thoroughbred horse came into view and was racing down the road. It was a runaway horse going at top speed and two black men followed close behind trying to catch up to the horse. At the end of the fence along the edge of the road, the horse made a quick turn up into the yard. My brother had been entertaining us with his guitar music. He threw the guitar aside and leaped from the steps just in time to grab the horse's bridle. I had never seen a horse so shiny and beautiful before. It was an exciting experience watching my big brother as he restrained the thoroughbred.

My sister and I cut our visit short that day and kindly thanked the lady for allowing us to satisfy our curiosity and yearning to return to our childhood days, if only for a brief time. Afterwards, we drove on up the road to where we thought a lady named Mrs. Daley once lived. I remembered her house sitting back from the road on acreage that looked like the small farms I had seen in my fairy tale books. Mama would send my older sisters to Mrs. Daley's to get milk and butter. Sometimes, Wanda and I got to trail along with them. A picket fence covered in rambling roses bordered the front yard and a row of hollyhocks ran alongside. Mrs. Daley lived in a small Victorian cottage. She would invite us outside where there was a stream twisting and turning through her back yard like a narrow canal. Paddling in the water was a mother duck and her tiny yellow ducklings. We had never seen anything that pretty.

Janette and I were quite disappointed when we discovered the small Victorian house was no longer there, but my excitement resumed as we climbed the hill to find the elementary school Daddy had built. Again, that hill didn't seem as steep as I remembered, but there before us stood the sandstone, three-story schoolhouse, neat and clean and well-preserved. The doors were open so we went inside. We could see into the classrooms through the glass windows of the doors. Everything had had a fresh coat of paint in preparation for the new school year.

Elementary School, Campton, KY, built by WPA 1942

I recalled going up to the construction site on Sunday afternoons where Daddy let our bird dog, Kate, and Maggie, the Irish Setter, run across the field while Wanda and I climbed up and down the stacks of lumber. The years had not changed the sandstone elementary school. It looked the same as it did more than 60 years ago when it was first built.

I came away from the small town that had been so dear to my heart realizing what time had done to change it. The yellow Queen Anne style house was no longer recognizable. The side yard that once grew golden grass wasn't nearly as big as I remembered. The sidewalk was half as long and there weren't as many steps leading up to the now-very-tiny front porch, but the trees along the edge of the road were ever as big. They had tripled in size and towered above what I remembered as being a vast expanse of grassy lawn. Although nothing looked the same, I still held onto my dream of the yellow Queen Anne house with the beautiful banister railings, its French doors, the golden grass, and the tiny white rabbits that hovered under the big rock by the outhouse. In my mind I could see my sister, Wanda, sitting at the beautiful cherry secretary, humming as she scribbled in her writing tablet. I could play paper dolls on the side porch then walk down the dirt road to Mrs. Daley's beautiful Victorian home and watch the ducks swimming in the water. The small church we attended a couple of blocks away is still there and a new church has been built beside it.

How different the world looks when seen through the eyes of a child.

FOLLOW THE WHITE TRUCK

I had just gone through a carwash with my Buick Sedan and was driving down Interstate 75, heading south to my friend's house. She had invited me to join her for a trip to High Point, North Carolina, on a buying spree. The furniture district was having a big show and she planned to buy a few new items for her decorator shop. Her shop carried high quality merchandise and I loved browsing through the beautiful decorator and furniture items each time I was visiting.

I had never been to High Point before and I was very excited and anxious to see what was in store for me on this trip. Naturally, I wouldn't be purchasing anything but I certainly would have the time of my life just looking at everything. The huge building that was our primary destination was about four to six stories tall and any decorator item that had ever been manufactured would be seen on this trip. To top it off, every booth or furniture display would be treating the customers with snacks and drinks. It was going to be a fun weekend.

I was supposed to meet my friend at ten o'clock that morning, and wouldn't you know, I was running late and trying to make up for lost time. At the time I didn't own a cell phone so I couldn't call ahead and let my friend know when to expect me. I'm usually a very prompt person. When I say I'll be there at ten o'clock, I'm there at five minutes to ten! I had already driven about eighty miles or more and only had a few miles left to go. I knew the exit ramp was right up ahead a short distance and I'd be home free after that. A few more miles down the winding country road and I would be pulling into my friend's driveway.

I was following an eighteen-wheeler in the right hand lane and couldn't see the road signs ahead of us on the interstate. I was afraid to pass the truck for fear I would miss the exit ramp. Actually, my concern was more with arriving on time than reading the road signs. Suddenly, the big white eighteen-wheeler gave his turn signal and took the ramp to the right of the highway. I followed close behind thinking we had reached the ramp sooner than I had expected. The driver of the truck reduced his speed to a crawl and suddenly I realized where I was. "Oh, no!" I had followed the huge transfer truck right into a weigh station. How could I have been so stupid? I began looking every direction to see if anyone had seen me! It seemed the natural thing to do!

There was no way I could go around the truck and get back on I-75 because it was a one-lane narrow drive with curbs on either side. Let me be the first to tell you, "You can't drive over those curbs!" As the truck pulled up and stopped, I could see the driver's face in the large mirror beside the window of the truck. There was no doubt about it—I could have counted every tooth in his head at that moment. He was grinning from ear to ear. I was stuck behind him in my pretty white Buick LeSabre and going absolutely nowhere! I could feel my face glowing in color. The same thing happens when I stump my toe and fall face down on the sidewalk. It isn't the pain from the fall but the embarrassment of being seen by someone; that is the killer.

Time is like the seven-year itch when you find yourself in a situation of this nature. What can you do while you wait—"Nothing", absolutely nothing except whisper, "Shit, Shit, Shit" while you bite your lip and tap your fingers on the steering wheel.

Next thing I knew, another big white tractor-trailer truck pulled up right behind my pretty white Buick. This time, I looked in my rearview mirror and could practically see the cab of his truck shaking, the driver was laughing so hard. At this point, I wasn't exactly seeing the humor in the situation, and why was it taking the first driver so darned long to do whatever it is they do in a weigh station? I wanted out of there. The two men were having too much fun at my expense. Wouldn't you know, to add pain to misery, suddenly, a young man stepped through the door of the small building a few yards over from the one-lane drive. He looked my direction, of course, scratched his head, and I didn't even try to imagine what he was thinking. He gave me a broad smile, and I lifted my hand and gave him a thumbs-up signal. He obliged with a big wave of his hand.

Finally, the driver in front of me with the set of sparkling white teeth began pulling out. Surely he could go faster than that no matter what kind of load he was hauling in the bed of his truck. When he was far enough ahead for me to go past him, I shot around his truck like I was on a Nascar race track. I didn't dare look at the big sideview mirror. I already knew what I would see—that same set of brilliantly flossed teeth, and I didn't want to see what color his eyes were either. Two miles ahead, I saw the ramp marked Exit 29. I signaled a right turn, praying the first big white truck would not follow suit. Something told me the driver might decide to follow me all the way into town just to see where I ended up. He was really enjoying my dilemma.

I pulled into my friend's driveway, totally relieved that I had finally made it to her house. I hesitated about explaining my reason for being delayed, but gave in and told the whole story to her. She couldn't wait to tell her husband and he in turn, couldn't wait to tell his brother. I would, thereafter, be known as the lady who went through the Weigh Station. "She drives a white Buick LeSabre!"

All the way to North Carolina, I found myself eyeing the driver of every white eighteen wheeler. I wouldn't mistake those pearly white teeth!

WATCH THAT FINGER!

I was listening to a radio talk show where they were discussing who the best drivers were and who the worst drivers were. It put me in mind of a time when I was driving south across Jellico Mountain in Tennessee in my pretty white Buick La Sabre. Jellico Mountain was never my favorite road to travel even though it was a four-lane highway. I avoided going anywhere in the winter months that involved crossing that mountain especially if it was covered with snow and ice. There were drop-offs so steep that if you went over the side of the mountain, you may never be found.

My sister and I were returning from a weekend visit in Kentucky with my mother. It was late Sunday afternoon and we were tired and anxious to get home. After crossing the Tennessee line, we were cruising along in the passing lane at the very top of the mountain. An eighteen wheeler was beside me on the right, a passenger car ahead of me, and a very impatient driver was tailgating me, one of those people we have all met at one time or another who is the perfect persona of the word "redneck," automobile and all. He was driving one of the older rusty, diarrhea green models. I got the impression he was anxious to get home to the wife and kiddies because he kept honking his horn and riding the tail of my car. I was starting to get a bit nervous.

Honk, honk, honk! Where in the heck did he think I was going to go so that he could pass me and get on home where he could hassle his wife because supper wasn't ready when he got there? I would have been glad to move over to the right lane, but it was impossible. It was obvious I couldn't go anywhere out of his way unless I plowed into the wide median. And that wasn't gonna happen! After a few minutes of his practically pushing me into the car ahead, that driver finally picked up speed and signaled to get in the right lane.

What a relief! I hit the accelerator and moved on ahead of the car that had just moved to the right. I breathed a sigh of relief as ol' Bubba drove past me in his antique rusted diarrhea green Oldsmobile or Chevy. Of course, I was drained of energy and frustrated as well, so, as Bubba breezed by, staring at me like I was a swamp bat, I decided I would get the last laugh. Looking straight ahead, I lifted my left hand and up went my middle finger. I didn't dare look at Bubba as he cruised on ahead in the left lane.

It wasn't long until I noticed I was catching up with him. Hmmmm! He had reduced his speed and was letting me catch up with him. Uh Oh! I think I may have made a little mistake in giving ol' Bubba the Finger. Sure 'nuff, I was side by side with him and he was staring daggers at me. Now, that was bad enough, but we happened to be driving along the highest peak of the mountain and if your car veered off to the right, you became History! It was so far to the bottom, clouds were formed between the highway and the valley below. It was a long, long drop to the bottom of that cliff and it was too late to start praying and besides, I had my sister to deal with who was already lecturing me for giving the guy the finger.

That's when I started to sweat, heavy sweating at that! I'd never seen such a scowl and beady eyes in my life, sorta' reminded me of Charles Manson. And to top it off, there was my sister, shaking her finger at me and huffing and puffing as she squeaked, "You've done it now! You've done it now!" It was coming at me from both the left and the right. I looked at her and very emphatically said, "SMILE, and keep looking straight ahead. Don't you dare look at that guy." I put a grin on my face and kept talking to her like I was reciting poetry, never looking at the angry face I could see out of the corner of my eye. I couldn't handle both the redneck and the blabbing sister at the same time. Finally, ol' Bubba must have gotten bored because he couldn't get my attention, so he hit the gas. I breathed the longest sigh of relief of my life and yet, I could only think, "He's up there around the bend somewhere just waiting for me, probably hiding behind an overpass pillar at the bottom of the hill at Caryville. I figured if I could stay between two eighteen-wheelers, he wouldn't see me drive past him. I wasn't sure which was the worst—Bubba lingering out there somewhere, or my sister wagging her tongue at me in disgust. I made it down the mountain and past Caryville and then I decided I could let out that breath I had been holding back for the last two miles. I was home safe!

A reminder to you: "Keep that middle finger where it belongs when driving—attached to the steering wheel."

WHAT'S NEW TODAY?

This was to be my contribution to my last high school class reunion, but as circumstances would have it, I didn't get to offer my contribution, or perform, whichever way you want to look at it!

At a previous reunion instead of the humdrum introduction to the love of my life and telling how many beautiful children I had, I already knew my children were the most beautiful, and I had parted ways years ago with the love of my life so I decided to tell the group all about the neighbors on my street. I was certain they would be impressed because one of my neighbors was John Calipari. That gave me a chance to blow my horn, and another well-known Kentuckian who lived just across the street from me was Carl Hurley. Of course, they would all recognize the names and then I added one other neighbor who lived in a condo just below me. She was the current Miss Kentucky who would be going to Atlantic City for the Miss America contest. My story went over very well. I got lots of laughs and was even told I'd make a good standup comedian. Get that! Me—a standup comic.

As I've often said, most of the people living in my condominium are elderly, or maybe I should say, older than I am. Not many of them are in the best of health. Also, as I've said before, we have a weekly Thursday afternoon social hour which is well attended. That's where I get to share my stories, which they say I am good at telling. Now, I don't mean to brag. I just love to tell stories. They think I tell funny stories. What I have discovered over the years is that I don't require a wide range of tales because, as you well know, the aging process sometimes hinders the memory and since a few of our Thursday afternoon attendees are slowly acquiring dementia and Alzheimer's, it gives me an advantage. I can tell the same story week after week and they laugh just as hard as they did the first time they heard it. Someone had the nerve to tell me the reason they laugh so hard is because they know they have heard the story over and over and I think it's the first time I have told it!

Each Thursday, someone invariably asks me, "Have you taken any trips lately?" They think I'm a world traveler. Just recently, I told about an accident I saw in London and it drew their attention immediately. It never occurred to them that I was talking about London, Kentucky, the town I bypass on my way to all these reunions I attend. Even when I lived in Tennessee, I made weekend visits to my kids in Lexington. I remember once talking about going through London then I mentioned Athens and Versailles, and my coworkers were astounded at my travels, also thinking I was mispronouncing the name of the city, "Versailles." Should I have told them that these towns were all in Kentucky and Versailles in Kentucky is pronounced, "Ver-sales"? Ah! Why burst the bubble?

Back to my story. Picture this: There are 98 condos in the building occupying nine floors. I live on the eighth floor with the elevator located directly at my front door. Actually, my front door and my back door are only a few feet apart but I use the front door because the back door is blocked by kitchen clutter. As you well know, every home must have at least two exits in case of fire or other emergencies. Rest assured, the kitchen clutter won't stand in my way should the occasion arise where I have to exit by the back door.

Anyway, the point I'm trying to make has to do with the night the fire alarm went off in the hallway. In the seventeen years I have lived here, it was the first time I had experienced an actual fire alarm. It was about 10:30 at night and fortunately, I had not removed my hearing aids so I was able to hear the sound of the alarm. At that hour, I realized it couldn't possibly be a fire drill, which we have occasionally and they are usually held mid-morning. A notice of the drill is always posted on a bulletin board in our mail room.

I grabbed my purse with all my important items, my wallet, checkbook, driver's license, loose change, extra hearing aid batteries, tiny flashlight, glasses, Tums, and car keys then reached for an extra pair of eye glasses. In this case, I had not yet dressed for bed and looking fairly presentable, I stuck my feet in my walking shoes and reached for a jacket. It would be a long walk down to the first floor. I rushed down the hall towards the stairwell. It would have been much more convenient for me to take the elevator but we are not allowed to use the elevators when we hear the fire alarm. I hurried down the first flight of stairs and when I reached the 7th floor, there was a line of people ahead of me. Most were already in their night clothes, dressed for bed. I very patiently waited while three of the people with canes descended the stairs ahead of me. In front of them was a couple with walkers. Step by step I kept my place in line. I stood beside the neighbor from the ninth floor holding his big tall walking stick, something like Big John might use. In fact, his name is John and he's big.

Keep in mind, nobody knew where the fire was, if there was a real fire, and nobody showed signs of panic—except me and I was getting a bit flustered! At the rate we were going, I would be the last one out of the building, if I indeed made it that far! Would it be the proper thing to do if I slid between the people and hurried on down the seven flights of stairs to safety, leaving them to fend for themselves? When I looked in the corner of the stairwell, there sat a man in a wheelchair with his oxygen tank in his lap. Since I didn't smell smoke, yet, I kept my place in line. Now and then when we reached another landing, I peeked through the stairwell doors to see if there was smoke in the hallway.

By the time I reached the first floor, the lobby was filled with neighbors, and firemen were coming and going with their hoses and hatchets. I loved those big hats they wore! I still didn't know where the fire was.

I soon learned that one of our young residents had burnt popcorn in the microwave. Instead of opening a window to let the smoke out, he opened his front door and caused the fire alarm to go off. I decided then and there that I would never get stuck in the stairwell in the event of a real fire. I started collecting bed sheets. I knew I would need quite a few sheets if I planned to tie them corner to corner with the first sheet wrapped around the leg of my bed, and the rest falling through the window down to the street. I wasn't going to be found in the stairwell suffering from smoke inhalation and mangled by canes, walkers, and wheelchairs while all the little old people ahead of me were being rescued.

To keep things lively and interesting, I will tell you the story about the day I rang a doorbell and the lady who answered the door was wearing a shower cap and holding a towel in front of her. That proved to be an interesting experience. The interesting part was when she turned her back to me and I followed her into her condo!

I was given permission to tell this next story. I love it and so will you! My little elderly neighbor who writes articles for a local monthly magazine that is distributed to all of the residents in the building, was having a birthday. The staff at the magazine headquarters decided to give her a medic alert necklace for a gift and they would also pay the monthly premiums for the use of the necklace. She wore it home and later read the instructions that said the medic alert could be worn in the shower. Well, she was getting ready for her evening shower and decided to give the medic alert a try. The lady was hearing impaired and removed her hearing aids and laid them aside on the countertop before entering the tub. She bathed herself, reached for a large bath towel, and was stepping out of the tub when she heard a noise. It was the faint sound of what she thought was the fire alarm. The fire alarms are located in all of the hallways of the building. Still wearing her shower cap, she quickly dried herself off and wrapping the towel tightly around her, walked to the front door of her condo. She opened the door and peered out. This little lady, standing no taller than 4 feet, 10 inches on her tiptoes, with a towel around her, was staring up into the faces of six EMTs and firemen, all dressed in full gear—uniforms, big hats, hoses, hatches and the works. She meekly said, "Is there a fire in the building?"

One of the EMTs replied, "Ma'am, are you alright? Your medic alert went off! We tried and tried to call you on the phone and got no answer."

My neighbor doesn't wear her medic alert in the shower anymore!

Each day can bring on a new and different experience where I live. I remember the day someone placed a notice on the bulletin board in the mail room reading, "Would the person who stole my clothes in the laundry room please return them." The story is told that one of the residents went to the laundry room to remove her clothes from a dryer. She had her basket with her and emptied her clothing into the basket with the good intentions of folding the laundry items after returning to her condo. She removed the clothes from the basket and began folding them. It suddenly struck her that she didn't recognize any of the items she was folding. She had taken someone else's clothes. She returned them to the laundry room and placed them on a table where they could easily be seen.

These are just examples of what makes life interesting when living in a condo. On the 4th of July neighbors gather on the rooftop to enjoy the fireworks. At Christmas we have a community potluck dinner. Everyone dresses in their finery and the best of the best home cooking is shared by the residents. If you think living in a nine-story building with lots of elderly people is boring, think again. Yesterday, a resident fell headfirst on the sidewalk in front of the condominium. Today, she is showing everyone her black eye.

We have an excellent door man who assists the residents. He sees everyone coming and going. Each day when I go to the mail room to collect my mail, I stop and greet the door man and ask, "What's new today?" And he smiles and tells me!

MOUNTAIN LAUREL FESTIVAL OF 1936

There is a festival taking place in Pineville, Kentucky, a small town nestled in the foothills of the mountains. A breakfast under tents provided by the local hospital is a feast you don't want to miss. Sidewalks are lined with guests arriving to see queen candidates parading by in shiny convertibles. The townspeople open up their homes to young people taking part in the Mountain Laurel Festival. The main event is the crowning of the festival queen at Pine Mountain State Park, located high above the small town. It is one of the most beautiful natural settings you will ever find for a beauty pageant. The mountain laurel, one of the prettiest flowers ever created, is in full bloom around the amphitheater, and I can assure you that the prettiest of the pretty young ladies from colleges and universities throughout the state of Kentucky can be seen at this festival. A queen is chosen from candidates representing the schools. A princess is chosen from Kentucky high school representatives.

Of course, I have a reason for writing about the Mountain Laurel Festival. It goes back to 1936 when my sister, Ada, who is now 98, was a Princess candidate in the festival. The festival was started in 1931 and has continued for 86 years with the exception of the years during World War II. I would venture to say my sister is probably the oldest living lady who has participated in the festival. With bright eyes, she would tell you that there were ten girls chosen from her high school to attend the Mountain Laurel Festival as princess candidates in May of 1936. All of the matching dresses were pink, the color chosen for the young candidates to wear every year. The long formals were made of organdy and the sleeves and hem of each dress was a mass of double ruffles. The dresses were all handmade. Each girl was given a pattern and she had to find her own seamstress. A neighbor, Mrs. Daley, was an excellent seamstress and had made many of my sisters' school dresses. She was delighted when she was asked to make Ada's dress.

Ada Estep Witt

On the morning of the crowning of the Queen, the girls gathered at the school in downtown Pineville to be escorted to the amphitheater located a few miles up in the hills. Each car had a driver and carried three girls. To avoid getting their dresses wrinkled, the girls pulled the ruffles up around their shoulders. It was reported that as each car drove through the main street of town and up the mountain road, it looked as though it was filled with bright pink flowers and lovely smiling faces perched above the blossoms. It was an exciting day for each of the young girls.

The Princess candidates representing the high schools of Kentucky lined up in single file across one side of the amphitheater and watched as the Queen candidates approached following stepping stones protruding from the vine-covered side of the mountain. Each girl was attired in a beautiful white evening gown and carried a bouquet of mountain laurel. They paraded beside the manmade pool, which gave a mirrored reflection of their beauty in the rippling water. One by one, they gave a curtsy to the governor of the state. He was also one of the judges. My sister remembered the University of Kentucky band playing "A Pretty Girl is like a Melody," a most appropriate tune for the occasion as the girls promenaded up and down the aisles so those attending could get a better view of the candidates. A more beautiful sight you will never see.

The privilege of enjoying such an event and being a focal part of the festival was probably one of the most exciting things my sister and her friends would remember through the years ahead. It was her first time to dance to the popular music of the day such as "The Way You Look Tonight," "Let's Face the Music and Dance," and familiar tunes like "Pennies from Heaven." It was the beginning of the big band era.

I have attended two of the festivals, one when I graduated from high school and a second one when my own granddaughter represented Transylvania College as a queen candidate. It was one of the most enjoyable weekends I have ever spent. The amphitheater, again, was beautiful. No flower could enhance such an occasion like the beautiful Mountain Laurel. Like every mother and grandmother, I thought my granddaughter would be crowned Queen that day. She met all of the qualifications—beauty, poise, intelligence—and she had personality. Her curtsy revealing her beauty before the reflective pool of water stood out among the others. Although she did not win the contest, she was excited and proud to represent her college along with Kentucky's most beautiful girls. The Mountain Laurel Festival is one of the loveliest beauty pageants provided by the state of Kentucky.

IF I COULD...

If I could turn back the clock to another time in my life it would probably be the years immediately following World War II. It was peace time again. The soldiers had returned home from the war, those that had survived. Unfortunately, my brother didn't return but we didn't let our loss keep us from living life to the fullest. Holidays were very special to my family. When you get all the siblings, in-laws, and kids together, there is no time for sad stories or unpleasant emotion. It's total excitement as to who will arrive at Mama's house first for the holiday. I call it Mama's house because she was the one who kept things going and did all the planning. Daddy, of course, was there and if it was a Christmas holiday, he was responsible for going to the woods and cutting down the pine or fir tree for us kids to decorate. It took lots of prodding to get Daddy in the mood for taking his saw and climbing in his old pickup truck and heading for the woods. We kids stayed stuck to the living room window while it frosted over, waiting for Daddy's return. He wasn't too choosy about the tree he cut down, but we didn't care what it looked like; we could turn it into the prettiest tree in town with Mama's collection of old ornaments, and my sister and me covering the tree with mounds of icicles. Wanda would throw the icicles on in bunches and I would follow behind her, removing the clumps and very meticulously placing one icicle at a time on the tree. Naturally, she would say, "What difference does it make as long as you get 'em on the tree!" When we finished decorating the tree we had one last ornament to be placed front and center where everyone could see it. My brother who died in the war had bought the beautiful shiny blue ornament for Mama that said "Merry Christmas." It was the first ornament we had seen that had writing on it.

Four of my sisters had left the nest already and were all married and beginning their own families. My sister, Wanda, younger brother, Don, and I were the only kids still at home. We couldn't wait to see the sisters pile into the house with arms loaded down with presents, mostly for the three of us since we were still in the toy stage of life. Times were improving since we no longer had to live on rations and families were no longer suffering due to lack of jobs.

There was never a sister missing at a family gathering. They couldn't bear to think we were all there having a good time without them, and besides, the sister that was missing would be the one who got talked about! Mama could also count on help from my sisters where Santa Claus was concerned. Inez and Ada lived nearby so they had extra beds to take care of those that Mama couldn't bed down at night. As far as we kids were concerned, a palette near the warm morning heater suited us just fine and on many occasions the kids were willing to sleep at the foot of the bed.

Mama had already begun preparing for the crowd by baking her pies and special cakes. Nobody could make Jam Cake with caramel icing or Nutmeg Feather Cake like Mama did. She had acquired some of her recipes from Cissy Gregg's magazine section of the Courier-Journal Newspaper. Mama's favorite recipes were kept hidden in a drawer of her Hoosier kitchen cabinet, always handy when she was in the baking mood.

Elizabeth Estep, 1965

One by one the families arrived. As they walked in the front door, Daddy would say, "What're you doin' here, Sis?" as if he didn't know they were coming. It took two or three trips to the car for suitcases and presents. My sisters could make a wrapped package look so tempting; we couldn't wait to see what was inside the wrappings no matter whose name was on the tag. Little by little, the presents began piling up under the tree, but there was still extra shopping to be done before Christmas day. Afterwards, two or three would sneak into the front bedroom to wrap the new purchases. Wanda and I were so curious we would squeeze boxes and packages thinking we could guess what was inside the pretty paper. On one occasion, we waited until Mama and the older sisters had gone downtown to shop. The house was empty so we gathered the presents that held our curiosity and decided to open them. My sister had no doubt that we could open and rewrap the boxes and nobody would ever guess we had seen the items inside. Those were the days when gifts were wrapped mostly in white tissue paper and sticker seals were used to hold the paper together. Ribbons were then wrapped around the paper. While Wanda worked at opening the packages and carefully removing the seals from each end, I stood and wrung my hands and repeated over and over, "I don't think we aughta do this. We'll get caught. What if we tear the paper?"

"Ahh, they'll never know we opened the presents!" And she continued working her crafty little fingers behind the seals. One by one, we examined the gifts, and one by one, we slid the boxes back into the tissue and used matching seals to replace the original ones. Ribbons were re-tied around the boxes. By Christmas morning, the two of us knew almost every gift that was under the tree. We never revealed our mischief.

There were so many girls in the kitchen on Christmas day it looked like a restaurant kitchen. The green beans and potatoes got taste tested and salted two or three times by different sisters. My older sisters contributed dishes to the meal because they lived nearby and could do some of the cooking in their own homes. Mama hid desserts in the Hoosier cabinet so that little fingers couldn't explore, but it was the bigger fingers that were the most curious.

Mama had one of those old buffets that stood on tall cabriole legs and had a long mirror above the buffet with pretty pictures on each end. The buffet was where she stored her good linens and silverware. I loved fingering the lacy items on occasion so Mama let me set the big round dining table with her crocheted tablecloth and napkins. Our good dishes were mostly Homer Laughlin items trimmed in gold with pretty roses in the center of the plates. The dessert dishes and cereal bowls had come as premium dishes in cereal boxes, oatmeal, and soap powder.

The men stuck to the living room while the girls and women trotted from room to room in the house. You could find two or three in each bedroom talking and laughing. But at the last minute most of them were in the kitchen helping Mama with dinner. Dinner was almost ready when Mama had prepared the large pot of chicken and dumplings. My oldest sister prepared the best homemade rolls ever made. We never had turkey at holidays. Mama would have nothing but a large stewing hen, one big enough to feed the whole crowd.

Christmas at our house was basically the same from year to year except for the addition of one or two grandchildren. Everybody came! We laughed a lot and enjoyed being together once again.

After Daddy and Mama died, the gatherings at their house were no more. Time has changed the way people celebrate today. I miss those family gatherings and wish I could bring them back one more time. I wish today's young people could know the joy of those old-fashioned family gatherings. I sometimes hope the stories I tell will paint a picture in their minds and they will think about our family and wish they could go there just one time. If I could bring them back, I would!

PEPPERMINT CANDY—A TRADITION

It's uncanny how a thought can come to mind that takes you back to another time, another place, and another occasion. I saw a commercial on television displaying large red and white candy canes. A picture popped into my mind of the old fashioned peppermint candy sticks. I was a young mother living in Louisville, Kentucky. Every Christmas I traveled home to be with the rest of my family around the holiday. That trip was a Must!

It's been many years since the path home at Christmas took me through the small town of Lawrenceburg, Kentucky, but in those days, we drove the old road through Lawrenceburg, Harrodsburg, and Danville then on down through Crab Orchard. Mama's favorite Christmas candy was the tall old-fashioned peppermint stick. There was an old general store right in the center of Lawrenceburg and the only stop my husband and I made during the five-hour trip was at that general store. It would be dark when we got there but the store was still open. A pot-bellied stove sat in the middle of the room. The store sold the 12" tall, 3 – 5" thick red and white swirling striped peppermint sticks, the largest I had ever seen. Actually, they were the size of a small log. The peppermint candy was beautiful to look at and reminded me of the candy store in my favorite Christmas story, *Little*

Women. The peppermint stick was wrapped in cellophane with a big red bow tied around it.

Every year I purchased the peppermint log just for Mama. It cost about $5. It would replace the one from the year before that was nearly gone. Mama would lay a dish towel over the peppermint log and crush one end with her hammer. It provided enough small slivers and pieces to nibble on for several weeks then she would crush a little more and place in a covered candy jar. Every year Mama knew she would have a new supply of peppermint candy at Christmas and she made me feel that it was the best Christmas present she received.

The interstate has taken us away from the two-lane roads that led to those interesting little byways and small family stores that once kept the small towns alive. I rarely have occasion to travel that way anymore, but I can't help but wonder if that general store is still there. Does it still have the pot-bellied stove? Does it still sell the old-fashioned curly candy, peppermint sticks, and Werther's Originals? Those were the simple things that made Christmas.

THE CHRISTMAS BOWL

A landmark stands in every small town where teenagers congregate daily. One of those landmarks in my hometown was called Cottongim's Drug Store. When the last bell rang at school at 3:30, half the kids in high school headed downtown to the Drug Store. They bought a nickel Cherry Coke and a bag of potato chips and filled all the booths and stools in the little drug store. There they stayed until it was time to go home for supper. On occasion, my sister and I joined the other kids. I never had more than a nickel to spend so I bought a fountain coke and, like my friends, we sat and twisted the straws and drank our cokes and talked about anybody that wasn't there with us. Now and then, I would see the soda jerk prepare a banana split for a customer and my mouth would begin to water. I dreamed that someday I would have enough money to buy a luscious banana split with the vanilla, strawberry, and chocolate ice cream covered with the delicious toppings and finished with the cherries on top. They cost a quarter and I'd think it was Manna from Heaven if I could have one of those.

I would venture to say that every kid that grew up in the town could tell a dozen or more good stories about their days at Cottongim's Drug Store. It was the local hangout for many years.

It was about 1946 and only a couple of weeks until Christmas. I was ten years old. Daddy was going downtown to the drugstore to pick up some medicine from the pharmacy. I asked if I could go with him. We kids never went anywhere with Daddy unless it was to church on Sundays or the little eight-acre farm in north Corbin to ramble while Daddy worked his small garden. But that day, I wanted to go shopping with Daddy.

The drugstore was buzzing with customers and while Daddy was in the back of the drugstore making his purchase, I wandered over to the display window where they placed the pretty knick-knack items for gift-giving during the holidays. There were perfumes, and figurines, and so many pretty ladies' things from which to choose. I spotted a large clear-glass bowl decorated with transparent fruits around the edge. I thought it was beautiful. I wanted to buy the bowl for Mama for Christmas but I didn't have any money. Kids didn't receive allowances in those days and unless I saved the nickels and dimes Mama gave me for the movies, I had no money with which to buy presents. I waited for Daddy to come to the front of the drugstore and then I told him I wanted to show him something in the window. I knew I was taking my chances on showing the Christmas items to Daddy. I pointed to the pretty bowl and said, "Daddy, I would like to buy that bowl for Mama for Christmas but I don't have any money." He said, "How much is it, Sis?" Of course, I had already checked the price and told him it was $3.00. He reached in his pocket and unfolded three one-dollar bills and handed them to me. He said, "Get the bowl." I was so proud of my purchase that day and couldn't wait for Mama to see her beautiful present. It was the prettiest thing I had ever seen.

Fifty-two years later, Mama died. The pretty fruit bowl still sat on her dining room table. I was determined that the bowl which held such fond childhood memories for me would be returned to me.

Mama's Christmas Bowl, 1946

Cottongim's Drug Store, another landmark gone, due to Progress. Every person who lived in my hometown during the 1950s has a story to tell about this wonderful old drug store. Sometimes Progress kills the good things in life.

A GUIDING STAR

Let's drift back in time over a half-century ago, to a small town when the sidewalks of Main Street were swarming with shoppers at Christmas time. It looked like a carbon copy of the streets of New York City. You knew the clerks in all the stores, the tellers at the banks, and the shoppers as you passed them on the street. Newberry's Dime Store or Woolworth's were on Main Street with their long fountains where you could have lunch and a tall milkshake and then do your shopping. Children had their nickels and dimes, hoping to find gifts for their parents. Maybe Mom would get lace-trimmed handkerchiefs or a bottle of Blue Waltz perfume this year. It only cost a quarter. The drug stores still displayed special gift items in their windows to tempt shoppers passing by.

Several jewelry stores, ladies' dress shops and men's clothing stores lined Main Street, as well as shoe stores. Two or three department stores such as Belks, J.C. Penney's, Burr's and Mitchell Hardware were handy for household purchases. Anything you needed to buy could be found on Main Street in the small town. It was a delightful place to be during the holidays. Drive-through banks hadn't come into being then. People had to go downtown to conduct their banking and withdraw enough cash to purchase their Christmas gifts.

Unfortunately, the small town I remember doesn't exist anymore. Progress and expansion have taken over the easy going way of life we once enjoyed. Drive down that street today and the only thing you will see are empty buildings; no pedestrians busy shopping because there are no dime stores, drugstores, department stores, and shoe stores. Business has moved to the outskirts of town near the interstate highways. You can't walk to the A & P Grocery or Kroger, IGA, or Piggly-Wiggly. Even the A & P went out of business years ago. It was my family's favorite place to shop for groceries. Your small town dime store has become a super WalMart, a one-stop shopping place on the outskirts of town. You won't see any Mom and Pop stores today.

I will take you back to a time that seems long ago for many, but only yesterday for me. I had married and was living in Louisville, Kentucky. I had two children and a trip to Mammaw's house was a five-hour drive. That was before the interstate and a time when we followed the winding two-lane roads to go back home at Christmastime. You observed license plates of automobiles going south and noticed most of them were from Ohio, Michigan, and Illinois. They were going south, back home for Christmas with their families.

We usually left Louisville right after work on Friday which put us on the road for a five-hour journey. Traffic was heavy on the old state roads and that meant we would arrive at my parents' house about ten o'clock that night. We usually hit the long straight stretch of highway between Berea and Mount Vernon that ran parallel to the railroad tracks right about the same time as the passenger train on its way south. The engineer would see us racing down the highway trying to keep up with the train. He saw the little hands waving and hanging out the backseat window, and then he pulled down on the train whistle giving it all the power it had and began waving back to the kids. That was the big delight of the trip and they looked forward to it every time we went home.

A five-hour drive is a long journey for a couple of small children and mile by mile they would ask, "When are we going to get there?" I would begin by saying, "When you see the big star at the top of the hill, we will be almost to Mammaw's house." Again and again, "Are we almost there?" I would answer, "No, not 'til you see the star."

As we approached the small town from a far distance, they would again ask, "Are we almost there yet?" I always answered, "Look up! Do you see the star?" Their eyes would brighten and they would say, "I see it! I see the star. We're almost to Mammaw's house!"

Many people remember that star and many have the same memories of it being the symbol of Christmas in their small town. I still look up, hoping to see the big bright lights on top of the water tower. A young man fell to the ground and lost his life while changing the light bulbs on the star one Christmas. My mother was very fond of this young man.

Although many changes have been made in this community, one thing that will never be forgotten is the bright star that represented so many memories for people, and for my children. It also represented the star of Bethlehem. The bright and shining star at the top of the hill was a symbol of the birth of Christ and also, of a young man who gave his life for the happiness of the townspeople.

If you grew up in this small community those many years ago, you, too, have fond memories related to the star on top of the water tower…the star that guided my children to their grandmother's house; the star they still remember.

AN EARLY CHRISTMAS

I am one who fully believes that Christ remains in Christmas. He is the reason we celebrate. I also believe in Santa Claus.

It was 1962. Jan was six years old and Greg was three. We lived in a beautiful old stone house with a screened in front porch in Louisville, Kentucky. The house was in an old neighborhood. It had high ceilings and dark pegboard floors. It was one of those neighborhoods where there was an alley behind the houses that people used as a private drive to and from their own homes. Most of the garages in their back yards faced the alley.

First, I must explain how we handled the pre-Christmas day plans back then. We spent every Christmas with my family, a five-hour drive from Louisville. Yes, those were the days before "Interstate"! Today, the drive would only be three hours.

It was always a problem deciding where Santa would find the O'Neal children on Christmas Eve, in Louisville or at my parents'. Most likely, we would probably be at my parents' house with all of my family.

There were the big toys that couldn't be wrapped, and Santa never wrapped his toys anyway. Rather than go through the ordeal of trying to hide and haul the toys in the trunk of our car, we planned for Santa to come two or three nights early because we would usually be headed south down the two-lane road before Christmas Eve. It became more practical to take care of Santa's visit before leaving home. The children were too young to know that it wasn't actually Christmas Eve when Santa arrived at our house.

I had met my neighbors who lived in an older home across the alley behind our house. She was a sweet little old lady who often aired her handmade quilts on the clotheslines in her back yard. All I could do was admire them and express envy. Her husband played Santa at the nearby shopping center every year. I can tell you that there has never been a more appropriate Santa. I could even have been fooled by him. His wife saw to it that he fit the bill in every manner. He was a chubby white haired fellow and his costume was made to perfection by his wife.

It was about three days before Christmas. We had all been up and rambling through the house by six o'clock that morning. It was Christmas Day at our house. Jan and Greg had opened all their presents and were playing with the toys Santa had left under the tree for them. I can only remember one of the toys which was a Showboat with a small stage and cardboard characters. It was for Jan. Of course, there had to be metal Tonka trucks and cars for Greg. The beautiful huge fireplace had been built with stones hauled from Iroquois Park. The white mantle went from one wall to another and that is where Jan and Greg hung their stockings. The stockings were filled with fruits and candies and small hand-held trinkets.

While the kids played with their toys in the living room, my husband was loading up our car with luggage, presents, etc., for our weekend trip. None of their Christmas toys would be making the trip. The garage was behind the house beside the alley, like all of the other neighborhood garages. I went to the kitchen door and started outside to take things to the car when, who should I see but Santa Claus in full red costume walking up the sidewalk. He was on his way to the shopping center and decided to make a stop at our house when he saw my husband loading the car. I swallowed hard and started waving my hand, trying to get my husband's attention. He had to stop the little old man and tell him that he had already been to our house. I could just see him walking into my house and asking Jan and Greg what they wanted Santa to bring them! That would have been disaster! My husband managed to get the message as I swung my arms back and forth and mouthed the words, "Tell him he's already been to our house. Tell him what he brought the kids!" My husband stopped Santa midway up the sidewalk and I watched as he shook his head in agreement. I breathed a sigh of relief.

Santa came up the steps and I took him through the kitchen and into the living room. Jan and Greg were sitting in the floor when they looked up and saw the chubby white-haired man in red standing above them. You can't begin to imagine the look on their faces! Santa greeted them with a laugh, hugged each of them then took them on his knees. He asked if they liked the toys he brought them, naming the toys, one by one. I stood back and watched in amazement. It was a sight I would never forget. The surprise and glow on those children's faces were worth a million dollars. I can still hear them later saying, "Mammaw, did you know Santa Claus came to OUR house! We got to sit on his lap."

You may not be a believer of Santa Claus at Christmas but an experience like that one can turn you into a believer. It is worth going through the fantasy to see the joy that can be expressed by two small children when they have been visited by the Real Santa Claus. It is one of the delightful experiences in life that will always be in your memory. I wish all children could share in such an experience.

Jan O'Neal with her Chatty Cathy, 1961

MEMORIES OF CHRISTMAS

It was the early 1980s. I was living in Tennessee. Several weeks before Christmas the local newspaper included an ad that had a coupon for a Christmas ornament at Watson's Store in Oak Ridge. Each week for five and sometimes six weeks, a coupon would be offered for a ceramic St. Nicholas/Santa ornament at the special price of $2.99, regular price, $6.00. The collection was called "The Memories of Christmas." Limited quantities would be sold. Being one of those people who can't resist a good buy, especially if it is something that will eventually become a collector's item, I clipped the coupon from the newspaper.

As I recall, there would be forty-one ornaments in the entire collection, meaning the collection would not be completed for at least eight years. Old molds had been found and the Saint Nicholas/Santas were being reproduced from the molds. Each was five inches high and had the original attire and year for St. Nicholas stamped on the base. Included among them was the most famous Santa of all, dressed in red with white trim and dated 1925. Each figurine came with a card describing the ornament and listing the others that had been presented in prior years.

Every Monday on my lunch hour, my friend and I drove the eleven miles to the store in Oak Ridge to purchase our Saint Nicholas before the supply ran out. This process was repeated every holiday season for the eight-year period. By 1995, I had forty of the complete collection of forty-one Santas. Somehow, I missed the one dressed in all white and dated 1896. I searched and searched for him, at stores in Knoxville, Charleston, South Carolina, and even at the Christmas Shoppe in Gatlinburg, Tennessee. Many others were there, but not my missing 1896 Saint Nicholas. The first year, the Santas sold for a special price of $2.99. The price increased each year with the last ones selling for $10.00.

I continued the search for Saint Nicholas 1896. He was nowhere to be found. Christmas, 1995, I was decorating my sister's home for a special open house affair. This was one of the holiday traditions I had started several years earlier and that year, my sister wanted to have the open house for friends, family, and co-workers. It was a three-night event with lots of hors d'oeuvres and refreshments on hand.

On the third night of our open house, a next door neighbor attended the affair. She was quite impressed with the Christmas tree I decorated with all Santa ornaments, some of them being German glass ornaments given to me by my son's wife, Sharon. Included was my entire collection of Christmas Memories. I told the neighbor the story of how I bought the ceramic figures and when the collection was completed, I was still missing one Saint Nicholas; the one dated 1896.

The neighbor said, "I have about six of the ornaments and I place them along my stairs in the living room."

Later, my sister and I were in the kitchen cleaning up and washing dishes when there was a knock at the kitchen door. It was her neighbor returning to thank us for the invitation and she was carrying a small gift bag. She said she had enjoyed the open house so much and seeing all the beautiful decorations, she wanted to give us a small thank you gift. The lady handed the gift to me. I opened the bag, lifted out the gift box, and there was a Saint Nicholas dressed in all white. On the base was stamped the date, 1896. My collection, "The Memories of Christmas," was complete.

Memories of Christmas collection

THE EASTER BUNNY

Let's get away from the iPhone, iPod, Cyberspace, and all that electronic stuff that every kid is involved with and return to something like the Fairy Tales, Uncle Remus, Brer Fox/Brer Bear/Brer Rabbit, even a world of rainbows, leprechauns and the tooth fairy.

The Fantasy World is something you can create and build into anything you want it to be. For a child, this is what makes memories… good memories. Children hear the stories; they believe the stories, and then the day comes when they doubt the stories. Are they really true? Is there really a tooth fairy? "I'm not sure Santa Claus is real." Yes, Mom realizes her child is outgrowing the fantasy world and entering the world of reality. Tommy and Mary Ann are growing up.

I still believe in Santa Claus, the tooth fairy, and the Easter Bunny. Where would my children be today if it hadn't been for Bambi, Brer Rabbit, *Song of the South* movie with Uncle Remus? I remember when my son watched *Pinnochio*, his eyes were as big as saucers and glued to the cat watching the goldfish in the fishbowl. He was so entranced by the scene he didn't move a muscle. And, of course, Santa Claus the morning he appeared in my living room and surprised my children—an experience they will never forget! Childhood memories!

While moms are gathering the baskets to fill with artificial grass, plastic eggs as well as the hand-dyed eggs and all the surprise goodies for their kids, I will tell you a story. It is an Easter story that never gets old with me, and one of my favorites.

Jody was my neighbor. She was a very vibrant and energetic mother. She was full of imaginative ideas for entertaining children. Her husband was a resident in medical school at the university. He had already fulfilled his requirements in the military, completed college and medical school and was currently specializing to be a neurosurgeon. During his many years of continued education and medical training, Jody had given birth to four children, three boys and one little girl. I remember standing at my kitchen window on the upper level of my house where I could see down on Jody's back yard. She was busy as a beaver running in and out of the house carrying craft goodies. Large open boxes were scattered everywhere on the grass. With magic markers I watched Jody drawing wheels on the sides of the boxes then tying the boxes together with short pieces of rope. What was she doing? The boxes were placed in a circle and all at once it came together. Jody was creating a train for a birthday party for one of her children. Each child attending the party would have his own boxcar—so creative, so imaginative.

Since I had a regular job, Jody was babysitter for my first grade son, Greg, and Jan, who was in the fourth grade. They walked to Jody's house each day immediately after school turned out. As the Easter holiday was approaching, Greg was expressing doubts to her about his belief in the Easter Bunny. He had already told her, "I don't believe the Easter Bunny is real."

It was Saturday night. My niece was helping me prepare Easter baskets for Jan and Greg. I had dyed eggs for small baskets and collected candies and small inexpensive goodies to fill larger baskets as a surprise for the kids. The large baskets were placed beside the front door to be discovered the next morning when Jan and Greg woke up. The small baskets containing the dyed eggs were placed on the front porch.

It was about midnight when my niece left the house. I turned on the porch light for her to see her way to her car. She stepped out on the porch and said, "Pat, come here. There's something you need to see."

I stepped outside and discovered big white splotches on the porch, the front steps, all the way out my sidewalk and across the hood of my car then into the yard next door. I looked across the street and everywhere there happened to be children living in the home, there were big white splotches leading across the yard to their front doors.

I knew immediately...my neighbor had been performing her handiwork. I said, "Jody had to have done it. Nobody else in this neighborhood could think of something like that!" The lady had waited until everyone in the neighborhood had settled in for the night and then she went to work. She had filled a tube sock with flour and wrapped it around the end of a rubber plunger. She went up and down the street, door to door, stamping rabbit prints to each house. They actually looked like paw prints.

I had already hidden eggs in my yard for Jan and Greg to discover after they emptied their Easter baskets on Sunday. The next morning, I had forgotten about the handiwork by Jody, and Greg had gone outside to find his basket of dyed eggs and then look for hidden eggs. It was just seconds later that he burst through the front door and yelled, "Mom! Come and look! You won't believe...the Easter Bunny came last night. He left his paw prints all over the sidewalk. They are even on our front porch."

I returned to work on Monday and Greg returned to Jody's house after school that day. When I came home from work, the phone rang. It was Jody! She said, "I believe I renewed Greg's belief in the Easter Bunny. When he arrived after school at my house, he was almost out of breath in trying to tell me, "Ms. Megison, the Easter Bunny came to my house the other night and left his footprints on my front porch. He even hopped across the hood of my Mama's car."

Jody's efforts to make it a special Easter for the neighborhood children also made it worth the backbreaking steps from house to house with a bathroom plunger and a sock full of flour creating rabbit prints. The look on my son's face and the expression of surprise gave her more pleasure than she could ever have imagined.

The years went by. Jan was now the mother of two little girls. Greg became the father of two little boys. It was another Easter holiday and I was spending the weekend with my kids. Jan and I were talking and laughing about the Easter Jody became the Easter Bunny in our neighborhood. At midnight that night, Jan and I drug out the old bathroom plunger, found a tube sock and filled it with flour. Off we went across town to Greg's house. We sprinted from house to house around the circle where Greg lived. We noticed two baskets of dyed eggs placed beside the front door of his house. Performing the same act as my friend Jody from years before, we left rabbit prints across the yards and porches of the children living on the circle.

The next morning we received the expected phone call from two little boys. "The Easter Bunny came to our house last night and left his footprints in our front yard." Some things never grow old.

HIDDEN IN A CLOUD

Although I was in the process of writing my family history, trying to get all the details written down, especially those being told by my mother; there was still so much I didn't know. As we sat around my mother's bed at the nursing home talking about this 'n that, and mostly what we had learned on the Internet, I could see the look of dismay in Mama's facial expression. She didn't have a clue what we were talking about. Every word we said was foreign to her. We may as well have been talking Pig Latin as far as she was concerned. In fact, we were all so new at computer technology ourselves we were guessing at everything we said.

I would look at my mother and wonder what she was thinking when we got into a big discussion about computers. As we continue to progress in our knowledge of electronic technology, I think back about my mother. She's been gone 19 years now. How would she fit into today's world? She had lived in the mountains for many years where the only things she knew were farming, household chores, outdoor privies, raising pigs, chickens, cows, and whatever fruits and vegetables it took for the family's survival. It was years later before she saw electricity, a washing machine, a radio, or a telephone. Those things came along gradually and were accepted.

Mama's conversations were about people, places, cooking, and material possessions. More often than not, her daily life revolved around what she was going to cook for supper or what medication was proper for the kid in the family that was sick. Church activities played a major role and became a part of her social life as well. Mama never worked in the outside world. She had never held a job with a paying salary. She was just a simple lady who had birthed babies and learned the entire Dos and don'ts of everyday life. If we had to live today without electricity and modern technology, Mama would be one of few who would know how to survive.

Could my mother adapt to our modern times, talk of new wars, terrorism, and ISIS? She had seen enough war in her hundred years of life and knew what it was like to be on the losing end. She wanted no more of that. How would she accept the use of modern technology? The nearest thing she owned that represented inventions was her Kitchen Aid mixer and a microwave.

In today's world, her children and grandchildren would never have to come visit her. They would just "Skype" her! It takes a dictionary, a newly written dictionary, to be able to understand what people are saying nowadays. Although I can use a computer, my knowledge of its use is very minimal. I remember when I purchased my first computer. You know, that big TV screen box that took up half the kitchen table, with a "hard drive," a "printer and a scanner" each occupying the other half of the table! No, the kitchen table is no longer being used for eating; that is done on a TV tray in the den before your television set or personal computer.

What would Mama think when my daughter says, "If you can't find it, just Google it. If you can't find it that way, go up to the right corner and click on the little wrench, the three dots, the question mark, and one of them will tell you which "window" to open." Mama would be thinking, "Why do you need to open a window?" We also talk about "browsing" and "scrolling." Browsing, to my mother, would mean you were searching through her linens drawer for napkins or doilies. And searching "YouTube" would be totally ludicrous to her.

Can you imagine your grandmother hearing you say you had it hidden in "a cloud"?

Somehow, I am beginning to realize how Mama felt. Computer technology is outpacing me. I can't keep up. I still don't have an "iPod" or "iPhone." The little cell phone my kids insisted I carry for emergencies is good enough for me. I use it only for emergencies, and so far, I have had one occasion only where I was stalled in five-o'clock traffic in pouring down rain and had to call Triple A for assistance. While I was waiting, a police officer was kind enough to have me sit in his patrol car out of the line of traffic while I waited for a service truck. Other than that, I see no use for talking on a phone while driving my car. I am highly irritated when people sit beside me in a restaurant and "text" during the entire meal. Rude, Rude, Rude! I could go to the Ladies Room and stay during the entire meal and it would never be noticed. Oh, yes, I could write a documentary on that subject!

Little by little I have acquired enough computer skills to 'get by'. I remember when my friends and I were visiting Gatlinburg, Tennessee, some years ago. We had eaten at the Apple Barn in Pigeon Forge and my friend said, "Pat, I want you to go to the restroom with me. There's something I want you to see." Well, the heads turned and the eyes goggled. What could be so exciting in a Ladies restroom? What she wanted to show me was a self-flushing toilet. In my small world, that was a really big treat—stepping back and forth in front of a toilet and watching it flush without having to push a handle. What would my mother have thought of that? It would be as far-fetched as sending a man to the moon; and they had already done that!

I can just see my mother in the public restrooms at Dillard's or Macy's. After using the toilet she would start looking for a handle to push. "Where's the darn handle?" And then she would step forward and "swoosh," the toilet would flush. If that wouldn't be a shock to the system! Okay, that's taken care of, now I need to wash my hands. Can you imagine her surprise when the faucet has no handles? "Well, how do you turn the dad-gummed faucet on?" She looks to the right then the left, behind the faucet—no handles. By chance, her hand moves across under the faucet and water begins spraying into the sink. She washes her hands but the next big issue is—how do you turn the damn thing off?

Now, my Mama is used to reaching for a towel when she wants to dry her hands, but there on the wall is a black box showing a curved arrow saying, Wave your hand in front of the red dot. What red dot? The first time I experienced that, I kept waving my hands back and forth and waited for a paper towel to appear. When I told my son about the towel box, his response was, "Mom, you need to get out more often."

What would Mama think when the sign on the wall said "Place both hands inside two holes below?" I can see her face and hear her saying, "There's no way I'm stickin' my hands down in those two black holes!" And then she would watch as another lady placed her hands in the holes. A gush of hot air would blast her hands with force like a tornado? And to think, she had advanced from the two-holer outdoor privy to this—what they call modern technology!

Oh Lordy, what will they invented next? I have yet to figure out the "bidet." My friend has one of those in her bathroom and I just stand and stare at it.

It's bad enough visiting the Ladies Room every time you go to the mall to keep up with new inventions that have been installed, but when it comes to Computer Science, I have to call my daughter, Jan, every time I have an issue. Just the other day I somehow clicked on the wrong button and every word showed up in Portuguese. Since I can't read Portuguese, how was I going to know which icon to click to take me to the page for a solution? Jan tried to talk me through, but I couldn't find all those little symbols she pointed out so I was getting absolutely nowhere with solving my problem. I didn't know how to translate. Finally, she said, "I guess you'll just have to learn Portuguese." Somehow, I think she was a bit aggravated with me! I'll never catch up.

HOW FUNNY CAN IT GET?

The town comedian is usually the person you see every time you go downtown shopping, to the movie theater, at the restaurant, and grocery store. He knows everybody and everybody knows him. We had two or three like that in town but they materialized at different times of life. I went to high school with a couple of them and a week didn't go by that someone wasn't telling what that person said or did. Funny, always funny! If anything went on in town, they were right in the middle of it no matter the situation. These young men could turn every action around town into a comedy routine.

Harold, the young man who stayed with my family at night when Daddy was working out of town, was like that. Mama was always fussing at us girls for every little thing we did or didn't do, but never Harold, he could do no wrong. I have to admit, Harold went out of his way to please Mama and then he would round the corner making faces and groaning about what she asked him to do. I remember when the neighbors would drop by and the first thing they did was ask the question, "How are you today?" and Mama would tell them. Oh, yes, she told them, every little ache or pain she had had that week, and from there would be the stories of 'did I tell you about my operation?'

I don't know how many times I would say, "Mama, they don't want your medical history. Can't you just say, 'I'm fine, thank you'?"

After high school, Harold moved away. He went up north to find a job and was gone several months. The first time he came back home, he stopped at our house and when Mama answered the door, Harold said, "I come to tell you 'bout my operation." He could always make my mother laugh.

I remember the time he was clearing old Ms. Perkins, the wicked witch of the neighborhood's field of weeds; he spent a week laboring in the hot sun only to earn two dollars for the week. He marched up to Ms. Perkins door and said, "I come to get my two dollars for cuttin' weeds." She gave him a stern look and said, "Your brother borrowed a couple dollars from me. I'll just put it on what he owes."

Harold was steaming when he walked away from her house. He kicked gravel all the way home and kept repeating, "I'll get her. Just wait 'n see. I'll get my two dollars." He needed the money and he had worked very hard to earn it, so late that night, he pulled out a couple of his mother's bolster pillow cases; if you aren't familiar with bolster pillow cases, they are the ones that fit all the way across the head of the bed; he slipped into the middle of Ms. Perkins corn field carrying the pillow cases and filled them both with corn. Ms. Perkins never knew!

The amazing thing about the characters who become the local comedians is that they remember everyone in town and can tell a tale about each of them. We sometimes wonder how they can become so familiar with everything that goes on around town, but they do, and each incident becomes a new story and one for the books!

There was an older neighbor of ours who worked with my sister at the Grapette Company in the south end of town. Everybody knew and loved old Charlie. Charlie was dry and solemn of expression but every comment coming from him was comical, to the point of being the kind of humor that has you holding your stomach. My sister worked as the bookkeeper of the company while Charlie worked in the plant. Occasionally, on weekends, Bena Mae would take the Greyhound bus to Clinton, Tennessee, to see her boyfriend. Actually, by that time, he had become her fiancé because they had plans of marriage. My family had already met the young man and there was no doubt he was the most attractive man we had ever seen. He was a cross between Alan Ladd and a young William Holden, and they don't get any better looking than that. I remember the weekend he came to Corbin to meet the family. I don't believe he was quite prepared for what was in store for him, and it was probably just as well.

He had spent time in Germany and was at Normandy Beach on D-Day and had just come home. Jobs were hard to find. He was driving a taxi cab. Well, my oldest sister was a bit concerned about his choice of employment so she took him aside and away from the rest of the family to get to know him better, or you might say to interrogate him. Her first question was, "Do you plan on driving a taxi cab the rest of your life?" Any young man with above-average intelligence would have grabbed his hat and headed for the door! But not this handsome young man! He had fought bigger battles than this in the war.

My sister already had purchased a full set of Samsonite Luggage, the top of the line. If a girl had white Samsonite luggage, she was considered in vogue and really going somewhere! That morning Charlie said, "Bennie Mae, there's no point in you spending your money on bus fare, I'm goin' down that way. You can just ride with me and I'll drop you off in Clinton."

The plan sounded good, so Bena Mae, dressed to the nines and her hair looking shiny with its long dazzling curls, agreed to share the ride to Tennessee with Charlie. Charlie was driving his pickup truck which hadn't seen a cleanup job in several weeks and the tires were covered in dried mud. Before Bena Mae climbed into the truck, Charlie said, "Here, gimmee them suitcases. You don't wanna' get them all messed up so I'll jest put 'em in these here burlap feed sacks where they won't get dirty." Each piece of luggage was tied in a separate burlap bag and placed in the bed of the truck.

Bena Mae had plans to meet her boyfriend at the bus station and when they drove up in the pickup truck, she could see him standing beside his car off to one side of the depot. About that time, a Greyhound bus filled to capacity pulled into the station. Traveling by

Greyhound Bus Lines was the most popular mode of transportation after the war ended. Charlie's truck was right where the passengers were getting off the bus. My sister was in hopes of making a grand impression on her boyfriend and anyone else that happened to be in the area when she appeared with her white Samsonite luggage looking like a movie star. Just as she stepped out of the cab of the truck in her prettiest dress, Charlie removed the large red railroad bandana from around his neck and quickly tied it on my sister's head. While she struggled, he managed to grab one of the burlap bags, slung it over her shoulder and very loudly said, "Bessie Mae, ye' ack like ye' ain't never been to the city 'afore." Bena Mae was at the peak of embarrassment and mortified as she tried to pull away from Charlie. The passengers stood staring at them. If there was ever a thing called justifiable homicide, she felt that was the time for it. While she was trying to pull away and cursing Charlie under her breath, her handsome boyfriend was leaning against his car smiling.

Charlie was known for his antics and clowning around, but this time he had gone too far. My sister went weeks before she would speak to the man again. One thing was certain though; she and no one else could stay mad at Charlie very long.

YOU JUST HAD TO BE THERE!

It seems to be a characteristic trait in small towns that certain people feel obligated to attend every funeral service or visitation of the deceased, even if they never met the person or knew the family. I, for one, stayed away from funerals and vowed I would never attend one unless the deceased was a close family member. The very first funeral I attended was when I was in about the 8th grade of school and I went with a girlfriend. I didn't even know the deceased. It was not a pleasant experience!

It never occurred to me until many years later when close friends and family had passed away and I definitely was obligated to attend their services that I understood why certain people in town were at every funeral service. I learned this when my own father died. He was quite well known in town and had many friends, so the funeral home was very busy with townspeople coming and going from the funeral home during visitation. People I hadn't seen in years arrived. Friends from my high school days were there. We hadn't seen each other since graduation. Conversation and stories went wild. It was definitely a catching up time for old and up-to-date news. There was more action and talk than you would see at a family reunion. Visitation at the funeral home was almost like a party. One thing is certain, if you have missed out on the goings on around town for a number of years, go to a visitation at the funeral home. That is catching up time!

I found the same things to be true when my cousin died. I saw people I couldn't even recognize from the old days. There was so much to be learned and before long, the laughter began. I have discovered in the past few years, refreshments are now being provided at visitations.

One thing taken seriously by both my parents was their religion and their church attendance. There would be no laughing by us kids inside the Lord's house. I believe that's the reason my sister, Wanda, and I always sat behind a large column on one side of the church auditorium; so that when we got tickled, Daddy couldn't see us from the church choir loft. It wasn't easy to keep a straight face when the lady sitting directly behind the preacher on the first row of the choir began nodding her head and falling asleep. She nodded and slept through the entire sermon. I don't think anyone in the congregation could concentrate on the pastor's sermon.

It is common knowledge that when a family member has passed, it is difficult to control your emotions and keep your mind on the important factors of the funeral process. Among my sisters and me, we had the fear of breaking out in tears and that alone would be embarrassing to us. We stuck together at the visitation and again at the main funeral service. Control! We must be in control. Undoubtedly, someone would say something, or an unusual action would take place, and that would break the spell for all of us. Even at my own father's funeral, we sisters were sitting together on the first two pews at the funeral home when the sister next to me whispered something loud enough for all of the others and two nieces to hear that broke the chain of silence and we were so tickled we couldn't hold back the laughter. I passed out the tissues as quickly as I could and all of us covered our faces so the guests could not detect our laughter. They thought we were overcome with emotion and were crying. Goodness sakes alive, I began to wonder what Daddy would say if he saw us. And then I decided he would see the humor in the situation and hopefully, give us a broad smile. I know these things do happen where laughter takes the place of crying, and the only way it can be described is to say, "You just had to be there!"

It has always put me in mind of Mary Tyler Moore when she attended the funeral of Chuckles the Clown. Mary was a very emotional girl and she was prepared for breaking into tears during the minister's presentation. The minister began describing Chuckles and his work as a clown and the more he said, the more tickled Mary became. All of her coworkers sitting around her thought Mary very distraught, when suddenly she burst out in uncontrollable laughter. Well, that's just an example of what can happen when family members are so keyed up in their emotions. They break out in laughter instead of tears.

SEVERAL DEATHS HAD OCCURRED in my family during the years after Daddy died. Each was very emotional and overwhelming and then the time came when we were attending my mother's funeral. We were prepared for her demise because of her age. She was 101 and died peacefully in her sleep.

Again, we were all at the funeral service except my oldest sister who had already passed on. My mother was a person who had dipped snuff my entire life and longer. I never knew her to be without her Bruton's Snuff. She always carried a small tin of snuff in her apron pocket and sometimes rolled up in her dress sleeve. If you saw my mother, you also saw her little tin of snuff. She literally passed away holding her small tin of snuff.

The night before Mama's funeral we were at her house. In the kitchen on a shelf was the tin of snuff. My daughter, Jan, knew that Mama had passed holding that tin, so she decided Mama had to be buried with it. Like I said, Mama was never without her Bruton's Snuff. The next day everyone was preparing for the service at the funeral home. Jan had Mama's little tin of snuff in her purse. She said to my granddaughter, "We can't let Mammaw be buried without her snuff tin. She has always carried it with her no matter where she was."

So Jan, her husband Jim, and my granddaughter, Mollie, walked up to the casket and stood side by side while they said goodbye to Mama. Jan had handed the snuff tin to Mollie and while Jim and Jan kept watch on the others in attendance, Mollie quietly slid the little snuff tin behind the pretty pink satin curtain that hung across the inside of the casket. One more tiny shove to be sure it was intact, and then "PLINK, PLANK, PLUNK"—the tin hit the bottom of the metal casket and began rolling around.

Totally unprepared for this, the three of them began to panic. What would happen at the end of the service when the funeral director and his assistants lifted the casket to take it out to the hearse. Or worse than that, what would happen when the pallbearers pulled the casket out of the hearse at the cemetery and then heard the rolling around of the tin inside. The casket would be dropped, for sure! The three of them immediately hustled out of the sanctuary, down the hall, hysterically laughing, while cousins watched, wondering what, pray tell, was going on. Straight to the funeral director's office they went where they tried, through laughter, to tell the gentleman what they had done. He just smiled, told them that people bury their relatives with all types of personal items, and then said, "Don't worry! We will take care of it." Next, I saw Jan and my granddaughter standing in the hallway, laughing so hard they could hardly control themselves. Jan motioned for me to come out. When she told me about the snuff tin rolling around in the bottom of the casket, I could visualize the whole situation and it brought on more laughter. We couldn't let anyone see us laughing at my mother's funeral!

THERE GOES MS. VELMA

Everybody loved her. The small Tennessee town with a population of approximately 4,500 residents had known this lady for more than 65 years. She was a stranger to no one. She could probably tell you all their names and they, in turn, called her Ms. Velma. She was my sister!

My daughter, Jan, and I had driven through torrents of rain and fog to get there for her funeral. When we checked into the local motel, I told the owner we were there to attend a funeral. She said, "You mean Ms. Velma, I've known her for years. She was a wonderful lady. Everybody loved her!" My nephew, also arriving for her funeral, pulled into a local service station and asked for directions to the funeral home. The attendant said, "Oh, are you here for Ms. Velma's funeral?"

Mama named her Velma Lenore. That seemed such a big name for such a tiny thing. As she grew, all the neighbors said she was the kindest, sweetest child they had ever known, and she was! Mama never worried about leaving Velma outside in the yard to play alone. The child could find so many things of interest and loved playing in the grass and picking flowers. Dandelions, violets, and any little wild weed that had a blossom was a flower to her, including morning glories and honeysuckle vines that grew on the fence above the house. Day after day, she would walk into the kitchen with a handful of flowers for Mama to put in a vase. A vase was usually a pint size Mason jar filled with water and placed in the middle of the kitchen table. My sister loved to read and would curl up in the corner of our sofa at home and read every magazine or book she could get her hands on.

She was pretty, wore a beautiful smile, and had a gentle nature. She was also a talker; never at a loss for conversation! She could outtalk all of her six sisters. The small town of Smithville wasn't far from Nashville, home of all the country music stars, and many of them owned land in the nearby communities where they built their beautiful estate homes. My sister talked about the politicians, congressmen, and country stars living in the area. She had visited some of the homes and could tell you their life histories, and loved doing so as she would ramble on and on with stories about them. She had a great alto voice and enjoyed singing. Anytime she heard music she recognized, we could hear her voice in harmony, just as we once did when she sang with our older brother many years ago. She knew and sang all the country music songs. My sister was a small town country girl at heart. The old saying holds true, "You can take the girl out of the country, but you can't take the country out of the girl." I remember the time she called home and was so anxious to tell my mother, "I got to sing a solo in church today." At that time, she may have been nearing the age of 60.

After her husband was admitted to the local nursing home, she not only visited him every day, she went door to door greeting the other residents. Her husband died but Velma continued visiting the nursing home and every Sunday morning, she was there to see her friends before attending church services. Velma was faithful to her church.

My sister had more energy than anyone I had ever known. She could clear her plate and then ask if you were going to eat all of your food. Nothing on the dinner table went to waste. She would eat the leftovers. At 5 feet, four inches, she never weighed more than 110 lbs., other than when she was ready to give birth to each of her two children. While the rest of us girls were constantly on diets and trying to lose weight, Velma was bragging about having gained a couple of pounds.

I don't believe she had ever traveled outside the states of Tennessee and Kentucky except for the time she went to California back during World War II, in 1944.

There are many stories to tell about my sister, but I will focus on her driving skills. Velma was late in learning to drive a car and to my knowledge she never drove far from the city limits of where she lived. She was in her eighties and still carrying a driver's license. Unless there was at least six inches of snow on the ground or thunderstorms were approaching the area, my sister never missed a day driving into town. Everyone recognized her little sedan cruising down the streets of Smithville. "There goes Ms. Velma," they would say, each keeping his distance because they were all familiar with her driving habits. She had her own driving rules and the residents of the town were quite familiar with them.

Her husband's nephew was chief of police. As many times as Velma had been warned about her poor driving habits, nothing changed! One day a man called the police department and said, "There's a lady driving down the street and she is a danger to the town." The chief of police didn't need a description of the lady. He knew it was his Aunt Velma.

The street around the town square where the court house was located was entered from the right and drivers had to circle the court house in order to make a left turn. One day Velma was in a hurry. She didn't see any cars coming so she drove straight across in front of the court house going the wrong direction then drove straight ahead. A couple of ladies sitting on a bench in front of a small store looked up and one of them said, "There goes Ms. Velma." Everybody knew her car. On another occasion, she ran a stop sign on her way home. Her husband's nephew spotted her and started his lights flashing and drove up right behind her, thinking she would pull her car over when she saw him. He followed her car several blocks until she reached home. Velma pulled into her driveway and the deputy drove in right beside her. She got out of the car and said, "What are you doing here?" He replied, "Ms. Velma, didn't you see me right behind you all the way?"

"Well, I didn't notice. Why have you got your lights flashing? I didn't do anything wrong." He said, "Ms. Velma, you ran a stop sign back there and you should have seen me behind you with my lights on, and stopped your car. I won't give you a citation this time, but you have to observe the laws like everyone else!"

That's how it was in one small Tennessee town. "There goes Ms. Velma!" That was my sister, Velma! Day after day, she was out and about running errands, meeting people on the streets, and visiting the sick. So many stories were told about her. Everyone knew and loved her.

It had poured buckets of rain the day of visitation at the funeral home. The doors continued to open and close. I believe the entire town of Smithville, Tennessee, turned out for the visitation services, all of the people dripping wet from the rain. Each had a story to tell about Ms. Velma, their neighbor and friend. She was a lady who knew the people and the history of the community. She was a friend to everyone.

My sister died of ovarian cancer. That was five years ago. I can imagine the residents of a small Tennessee town looking up now when they see a turquoise Ford Escort driving by and they say, "That looks like Ms. Velma's car!"

I look back some 75 years with memories of my first day of school. I walked with my older sister, Velma, all six blocks to the elementary school. She held my hand every step of the way! And because she was by my side, I wasn't afraid.

GOING TO THE DOCTOR

Going to the doctor when I was a kid was something you did only if your arm was broken, you had appendicitis or you were getting your tonsils removed. I was scared of doctors; I don't know why since the only time I ever saw one was when he pulled me through the birth canal and the first thing I saw was gray hair, wire rimmed glasses, and squinted eyes looking like they were unhappy with what they saw. That expression could have been because this was about the seventh trip to our house for ol' Doc Smith. He visited so often to deliver another baby Mama had almost reached the point of setting an extra plate at the table for him.

We kids didn't go to the doctor when we were sick. It didn't matter how sick we were, Mama could fix it. She always had a home remedy for the condition except when it was measles, chicken pox, or the mumps. I never had the measles and chicken pox but I do remember ol' Doc Smith coming to the house to treat me for the mumps. That wasn't a happy experience. When I think about it, I still get that chalky taste in my mouth.

I think the next time I walked into a doctor's office was when I went to get my blood test three days before I got married. Even then, I didn't like the idea! From then on, I only saw a doctor when I was pregnant and made my monthly visits to make sure all was going well until the baby was born. That only happened with two pregnancies. My doctors were either middle aged or looking closely at retirement. Once a year I went to my gynecologist for a pap smear. That was long before mammograms were also required once a year.

I really never enjoyed having my privacy invaded by someone I hardly knew, or didn't know at all. I can tell you exactly the last time a physician made a house call to see me. My daughter, Jan, was about eighteen months old. She was in the middle of a bad series of illnesses. She had the German measles, the chicken pox and a bad case of strep throat all at the same time. She was still in diapers and taking the bottle. The child was extremely ill, and wouldn't you know, I came down with the hives at the same time. The balls of my feet felt like huge mosquito bites, my eyes were nearly swollen together and my hands were so swollen I couldn't bend my fingers, which meant I wasn't able to put a pin in the baby's diaper and close it. I was in a mess all around. At ten o'clock one night, my doctor knocked on the front door. He was on his way home from hospital rounds and I was his last patient for the day. That was the last house call I can remember.

I often wondered why all doctors were old, or at least they seemed old to me, until my husband and I moved from Louisville to Lexington and I had to seek a new OB-GYN doctor. I don't recall who made the reference, but I forced myself to make an appointment for an annual checkup and pap smear. I can tell you now, I praised the day when I no longer had to have pap smears. Climbing upon the table, sticking my feet in those stirrups which were nothing like the stirrups on a horse, and spreading my legs for an examination was undoubtedly the most humiliating thing a woman ever had to do; this woman anyway! What made it even worse was when I waited in the examining room to meet my new gynecologist, completely undressed and wearing the wraparound dressing gown that actually didn't wrap around quite far enough, and my new doctor walked into the room. That's when I needed a heart doctor instead of a gynecologist. My new doctor looked like he had just graduated from high school. There was no way I was going to be examined and given a pap smear by someone who was younger than I was. And I was 27, married, and had two children.

What happened to the old gray haired men wearing wire rimmed glasses, the grandfather type that I had gotten used to? It was a new day; a time to get used to the young physicians straight out of medical school. I was never so humiliated! I soon learned that if I stayed with the same family physician through the years, who started out as a handsome young intern in the beginning, I would get to watch him age, with his hair gradually turning from auburn or black to various shades of gray and eventually he, too, would be wearing the wire rimmed glasses. The next thing I knew, he would be retiring and moving to Florida. I was back to the new young physician straight out of medical school and beginning the same trail of breaking him or her in for the next few years. Unfortunately, I have reached an age where all physicians are younger than I am. If I live long enough, I will be breaking in another new doctor!

For the last twenty years I have watched my family doctor go through the aging process. His hair is a lighter shade of gray each time I visit him. I have grown quite fond of this man and he has adjusted to my cantankerous ways. I trust him and am beginning to see it won't be long now before he will be planning his retirement years.

I had an appointment recently with my doctor for blood work and checkup. He asked how I was. "Great," I said then we got into a discussion about AGE. I told him how I felt about the time I have left and what I expect from my remaining years. We talked about what is important as we get older and what our interests are for the future. I told him that I had taken up "cemeteries." He laughed and asked, "Are you searching for your ancestors?" I said, "No, I just like to go through cemeteries and read epitaphs."

I told my doctor another short story, and when I finished, he hugged me and said, "Patricia, you have just made my day." I had just received the best medicine that could be prescribed.

When I arrived at the doctor's office, the parking lot was filled and then the waiting room was also full. And yet, my doctor had time for a personal conversation with me. I apologized for taking his time and he said, "No, I enjoyed every minute of our talk. I look forward to seeing you again." I saw him wipe his eyes as I left the room.

THE NURSING HOME (1996-1998)

To finalize my collection of stories, I thought I would add a segment of my journal written during the last two years of my mother's life when she lived at Hillcrest Nursing Home.

Mama had just turned 99 before she entered Hillcrest Nursing Home. After a recent hospitalization and since her funds for hired help were running out, the decision was made to admit her into the nursing home. We realized she would have the care she needed there. Also, we soon learned she would be provided with three good meals a day.

I was keeping a journal of my weekend visits with Mama at the nursing home. I wanted to have a record of the time she was there and the treatment involved for her. She was receiving good treatment by the nursing home staff and I tried to look at the bright side of the situation when I visited Mama on weekends. I always humored my mother, which worked well for both of us. I received a report of the week's events when I arrived at the nursing home every Saturday morning. I was driving 70 miles from Tennessee. All six sisters and my niece, Brenda, were sharing in daily visits with my mother. I visited on Saturday and Sunday.

One of Mama's first in-house visitors was a friend and former neighbor of ours. He was a temporary resident at the nursing home. She said he visited often. One day, just before Easter, he had a plastic egg for Mama with a piece of candy inside. They were both hearing impaired so it was difficult for them to communicate.

"He calls me 'Honey.' " (characteristic of his entire family) "Can't hardly understand a thing he says, but I just shake my head like I can."

Former high school friends of my sisters often visited the elderly at the nursing home. When they learned that Mama was a resident they would stop by her room and talk to her. One of the men gave her special attention because she reminded him of his own mother who had recently passed away.

I was sitting with Mama on Saturday morning and she was telling me about all the visitors she had entertained during the week. "People come to visit me all the time. Young men! They just hug and kiss on me—I don't know who tha' hell they are!" Using foul language was new to my mother and the way she used it always made me laugh.

Mama attended a couple of the religious services in the dining room on Sunday morning. I asked, "Mama, do you enjoy the sermons on Sunday?"

"I guess. Can't hear a thing the preacher says though. There's more women there than men. Ugliest bunch of men I've ever seen. Ever'one of 'em is like this." (She slumps her head down on her chest and closes her eyes.) Again, she made me laugh. Continuing my conversation, I said, "Mama, I bet you're the oldest person here."

"I may be, but I'll tell you right now, I sure ain't the ugliest and I don't have the most wrinkles. Do you think I'm as wrinkled as those other women?" rubbing her fingers up and down her face and neck. I didn't dare disagree with her. Later in the day I wheeled Mama to the dining room to play the piano. The room was unoccupied. She tried to play two hymns. She had learned to play by ear as a young girl. Her hands shook, but she did quite well. I told her if she practiced, she could play for the religious services on Sunday. She laughed.

Her manner of speaking was often humorous. Someone commented about how nice the facilities were and how comfortable her bed looked. She responded without hesitation, "Well, if it looks that good then you git' in this bed, and I'll go home!"

When trying to persuade her to eat, my brother looked at her food tray and said, "That food looks great." She pushed the tray forward and blatantly said, "Then you eat it!"

I met a sweet lady, age 92, Winnie Nelson. She was the granddaughter of a local minister for whom the town of Corbin was named, James Corbin Floyd. Winnie had been at the nursing home eleven years. She was one of the few elderly ladies alert and able to communicate with others. Each day Winnie wheeled herself into the dining room where I occasionally shared her table for lunch. Her pleasant personality and positive attitude set her apart from other residents. Winnie always had a smile and a good word for the day. At the end of each meal she would always say, "Why don't you come down to my place and sit a spell and we'll talk?" This sweet little lady read her Bible faithfully every day. She talked continually. She told me that in 1937, she lived down the street from us. She remembered my family. (I don't know why, but it seemed that everybody always remembered my family!)

Winnie's brother visited her every Saturday, like clockwork. I got the impression Winnie was educated and came from good breeding.

I continued my weekly visits with Mama and oftentimes I could hear Gertie yelling as I entered the lobby and rounded the first corner of the long corridor of the nursing home. I knew it was Gertie because she was the only Alzheimer's patient who erratically yelled loud enough to be heard throughout the building. A person visiting the facility would remember seeing Gertie, even if they took little notice of anyone else. I could see her sitting on her favorite camel-back sofa at the far end of the hall, dressed for the day in one of her pretty cotton dresses with her chubby knees exposed below the hem of her dress. She wore knee-high stockings and white slip-on canvas shoes.

It was difficult to guess Gertie's age. She never smiled. Her long silvery-gray hair was usually combed smoothly to the crown of her head in the shape of a biscuit. She shuffled along the hallway hour by hour each day, entering the residents' rooms. When she ventured too far from the nurses' station, one of the nurses went looking for her and led her back to the sofa. Gertie had to be hand fed by one of the aides.

I had had no previous contact with patients of Alzheimer's disease and knew nothing about how to deal with them. Gertie was my first experience. I had no knowledge of how long she had been at the nursing home. I only knew that when visiting Mama every Saturday and Sunday for three months, I had never observed any relatives or friends visiting Gertie. I was told that she had ten children and none of them visited her.

Weeks turned into months. I continued writing in my journal, noting as many of my mother's activities as I could. Another visit brought me to learn that sweet Winnie had died. She had become such a dear friend.

One day I met a man in the activity room where there were books and a television. The man was in a wheelchair. Something about him looked very familiar and so I asked his name. He said "Harold French." Of course, I remembered him from my high school days. He owned French's Shoe Store downtown. My sister, Wanda, and I traded there often. It was the best place in town for a good buy on shoes.

Each week after that, I made an effort to talk with Mr. French. He was a very friendly person, always smiling, and seemed quite satisfied with his stay at the nursing home. Every Saturday morning at a certain hour he posted himself in the lobby beside the telephone. He waited and then the phone would ring. It was always one of his sisters from Ohio. When their conversation ended, Mr. French continued to wait beside the phone. Again, the phone would ring. This time it would be his second sister, also calling. The routine never changed. The sisters called faithfully every Saturday morning.

A year had passed and on Mama's 100th birthday, I planned a big party for her to be held in the dining room. A friend made the prettiest birthday cake I had ever seen. We had punch and other refreshments. A lady from the little church Daddy had built brought a beautiful bouquet of orchids from her husband's greenhouse. Using the nursing home's helium tank, my sisters and I blew up 100 balloons for the party. The dining room looked festive and the nursing staff was very cooperative in helping us with the party. Residents were invited and invitations had been sent to relatives and friends at Mama's church. My sister, Wanda, was helping get Mama dressed and a friend, who sold Mary Kay products, was on hand to apply Mama's cosmetics. "Are you gonna fix my eyes like Tammy Faye's, with artificial eyelashes?" Mama tried to pretend she wasn't excited about the party, but we could see she was looking forward to it. She said, "I don't know why you're going to so much trouble. Nobody'll be at the party. All the people I know are already dead!" As many as 100 guests arrived at the celebration. When the party ended everyone went outside the building and let the balloons go into the air. Each balloon had a note attached reading, "If you find this balloon, please call this number and wish Elizabeth Estep a 100th Happy Birthday." The balloons flew through the air following the cold breeze.

A few days later the nursing station received a phone call from a lady living near the Blue Ridge Parkway in Virginia, wishing my mother, Happy Birthday. I was thrilled!

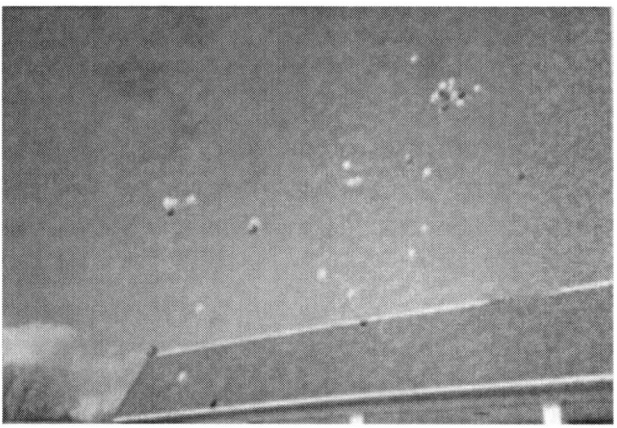

100 Balloons at Elizabeth Estep's 100th birthday party

Dr. Turner put Mama on a catheter, changed her medication and began giving her Prozac. There was a tremendous change in her personality. She was pleasant each time I visited her. She never complained about physical pain, but occasionally asked for a nerve pill, which we gave her in the form of a Tic Tac. She said, "Now, don't let the nurse know you are giving me a nerve pill." Occasionally, my sister, Wanda, would pass the nurses' station and remark, "I gotta' go to Walmart and get Mama's prescription filled for Tic Tacs. She's almost out."

One day Wanda handed her two Tic Tacs and she demanded, "I want four!" Wanda said, "I can't give you four pills." Mama stiffened and smugly replied, "Don't you know, I'm addicted?" Mama asked Dr. Turner why she couldn't have additional medication. He told her he wasn't allowed to give her any more. The government (Medicare) wouldn't allow it. She looked up at him and said, "Send them to me. I'll straighten them out." He turned to me and said, "And I believe she could!"

Arriving at Hillcrest on another Saturday morning, Mama was in her chair and the first thing she said was, "That ol' bitch won't let me go back to bed!" The aides and nurses took the residents' comments in good humor. Mama had been sleeping too much. She needed to stay awake. I ran into a therapist in the hallway and related Mama's comments. She said, "I'm that ol' bitch!"

I was told about the fluffy scrambled eggs she had for breakfast. But, "the sausage must have been made out of goat's hide." She was in a good mood both days that weekend. Since her medication had been changed, she didn't complain nearly as much, even though she slept more. She had an enjoyable sense of humor when she was feeling good.

Another year passed and I continued making my weekly visits. On Mama's 101st birthday, she wasn't feeling well so we held a small party in her room, serving punch, cake and ice cream.

It was the weekend of July 18, 1998, six months later. I arrived at the nursing home early on Saturday morning. I noticed shortly after I got there that Mama didn't seem to be herself. She wanted to sleep most of the time. I encouraged her to get out of the bed and sit in her chair. When her meal arrived at noon, she would lift her fork to her mouth and couldn't seem to take a bite. I took the fork from her hand and tried to feed her. She just couldn't stay awake to eat. After a few bites of food, I gave up trying to feed her. She wanted to go back to bed.

On Sunday, she still seemed too sleepy to sit in her chair. This wasn't like my mother. She wasn't one who wanted to sleep all the time, and she had not received medication that would cause her to sleep. She ate very little lunch then asked to go back to bed.

My brother came to replace me on Sunday afternoon. I had to leave for my trip back to Tennessee. I told him that Mama had slept most of the time I was there.

On Monday, July 20th, my sister called to say they had taken Mama to the hospital. They thought she had had a stroke. She was placed in ICU. On July 23, 1998, my mother passed from her earthly family on to her Heavenly family.

A LONG-AWAITED JOURNEY

There were phone calls inquiring about the surviving relatives of Howard Estep who was killed in World War II. Then came letters from another man providing documents concerning Howard's death. A few days later I learned that investigation was going into finding records providing information regarding the cause of a plane crash that occurred in Rapid City, SD, in 1943.

It had been fifty-five years since the crash of a B-17F Bomber at Ellis Air Force Base, Rapid City, SD. Six of ten airmen perished. One of those six soldiers was my brother, Howard Estep. In a two week period, three planes had crashed in the Badlands killing 20 young men.

A young man from New Jersey was a researcher of military airplane crashes. He had found the records regarding the B-17F crash that occurred on June 17, 1943, documents that were never received by any of the families. The only information my parents received was that a B-17F bomber was flying too low and crashed into the side of a mountain. It was August 1998, three weeks after my mother was placed in a grave beside my father that I boarded a plane with six other people at Nashville, Tennessee, heading for Rapid City, South Dakota.

I REMEMBER IT SO WELL. I had just turned seven when the news came. I, like every young child, looked up at that big brother in military uniform as the tallest, the bravest, most loving person in the world. He could make me laugh and also wipe away my tears. He was my idol. And then there was that dreaded telephone call in the middle of the night from an Air Force commanding officer. I would never see my brother again!

FOR FIFTY-FIVE YEARS, I missed my big brother and often cried when his name was mentioned. Eight of us arrived at Ellison (formerly Ellis) Air Force Base to meet the VIPs. They were expecting us and we were treated with the utmost respect. My friend had carried his father's flag and it hung at half mast for two days. Dinner was provided, and we were served a VIP breakfast the following morning. Immediately after the breakfast we were taken to the airfield to enjoy an air show presented by a well-known group called Dakota Thunder. It was a fabulous show. They said there were as many as 50,000 people in attendance. We were honored with front row seats. Suddenly, from out of nowhere, someone tapped me on the shoulder and said, "Are you the lady whose brother was named at the breakfast this morning?" I answered, "Yes," and she continued, "My husband's relatives are from Tennessee and their names are "Estep." I wanted to meet you in hopes that we may have a family connection." Fifty-thousand people, and she was able to plow through the crowd and find me. I was overwhelmed. I never dreamed such a thing like this would happen, especially so far from home.

Riding a shuttle across the airfield, a young man asked me the purpose of our visit to the air base. I explained that we were researching the crash of a B-17 during World War II. He listened with interest and said he thought we should be interviewed by the local newspaper. He made the phone call and that evening a young reporter met us at our hotel. Our story would appear in the news the following day.

There were many ongoing details, but the next morning we were guided to the old runway that had not been used in years. It was the runway where my brother's plane crashed. Grass was growing in the cracks of the landing strip.

This is the story we had been told by one of the airmen who survived the crash: It was twelve o'clock noon. Ten men were on board for takeoff. The pilot taxied down the runway about 300 yards but could not get the B-17 bomber off the ground. It was too heavy. Rather than applying the booster charges, he decided to abort the flight, having spotted a large field ahead. But what the pilot did not see was a pond near the end of the runway. The plane skidded across the field and over the pond then nose-dived into the opposite bank. The plane exploded. The pilot had not been told that extra ammunition was being loaded on the aircraft, three huge fuel tanks and 25,000 rounds of ammunition were in the cargo section of the aircraft where my brother, as crew chief, was sitting. The pilot, co-pilot, and two other airmen escaped through a large hole in the cockpit of the burning plane. The gunner climbed through a small window but died later of 80% burns. The five men in the rear of the plane died instantly. It took two days for the investigators to find any evidence of my brother's body. All of his personal belongings were lost in the explosion.

AFTER VIEWING the photos and blueprints of the airfield, we had spotted a small white frame house in the middle of a farm a short distance away. The house was shown in the photographs. We could see the spot where the B-17 made its final impact located beside a deep crevice at the edge of the farm. Climbing into the rented van, we headed across the farmland towards the little white house. Nobody was home so the three men in our party headed across the grounds toward the bank beside the crevice. Mike, our researcher, had brought a metal detector and a heavy plastic garbage bag with him. A few minutes later the men returned and I nearly lost it when I saw what the bag contained. By digging along the surface of the ground with their hands, they discovered shrapnel and burned pieces of metal from the airplane crash. Mike was holding several spent bullets dated 1942.

Spent 1942 bullet, Scrap metal from plane crash

My mind was in a daze as we drove back to our hotel that evening. The next morning we headed to the airport for our return flight home. We had accomplished our goal. After all those years, two families were able to close the books on the airplane crash that occurred on June 17, 1943. For six of our party, the airman who died of 80% burns was the husband and father. For me, it was my brother. Mike would return to New Jersey with enough material to reproduce the events of the long-ago tragedy.

But the story doesn't end here. Two days after arriving home I received a phone call from the newspaper reporter in Rapid City. Her name was Heidi. She said that an elderly man called her saying he had read our story and wanted to report that he was visiting his uncle in the little white house on the farm the day the B-17 bomber crashed. As a young man, he was a witness to the accident. He had arrived to tell his uncle that he had just joined the Navy and was leaving the next day for basic training. The two men were having lunch when they heard a loud crash that shook the house and rattled all of the windows. Running out the door and across the field they could see black smoke barreling from an airplane. They fell to the ground to avoid the bullets that were exploding like popcorn. I later called the man who had witnessed the accident and he gave me a detailed description of the events that occurred on that fatal day so many years ago.

The books are now closed and the only items that remain as evidence of my brother's life are the memories, a few photographs, and a shoebox filled with his letters to my mother. A spent 1942 bullet and two pieces of melted metal from the lost plane, these, along with my box of tattered letters are the remains of my brother's life.

MAMA'S BUTCHER KNIFE

Sometimes I think there are too many things from my early life that I have forgotten and wish I could bring to mind. But, then again, there are some thoughts that never seem to leave me. This is one of the ever-present memories…

I was going to visit my oldest sister. She is 98 and still living alone. Her health is as good as can be expected for a lady her age, but she has trouble eating.

She can still prepare simple meals for herself, but she cannot chew raw foods and most meats. Meatloaf is one of the few meats she can eat because it can be mashed up with other soft foods. She loves fresh tomatoes and keeps a few sitting in her kitchen window during the summer months.

The last time I visited her, I loaded the car with dishes I had prepared the night before, things I knew she would like. When my niece and I arrived, another sister came by to have lunch with us. We spread the table with the dishes I had cooked.

Elizabeth Estep. In her kitchen, age 70

Today, I am doing the same thing – cooking! I walked into my kitchen and pulled out my bag of Idaho potatoes then reached for the big chef's knife that I use daily. I realized right away that the knife needed sharpening. I have used the same small sharpener for years and as I pulled the knife back and forth across it, I could see my mother standing at her kitchen stove with her huge handmade butcher knife in her hand. Our next door neighbor had made the knife for her long before I was born. It was used for all of her cutting. She never used small paring knives like most of us have in our kitchens today. I can see the chicken in the sink where she has just cleaned and plucked its feathers. She reaches for her knife and begins sliding it back and forth over the edge of her big iron skillet to sharpen it. You could hear the musical sound as she turned the knife from side to side. By the time she finished, the butcher knife could split a hair and she was ready to cut up the chicken for supper. This was where Mama's expertise came in—she could cut a chicken into more parts than the practiced butcher in the meat department at the A&P.

Many times, I watched my mother slide her knife down the length of an ear of corn with the ease of a feather, preparing the corn for frying. Her glasses would be spattered with the milk from the corn where she had scraped the cob, and her black hair falling on her forehead was covered with the small bits of corn kernels. Corn shucks and silks had blown all over the front porch and I sometimes wondered if having fried corn for supper was worth the mess created in preparing it. Take my word for it—it was!

The big enamel pan on the back porch that we called the dish pan held heads of cabbage and I can see Mama swinging her butcher knife and cutting the cabbage in sections, getting them ready for chopping and making sour kraut. She would hand me the core of the cabbage to eat as a snack. I always salted the core and it was as good to me as a Baby Ruth candy bar.

As I stand at my kitchen sink, I peel potatoes with my chef's knife, cut them in cubes, and put them on the stove to boil. My mashed potato casserole topped with melted cheese will soon be ready and all it needs is re-heating in the oven later. My sister loves the potatoes. She had never eaten them fixed that way before.

My cabbage for coleslaw has been shredded, very fine, just for my sister. It isn't easy shredding a full head of cabbage. There are bits and pieces all over the floor and my arm is sore from sliding the cabbage up and down my grater, but there will be enough for leftovers. The last time I took coleslaw to my sister she said it was the best she had ever eaten. And like Mama, meatloaf is one of her favorite meat dishes. I haven't made the meatloaf yet and I am hoping it turns out good. The taste varies from one time to another. I will probably wait until I get to my sister's house to make the cornbread. It is much better when taken right out of the oven. The advantage to these dishes is that they are still delicious as leftovers and my sister can eat them in small portions for three or four days just like Mama did when I made them for her.

My sister uses a cane and we don't do anything strenuous when I go back home, but we might hit one of the farmers' markets and buy a few fresh tomatoes and home-grown peaches.

Mama's old butcher knife has been long gone for many years now. The screws loosened and it just plain fell apart, but there's still the old eggbeater, the handmade rolling pin I watched her use to make bread and the biscuit cutter for the large pan of biscuits. The new chef's knife that I use today in making coleslaw for my sister will someday be added to the memorabilia along with the small iron skillet that turns out perfect cornbread. These are a few of the simple things that create our memories.

HER LIFE IN A NUTSHELL

During all those growing up years, she was just Mama, doing what all mamas do —getting us kids up in the morning in time to eat a hot breakfast of bacon and eggs, and of course, oatmeal, before we lit out the back door on our way to school. We never questioned who put the clean white sheets on our beds every week, did the laundry, kept our house spankin' clean every day, and had supper on the table at six o'clock every evening. That was Mama's job. She did all these things without giving thought to whether or not she wanted to do them. Housework was done on a daily basis. We kids just took for granted all these things would be done. That was what she was supposed to do.

Mama died in 1998. That was nineteen years ago. Her kidneys shut down and her heart just gave way. She had run out of strength and energy after 101 years. She had tackled and accomplished every task that could be expected of a mother. It was time for her to move on to a better place. She had fulfilled her duties as a daughter, a wife, mother, grandmother and great-grandmother. And, I should add, the favorite aunt of many cousins in the family. She had become the head matriarch at every family reunion. She was the reason all the cousins attended. They wanted to see Aunt Lizzie, the sole survivor of her line of descendants. All of her siblings and Daddy's eleven siblings had already passed on.

I remember the multitude of stories she told me, time and time again. As a young girl, I didn't realize how much her family tales would mean to me when I grew older. And I didn't appreciate the life she led, the many experiences and heartaches that dominated her life that none of us in this day and time could even imagine overcoming. One day, I sat my son down and told him the story of his grandmother. He was amazed at the battles she had overcome and the many ruts in the road she had had to triumph over in all of her years. I told him about her childhood as one of thirteen siblings, living on a Virginia/Tennessee farm in the Appalachian Mountains, working in the fields alongside the men to grow gardens in the summer. Farm chores were no different for the girls than they were for the boys. There was no time for an education after the sixth grade of school. This was her biggest disappointment.

Mama was one month away from her 19th birthday when she was married in 1915. Her elopement and wedding took place on a cold December day with 12 inches of snow on the ground. I remember being told about the railroad house she lived in while Daddy worked for the L&N Railroad Company. In order to live rent free in the house, she had to take in boarders working for the railroad. She was responsible for their laundry, three meals a day, and clean beds at night. During that era, she was carrying her first child. Mama knew what it was like to battle floodwaters while walking the floor with a newborn baby. Daddy was called to duty by the railroad during the torrents of rain and flooding.

Later, my parents experienced the Influenza Epidemic of 1918 with both of them and their first-born child lying lifeless and helpless along with everyone in her family and all of the residents of the community sick and dying, one by one. Her second baby was born with the flu.

The birth of her first blue baby was unexpected and quite traumatic. Two more blue babies then the death of a two-year-old child created the start of the family cemetery nearby. Neighbors constructed a small casket for the baby girl while Mama sat at the bedside of two other children, my brother, Bug, and my sister, Ada. The doctor stayed with them anticipating their deaths at any moment.

The Depression years came along and Mama worked at tightening the belt and pinching pennies during the hunger years with lack of food and money while Daddy had to search for new jobs. He was always gone. His work kept him away from home most of the time. Problems arising at home had to be handled by Mama. She was nurse and caretaker of all of us kids. Neighbors called on her when their children were ill. She knew all of the home remedies. Mama never had driven a car in her life and we kids laughed when she decided she was going to learn how to drive. By then she was probably sixty-five. We also laughed when she expected Daddy to be her instructor. Lordy, Lord! Daddy, himself had never learned to drive the proper way. He didn't know there was such a thing as turn signals to be observed. When he bought his first car, he had never driven one and there weren't enough car owners to require traffic lights and turn signals.

Mama never had a regular paying job in her life, but I figured she had one of the hardest jobs there was, and never received a dime for her labor.

One thing about Mama was that regardless of how little food was available for her own family, she could manage an extra plate of food for a neighbor who was seeing hard times. There was no doubt she was the best cook in town. I can remember as a child carrying a large platter of meat and vegetables to a needy family in the neighborhood.

She watched her own brother go off to war during the First World War. He returned safely. That was the war of the Soldiers Flu, the epidemic that killed millions of people. Then years later, along came World War II. It was a terrible time for all people. Mama managed the ration stamps in a manner that provided the needs for the whole family. She scrimped on flour and sugar and food items, saving sugar for special treats such as candy and cookies to send to my brother who had joined the Army Air Corps. There was the constant worry of him being sent overseas to fight the Japanese. Again, Mama had to face the death of another child. My brother was killed in a B-17F bomber. His death at the age of 21 took a toll on Mama, but she remained strong for the rest of the family. The war years were nearly unbearable in every way for every family.

Each of her children left home one at a time. The last to leave the nest were my sister, Wanda, my brother, Don, and me. The house was empty and quiet. My two oldest sisters and my brother, Don, continued living in the same town with two of them in walking distance of my parents' house. I haven't given Daddy much credit in my stories, however, he was there overseeing the financial end of the household, bringing the paycheck home every week after laboring in his construction work. Daddy retired and the only time the rest of us kids were at home was for holidays and weekend visits. Time passed, my parents grew older, and then Daddy was diagnosed with pancreatic cancer. Two years later he died. While Mama watched as he was lowered into the ground at the cemetery where four of her children were buried, a phone call came with news that her sister, Cassie, had just passed away. I remember Aunt Cassie as being the sister with strawberry blonde hair and lots of freckles when she was young.

Mama was totally alone at home at this point. Things went fairly smooth for several years and then she was diagnosed with colon cancer. Surgery was required and from then on she would wear a colostomy. A few more years went by and then my oldest sister, Inez, who lived across the road and was her primary caretaker, died of cancer. Mama had experienced the deaths of my dad, his siblings, and all of her siblings and now, in the autumn of her life, she was undergoing the pain and suffering of her children leaving her side. Mama was 97 when two grandsons died tragically in separate incidents. When a sister said we should keep the news from Mama about one of her grandsons, my niece said, "We can't do that. She has suffered more than we could ever know and she is stronger than all of us put together. She must be told."

So, at the age of 99 Mama entered a nursing home facility and by the age of 101, she had given her all. She was ready to leave the remainder of her children who could all take care of themselves. It was time for her to go to a better place where she could be with the many happy family members who had waited so long for her to join them. Mama had paid her dues. She was ready to sit in her rocking chair beside Daddy, my sister, Inez, my brother, and all the little babies she only got to hold in her arms for a brief period of time. With her needle and crochet thread she can work her hands back and forth and look in the face of her angelic mother and all of her siblings and say, "I'm home now."

Mama had a happy life. She was ready to leave her worldly home and join the many loved ones she had missed for so long. The family she left behind was happy for her. We knew it was time for her to go. She had given her all.

Today, two more of my sisters have joined the Heavenly throng. The old wooden swing still hangs at the end of the front porch at Mama's house. You rarely see anyone sitting in the swing but if it could talk, there would be no ending to the stories it could tell from days gone by.

I miss Mama; I miss Daddy! I miss walking through the house with the smell of Mama's cooking in the kitchen and Daddy looking up and saying, "Well, hello Sis! What are you doin' here?" I miss the summer evenings when all of us kids sat on the front porch laughing and singing, and telling childhood stories.

The four remaining sisters, Ada, Janette, Wanda, Me (Pat), and my brother Don, are getting older now and in the next few years we will join Inez, Velma, Bena Mae, and my sweet brother, Bug, who has been gone so long.

Soon, we can sing, "When we all get to Heaven, what a day of rejoicing that will be…"

Elizabeth Estep, 1897-1998 Painting by Frank Stone, Lexington, KY

AFTERWORD

I leave behind my collection of short stories with the assurance that they will be read and passed down to my grandchildren so that stories and fond memories of life in the old days will live on through time.

ABOUT THE AUTHOR

Born and raised in the foothills of southeastern Kentucky, Patricia Estep O'Neal reveals segments of her family life as the tenth of thirteen children. Family life began when her parents lived on large farms in Tennessee and Virginia. Their move to a small Kentucky town was where they raised their children. World War I, the Depression years and World War II brought hard times and sadness, leaving scars on this family. Patricia tells about life as the youngest of seven living sisters, two brothers, the hard times and the fun and laughter shared with them. The friends she started the first grade of school with became the ones with whom she graduated high school. The bond between them grew. Patricia's social life consisted of inner action at school and church with family and friends.

    Her mother spent many hours telling stories about life in the hills where the farm was divided by the state line between Tennessee and Virginia. She would tell about grandparents' experiences during the Civil War. The family stories were recounted often, and little by little, they made an impression on Patricia. Today, she has written a collection of short stories. You will enjoy a fraction of history, childhood tales, laughter and tears as you read and relate to the life of this small-town Kentucky lady.

ALSO BY PATRICIA ESTEP O'NEAL

Room at the Foot of the Bed

CPSIA information can be obtained
at www.ICGtesting.com
Printed in the USA
LVOW11s2114181217
560207LV00004B/316/P